Where the Salmon Run

The Life and Legacy of Billy Frank Jr.

Where the Salmon Run

The Life and Legacy of Billy Frank Jr.

Trova Heffernan

THE WASHINGTON STATE
HERITAGE CENTER

LEGACY PROJECT

in association with

UNIVERSITY OF WASHINGTON PRESS, Seattle and London

Library of Congress Control Number 2012934508
ISBN 978-0-295-99340-9

Washington State Heritage Center
Office of the Secretary of State
P.O. Box 40222
Olympia, WA 98504-0222, USA
www.heritagecenter.wa.gov

University of Washington Press
PO Box 50096
Seattle, WA 98145, USA
www.washington.edu/uwpress

FOR SUGAR, TANU, AND WILLIE

"I'M DEDICATED TO MY CHILDREN . . . AND NOT ONLY MY
CHILDREN BUT EVERYBODY ELSE'S. WITHOUT MY FAMILY . . .
I COULD'VE NEVER DONE ANY OF THIS."
— BILLY FRANK JR.

Contents

Preface

From time immemorial, the original inhabitants of the Pacific Northwest have been recognized as eloquent orators. Written documents and records, however, can be lacking. To capture the contribution of the subject, *Where the Salmon Run: The Life and Legacy of Billy Frank Jr.* relies on oral history interviews with the Nisqually elder and those who know him best. Conversations with family, allies, and onetime combatants illuminate a divisive chapter on the rivers of this region and a story of the salmon that continues to this day. This book is told largely from the perspective of Billy Frank Jr. and other tribal leaders. It is in no way a comprehensive history of the fish wars or the co-management of natural resources that followed.

Where the Salmon Run

The Life and Legacy of Billy Frank Jr.

Prologue

Spawning salmon will not go unnoticed. The fish travel saltwater highways of the ocean and transform into something of a spectacle. Their bodies turn varying shades of red. Their noses curve into hooks and large swells form on their backs. Approaching death, their once healthy bodies deteriorate. The fish die and a new cycle of life begins.

Salmon are miracles of the ocean, crossing for years thousands of treacherous miles along the West Coast of North America. They are well equipped for the journey. Muscular bodies and caudal fins can lift the fish to unbelievable heights. They clear waterfalls and swim against ocean currents and river flows. Salmon can smell a single drop in 250 gallons of water. This keen sense of smell guides the fish back to their spawning grounds, where they carefully bury their eggs in gravel nests. But out of a thousand eggs, only a fraction of adult salmon will survive the journey.

For all their strength, salmon cannot overpower the ravages of humans and the seeds of development, which have wreaked havoc on their environment. To live, salmon depend on cool, clean water and secure stream banks. Deteriorating habitat and overfishing have devastated runs. International vessels and fleets have intercepted huge numbers of fish. Dams have blocked passages to spawning grounds. Turbines have disoriented the salmon and marked them as easy prey.

Early logging robbed the water of shade and nutrients, leaving behind a dirty residue that spreads through streams like a moving cloud, threatening salmon eggs.

For every mile the salmon have traveled, Billy Frank Jr. has taken a step. He has swallowed his pride, let go of the past, and formed the unlikeliest of alliances to ensure that salmon survive. "The person who had to walk the farthest is Billy Frank," attests Bill Wilkerson, a former director of the Washington State Department of Fisheries, "and he has never stopped."

"I've heard of Uncle Billy my whole life," a Native radio commentator from New York once said. "He lives on the water. He knows the earth. If the fish can't live, we can't live. It's that simple."

Introduction

Billy Frank Jr. is a fisherman, and when he dies he hopes that's how history remembers him. He is not a casual angler who passes sunny afternoons away in search of tall tales and kings. Fishing is part of Billy's DNA. It dominates his history. It defines his future. Billy has a visceral need to protect salmon and scars to show for his trouble. In a society fascinated by advancing technology, Billy will take you back to nature. He will show you the great rivers where the salmon run, and he will tell you the story of his mysterious fish.

In fact, Billy's entire life is rooted in a war over the fish, brutal clashes that reached a fever pitch in the 1960s and 1970s. Havoc on the water aroused the attention of the country. Some even called it the great fish war of the Northwest.

The great fish war did not deal only with salmon. While the state of Washington called the crackdown on Indian fishing conservation, Indians called it racism and an abrogation of a treaty. To Native Americans, fishing is a sovereign right. They ceded land to the U.S. government, but they never gave up their right to the fish. They reserved this right in a treaty and depended on the promise made by Isaac Stevens, superintendent of Indian Affairs: "I will write it down in the treaty that you and your people have the right to take fish at these old fishing places, and I pledge the Americans to keep this promise as long as the mountains stand, as long as the sun shines, and as long as the rivers run."

Whites questioned rights that allowed Indians to fish in ways they couldn't. They scornfully labeled Native Americans "super citizens" and accused them of destroying the runs. The feud on the riverbank raised powerful questions about the definition of Indian treaties and promises between nations.

DECADES AGO, in a far different America, a federal Indian movement swept the country. Unknown fishermen held up their treaties and took a stand. One was a Nisqually Indian named Billy Frank. "I wasn't the Billy Frank that I am now," the Nisqually tribal leader told reporters in 1984. "I was a bitter person." Says friend Tom Keefe, "When I look at Billy Frank, and I guess I know more about him than most people, I can say there is a guy who decided that he could change the world by changing himself."

AT EIGHTY-ONE YEARS OLD, Billy wears his long gray hair in a ponytail and carries a message of perseverance around the world. Leaders of every persuasion hear the story of the Indians from an Indian who knows. "My people are still here!" he tells them again and again and again.

Billy is a onetime hell-raising Nisqually Indian and a present-day statesman. Old stereotypes that branded Indian people as lazy, ruthless savages seem preposterous when you meet Billy. The hardworking elder has made bridge building with dissenters an art. At the height of the fish wars, with battle lines drawn between the state and Indian fishermen, a staffer for then-Governor Dan Evans pronounced Billy as "friendly as an old shoe."

Billy's prolific family tree is filled with leaders, and he has lived his life following in their footsteps. He stands when he speaks, just like his father. "We've got to get together," friend George Walter demonstrates at an Olympia coffee shop with his arms encircled. "This is the gesture when he approaches you, and it's also his gesture for the world."

With Billy, the analogies never end. He's like a mammoth cedar tree with roots that spread far and wide. He's like the Pacific salmon, because he survives, returning, without fail, to the river that has marked his life.

Real life handed Billy jail sentences for exercising his treaty rights, but no monumental chip weighs him down. He could have retreated behind the walls of his Indian tribe, but he spoke out. He could have brooded in an 8 x 10 jail cell, but he found humor instead. Behind bars so often he earned a promotion to jail barber, Billy quipped: "I don't know if I'm getting better or worse [at cutting hair] but I don't think I'll run out of customers."

Billy is the youngest child of a vigilant mother who taught him to respect women. He is the son of a Nisqually elder who taught him the story of his people.

Should you talk salmon or treaty rights, warns Charles Wilkinson, a long-time friend, don't underestimate the hard edge of Billy Frank. "You can't understand Billy by just thinking of him as a hail fellow well met that everybody loves. He also can be one tough son of a bitch when salmon are involved and Indian rights are involved. And that's part of his greatness."

BILLY IS ALSO FAMOUS for his salty tongue. "I don't know if you remember where you were on your 75th birthday, do you?" Christine Gregoire, governor of Washington, eyes Billy before a thundering crowd. "I do. You were in my office, pestering me about something, complaining about something. I actually don't remember what that was, because it's not all that infrequent. But you were in rare form that day. I'm told that on the way out of the office someone—who will remain nameless—had two comments. He said, 'That was an amazing meeting. I think you may actually have changed her mind.' Billy smiled and said, 'You win one every once in a while.' Then the friend said, 'But the really amazing thing was that you spent 45 minutes arguing with the governor and didn't cuss once!'

"'Goddamn it. I didn't, did I?'"

It is often said that Billy's last name describes his attitude, and that day in the governor's office, the straight-shooting Nisqually lived up to his reputation. "I want respect for my people. I want respect for our culture. I want respect for our natural resources."

For all the complexities that surround Billy's life work, his guiding philosophy is simple: live in balance with the earth; there are consequences for tampering with nature. Tell the truth, even if there's nothing more difficult. Treat people with dignity, including your enemies.

Billy's passion is the work of many lifetimes. His journey has been slow going, tough going, and sometimes, not going at all. "They're always coming after me," Billy says of critics. Squabbles are so common in Indian Country that sometimes even the courts throw up their hands at the infighting. In the 1960s, Nisqually leaders labeled Billy a renegade. "He was ostracized by his own tribe and that just made him tougher than the dickens," says Guy McMinds, a Quinault tribal leader. Sometimes, Billy is begrudged for getting *too* much credit.

The history between the smoke shop owned by Billy's family and the Nisqually Tribe is long and difficult. "There may never be peace," says family. "There's some people that don't support him," acknowledges Zelma McCloud, onetime Nisqually chairwoman, "but not that many. He'll go down in history . . . like our Chief Leschi." To this day, opponents in a landmark court opinion over fishing rights claim the sweeping decision tipped the scales too far toward the Indians.

BILLY IS A MASTER of forgiveness. "Dad never did want to go around and start trouble," says Sugar, Billy's oldest son. "He always tried to settle it. . . . He's strong. He can have people yell and scream and call him all kinds of names and he just smiles and walks away." "It doesn't matter how people treat him," agrees Willie, Billy's youngest child. "He's always going to treat them with respect."

Even so, Tom Keefe says Billy understands the anger that many Indian people hold. "There's a side of Billy that, when the doors are closed and it's just Indian people there, I am reliably informed he is capable of articulating the anger and the bitterness that resulted from years of oppression by state authorities. But I don't think it dominates his life or has dominated his life. I've seen him really grow as a person, like you would hope any person would be capable of doing if they set their mind to it."

The elder takes the good and bad in stride. His role as the consummate bridge builder has taken him from a concrete bunk at the Pierce County jail to a public stage where he accepted the Albert E. Schweitzer Prize for Humanitarianism, an honor bestowed on the likes of Jimmy Carter, the president, and Desmond Tutu, the archbishop. The onetime underdog has crisscrossed the globe in defense of Indian people and earth. His footprint can be found from the halls of Congress to Alaska's Prince William Sound, where Billy helped tribes recover from the *Exxon Valdez* oil spill.

"The fight is never over—the fight for who we are and our culture and our way of life," he says as his dark eyes light up. He clenches his fists. He smiles at the thought of his indigenous brothers in Alaska and across the world rattling the cage. Billy has been rattling cages since he was fourteen years old.

How did he do it? Therein lies an extraordinary and controversial tale of courage, determination, and a guiding belief that it takes a village to move history.

Willie Frank Sr.

Chapter 1

Spirit of the Father

Gramps found himself on the witness stand and he must have been 103 years old. He wore his trademark Native vest and no shoes. Thick socks covered his feet. Willie Frank Sr.'s hair, snow white and somewhat askew, topped a slender frame. Deep lines etched across his face revealed a lifetime on the river. His mouth curved inward. His brows furrowed. His intense eyes held stories and secrets. Any Indian worth his salt knew Gramps. Many people called him the last full-blooded Nisqually alive.

"If this Nisqually elder can't go to the court, the court will go to him!" Stephen Grossman was insistent. The administrative law judge presided over court that day to hear Gramps's words himself. It meant abandoning the formal courtroom and traveling south to Gramps's home, a legendary place known as Frank's Landing. Court came to order as the Nisqually River rushed below the foothills of Mount Rainier, cutting a jagged line for eighty-one miles before pouring into Puget Sound. The temperature crept upward. It was a warm August day in 1982. "This hearing is being held at Frank's Landing in the home of Mr. Willie Frank Sr. to accommodate the witness, the reason for which will become obvious on the record," Grossman announced.

The elder sat on the de facto witness stand—a favorite wooden chair—flanked by lawyers, a court reporter, and the judge. Gramps defied his years and sat straight as a rail. Discomfort may have accounted for his stiff posture. The elder never did trust the whites. He often fell silent in their presence. "He used to laugh that they carried their brains in their pockets. If they had to remember something, they took out some paper to look it up first," recalled Susan Hvalsoe Komori, a former attorney for the Nisqually Tribe.

There aren't many who would maintain the wherewithal to testify at 103 years of age, and even fewer with the gravitas to sway a judge. But Gramps possessed both. His opinion on the matter at hand meant something to the judge. At two city dams on the Nisqually River, salmon and steelhead were dying in the sharp turbines, steep climbs, and powerful water surges.

Facing a dwindling fishery, the Nisqually Tribe sued the city of Tacoma for past damages and changes to federal license requirements; it sued the city of Centralia in order to place the city dam under federal regulation. To convince Grossman, the Nisqually Tribe had to prove the river was historically navigable and vital to its people. Gramps, born about ten years before Washington became a state, was called to the stand. He had lived his whole life on the banks of the Nisqually. In his elder's voice, he would joke, "Me and the river are the oldest things around here, I guess. The river was here a long time before I came, and it'll be here a long time after I'm gone." As the court reporter tried desperately to decipher an unfamiliar speech pattern, Gramps weighed his words deftly, sometimes drifting into Nisqually dialect. Frequently, he tilted his head back and closed his eyes, as if flashing through the years. A rush of memories came. "You could watch his face as he talked and feel as though you could almost see what he was describing, as he was obviously seeing it again himself," Hvalsoe Komori recalled.

Gramps was a born storyteller revered across Indian Country. His powerful tales lingered in the mind and traditionally included far more than the navigability of the river. As Gramps spoke, you could see his Nisqually ancestors crossing snow-capped mountains

HARRY BENSON

Willie Frank Sr. rocks granddaughter Merita Miguel, fifteen months, in this image for Life *magazine taken by world renowned photographer Harry Benson. "[He] reached back almost to treaty times and brought forth so much in the character, and the history, and the mentality of the Salish Indian people," says family friend Hank Adams.*

and erecting villages in the shadow of Tahoma (Tacobet), the massive volcano non-Indians call Mount Rainier. You could find them rejoicing in the salmon, the mystifying fish that braved a precarious path to sea and faithfully returned.

WHEN THE FIRST SALMON came home to spawn, drum beats echoed across the riverbank. The Nisqually praised the spirits. Children arrayed with red ocher and bird down gathered at the water's edge.

Outstretched arms passed the first salmon up the riverbank to a crackling fire pit. Practiced hands painstakingly separated flesh from the spinal column. The meat, secured to skewers, cooked high above a steadily burning fire. A mix of cedar and smoke wafted through the air. The intricacies of the ceremony are recalled in *Uncommon Controversy: Fishing Rights of the Muckleshoot, Puyallup, and Nisqually Indians*: "It is then parceled out to all, in small morsels or portions so all can participate. Doing this, all bones are saved intact. Then in a torchbearing, dancing, chanting, and singing procession, they proceeded to the river where they cast the skeleton of the salmon into the stream with its head pointing upstream, symbolic of a spawning salmon, so the run of salmon will return a thousand-fold." The salmon blanketed the river upon their return from the sea. There were so many fish, the Nisqually could cross the river on their backs.

But a quarter century before Gramps was born, thunderous storm clouds gathered. The bright light of the Nisqually way of life dimmed. Gramps felt that he was there watching through the thick trees. That's how often his father told him the story.

GRAY SKIES SETTLED OVERHEAD and held the region in its predictably drizzly state. Isaac Stevens—fiery, smart, and full of zeal—prepared for an unprecedented land deal.

At thirty-five, Stevens had survived a harrowing past. Born the third child of seven, he was so fragile as an infant that his parents feared he might not survive. Mild pituitary dwarfism accounted for his large head and his shorter legs. Stevens stood roughly five feet tall. His keen intelligence complemented his commanding presence. Stevens had graduated first in his class at the U.S. Military Academy at West Point. President Franklin Pierce rewarded Stevens for his political support by appointing him Washington territorial governor and superintendent of Indian Affairs. The Massachusetts-born Stevens had never before set foot in Washington, nor had he acquired much knowledge of Northwest Indian tribes. But he never lacked for ambition.

Stevens neared Nisqually Country on an errand for the U.S. government in the winter of 1854. Enticed by the Donation Land Act and its promise of 320 acres for white men, non-Indians had been encroaching on Indian land. Stevens had come to do away with Indian ownership and open the West to American settlers.

Smoke from burning fires hung in the air at the council ground at Medicine Creek. Bands and tribes, including the Puyallup, Nisqually, Steilacoom, and Squaxin, greeted the visitors in anticipation of lavish gifts and a great feast. When the Indian leaders were presented instead with molasses and tobacco, they were taken aback.

Council convened. Benjamin Shaw read the treaty terms in Chinook Jargon, a nineteenth-century trade language with a vocabulary of three hundred words. The Indians would be paid for their land and moved to reservations. They would maintain their fishing rights, however, in usual and accustomed places, even those located outside reservation boundaries. It is highly unlikely the Indians understood what Stevens proposed. While whites sought prized acreage in the name of the United States, the tribes valued their hunting and fishing rights. They wanted to live freely on their land, as they had for thousands of years.

The meeting broke for the night, and by the next day, December 26, 1854, the deal was done. Sixty-two leaders signed the Treaty of Medicine Creek (or She-Nah-Num), the first in a series of agreements ceding Indian land in present-day Washington to the United States. The Treaty of Medicine Creek was subsequently ratified by Congress on March 3, 1855.

Assessments of Stevens's character run the gamut, from a dedicated soldier carrying out the wishes of his government to "a man who would stoop to any method to accomplish his objectives, with his ambitions overcoming all scruples." History would later dub Stevens a "young man in a hurry" for his fast-paced excursions across the territory. At the close of his treaty negotiations with Pacific Northwest tribes, the governor's real estate deals on behalf of the United States, totaled sixty-four million acres. He had brokered ten treaties in all, including three made jointly with Joel Palmer, the Oregon superintendent of Indian Affairs. The new Nisqually Reservation encompassed roughly 1,280 acres of rock and timber, unlike the grassland at the river's edge where the Nisqually people had always lived.

"Whatever these chiefs did during that day, they protected the fishing," says Georgiana Kautz, a Nisqually Indian. "They protected the hunting, the gathering rights, the shellfish. All of these things they knew in 1855. I think they were amazing, you know. They really were." Stevens had a script in hand and stuck to it, charges attorney Charles Wilkinson: "The United States not only got the land, they got it without a war."

"You have Governor Stevens stating and submitting the treaty [to Congress] for ratification," says historian Hank Adams, "informing the United States that the Indians catch most of our fish, as well as clams and oysters. This represents the part they play and ought to play in the labor and prosperity of the territory."

The negotiations would prove a source of continuous debate through the ages. How much did the tribes truly understand? Did Nisqually warrior Leschi actually sign the treaty?

Unhappiness spread across Indian Country. Peace between whites and Indians crumbled. Word spread that Leschi was "stirring up trouble with other Indians." Stevens offered fifty blankets to "any Indian who could lead him to Chief Leschi." The superintendent got his wish. Leschi's nephew, Sluggia, duped the leader into surrendering. He misled the chief into thinking whites were ready to talk peace. The nephew paid for his betrayal. In 1857, Wa He Lut, a Leschi warrior, got even. He shot Sluggia and pushed his body off a cliff.

In November 1856, Leschi's brother, Quiemuth, grew tired of fighting the whites. He asked James Longmire, a pioneer, to take him to Governor Stevens. Quiemuth surrendered and sat in the governor's living quarters awaiting jail at Fort Steilacoom the next day. Dawn broke in a morning chill and evidence of the battle clung to his shoes. As Quiemuth sat by a crackling fire, Stevens retired to bed.

The sound of a gunshot soon cut through the air.

"I saw by the dim firelight a man fall and heard a deep groan," stated Longmire. "I ran to the falling man and found it was Quiemuth, speechless and dying. At this moment the governor rushed in, saying as he saw the dead chief: 'Who in — has done this?' I replied I did not know." Quiemuth's body was sprawled across the carpeted floor of the governor's office with a gunshot wound. A fine blade pierced his chest. The alleged killer, Joseph Bunting, was arrested, but let go due to "insufficient evidence."

More than a year later, Chief Leschi appeared emaciated and ill. Two members of the territorial militia, Joseph Miles and A. Benton Moses, had died during the Indian wars, in a swamp in 1855. Prosecutors charged Leschi with the murder of Moses. Leschi "with malice aforethought . . . did discharge and shoot off his gun" at Moses, attorneys said. After two trials, Washington Territory prepared to execute Leschi. As he took his last breath at the gallows before three hundred people, the Nisqually Indian proclaimed his innocence: "I went to war because I believed that the Indians had been wronged by the white men . . . I deny that I had any part in killing Miles and Moses . . . I did not see Miles or Moses before or after they were dead, but was told by the Indians that they had been killed. As God sees me, this is the truth."

"I felt then that I was hanging an innocent man and I believe it yet," wrote executioner Charles Grainger. The former British sailor treated Leschi fairly and won his respect. At the hanging, Leschi spoke highly of Grainger, and no one else.

Outraged by the conviction and execution of Leschi, the Nisqually inscribed on the monument at his gravesite, "Leschi, Chief of the Nisquallies, Martyr to Vengeance of the Unforgiving White Man was Hanged 300 yards S.E. from Here Feb. 19, 1858."

THE INDIAN WARS had ended, but conflict remained. The lucrative fishing industry attracted non-Indians to Washington rivers. Eventually, fish wheels, traps, and canneries dotted the landscape. The first cannery on Puget Sound opened in 1877. The industry was a businessman's dream—every dollar invested in a Puget Sound fish trap returned $2.50. By the 1870s, however, the great fish runs of the Northwest started to diminish. Statehood brought fishing regulations and a commercial licensing system to apply uniformly to all off-reservation fishermen. By the 1890s, the state banned weirs, required a license for off-reservation fishing, and closed rivers to salmon fishing at usual and accustomed fishing grounds of the Indians. "A salmon bound for its native stream was much more likely to end up packed in a can before it could reach the nets of the Indians or its birthplace," writes Faye Cohen in *Treaties on Trial*. Salmon-rich waters of the Northwest were losing their fish.

The assumption in 1854, that the salmon-rich Northwest could never become salmon-poor, proved dangerously incorrect in time. Demand for salmon and friction between Indians and non-Indians sent treaty fishing rights to the U.S. Supreme Court seven times in seventy years. The origin of those court battles was language in the Treaty of Medicine Creek brokered on the delta in 1854.

AMONG THE MANY MYSTERIES of Indian Country is the exact birth date of Gramps. Not that it matters much. The Nisqually Indian provided far more answers than questions. His body of knowledge predated statehood. Over the course of his 104 years, the Wright brothers invented the airplane, Americans explored their first personal computers, and the once strong runs of Pacific salmon landed on the Endangered Species List. Gramps had seen it all, and he could tell you how it used to be.

Sometime in 1879, Gramps was born Qu-lash-qud in the village of Yell-Whahlse. The former home of Chief Leschi sat on the south side of Muck Creek prairie, roughly eight miles from the mouth of the tributary. Throughout history, Indians had speared and trapped their fish along the creek. Well into his later years, Gramps remembered the mix of forest, wetland, and prairie grass that dominated his childhood. He remembered Muck Creek in the old days. "This, ah salmon, he comes up the river once every four years and they come up just by the thousands, white man call them humpback salmon; well, the Indian call them hadu, and they just fill the river to spawn. Then they seem to die, after they spawn they die, yeh. The only salmon that went back out was the steelhead; he never die, he went back out to the ocean, I guess, wherever he came from."

Qu-lash-qud was raised by his father; his mother, Sarah Martin, died when he was young. Qu-lash-qud and his remaining family shared a longhouse with four other families. It had a dirt floor and an open fire. Ferns in his sleeping bunk kept him warm. The young lad lived off the river and the land, getting his fill of fish, huckleberries, and other fruit.

Qu-lash-qud watched the women bake bread over an open fire. They maneuvered sticks to hang salmon from the roof. The fish dangled there, above a smoldering fire, for days at a time. In a week or so, heat from the stoked fire dried the salmon to the bone. The women sent Qu-lash-qud off to the river. He tied the fish to a bale of hay and left them to soak overnight. By dawn, the salmon were so soft you could eat them without teeth.

When he wasn't soaking salmon, Qu-lash-qud often stood behind his father, Kluck-et-sah, on a galloping horse. They'd ride together up and down the winding trails around Puget Sound, disappearing into clusters of dense trees. His father also taught him to fish. They'd climb into a shovel-nose canoe and drift for miles, scooping up the salmon.

At Thanksgiving, they shared feasts. "All the creeks were just full of fish," Qu-lash-qud told a filmmaker, Carol Burns, years later. "Every year they come up to spawn, and on Thanksgiving we all lived up on the prairies and we'd come down and camp on a creek and build a fire and catch the biggest dog salmon and bake them Indian style with the stick and we'd have our Thanksgiving dinner."

With his mother gone, Qu-lash-qud looked to his Aunt Sally as a female mentor. He called her Grandmother. One day, Qu-lash-qud and his friend drummed and played where the elders gathered to pray. The boys started to feel sick. "We don't feel good," they complained

NISQUALLY TRIBE ARCHIVES

After the death of his mother, Sally Jackson became a maternal figure to Billy's father, Willie Frank Sr.

to Grandmother. "Don't know what's wrong with us." "You're down there making fun . . . where we pray down there," Grandmother scolded. "We got these sticks that are powerful. You guys are down there and you're making fun . . . that's why you don't feel good."

Qu-lash-qud was just a kid the first time he spied a white man. A group of whites "menacingly approached" the longhouse and ransacked the place while the boy watched through a crack in a rain barrel. The memory of the armed horsemen never left his mind. "Gramps would sometimes have fears and he'd relate back to raids against Indians when he was a little boy," Hank Adams recalls. "White marauders would come in with guns and be threatening Indians, or beating Indians. He'd talk about hiding under barrels and hiding under different things. This would be in the 1880s and 1890s."

Throughout his life, Qu-lash-qud told chilling stories of disease ravaging the Indian people. "Let me tell you about this one—what I heard. A ship come here on Puget Sound and the ship was throwing brand new blankets, suit of clothes, underwear and the Indians on the shore got in their canoes and went and got all that stuff. And brought them ashore. And come to find out all those clothes and blankets were smallpox. The ship had smallpox. And so all the Indians got smallpox, from the mouth of the river to La Grande. They all died off. Smallpox killed them all. See when I come to, there was just a few Indians. I'd say just about 300 living on the reservation."

The staggering losses drove many to drink, writes Norman Clark in *The Dry Years: Prohibition and Social Change in Washington*: "In their sorrow . . . the Indians finally reached for the bottle of rum which the fur traders had been offering them. In the white man's liquor they found a source of ecstasy and release from their grief." "Pretty soon American come over in wagon trains and they had bad whiskey," said Qu-lash-qud. "Indians now fight and kill each other after they had bad whiskey American brought over."

THE FREE EDUCATION promised in the Treaty of Medicine Creek, in fact, carried a price. American Indian boarding schools opened to throngs of supporters who hailed them as a means of survival, and legions of critics who denounced them as cultural genocide. Richard Pratt, founder of the first off-reservation boarding school, at Carlisle, Pennsylvania, unapologetically avowed, "A great general has said that the only good Indian is a dead one. . . . In a sense, I agree with the sentiment, but only in this: that all the Indian there is in the race should be dead. Kill the Indian in him, and save the man." Pratt set out to kill the Indian by teaching Indians to be white. Uprooted from homes and taken from their reservations, Indian children bore the brunt of a profound culture clash. They were silenced from speaking their Native tongue and urged to worship an unknown god.

Along with schoolwork, teachers handed out new names. Most came from American politicians and did not reflect Indian history or heritage. "At Fort Peck, we had a Grover Cleveland. We had the Thomas Jeffersons. We had George Washingtons and we had John Adams. And these are all new names," recalls Hank Adams. In fact, Adams himself is an Assiniboine-Sioux from Montana, the great-grandson of Digs the Ground, an Indian renamed John Adams in boarding school.

One day a granduncle took Qu-lash-qud by the hand to St. George's Industrial School for Indians, a Catholic boarding school located in Milton. Qu-lash-qud was told to take the Indian out of everything, except the color of his skin. He dressed like a white man. He cut his hair short like a white man's. His teachers gave him a white man's name. Willie Frank rolled right off the tongue, and it was a logical choice. His father, Kluck-et-sah, shoed horses for a white man named Frank. Then and there Qu-lash-qud ceased to exist. He was Willie Frank.

BILLY FRANK JR. PERSONAL COLLECTION

Forced to cut his hair, silence his tongue, and learn the American way, Willie Frank Sr. took up the big horn at boarding school and played the "Star-Spangled Banner." Seated, middle row, fourth from left.

AT BOARDING SCHOOL, Willie Frank even learned about the whites' God and their heaven. "If you die, you go to the great place that's got everything," his teachers told him. The religion never made much sense to Willie. He already lived in paradise. The mountain fed the river. The river and the land fed his people. Every year, the salmon returned, darting upriver to spawn. And Willie was alive. No. He didn't need the whites' faith. "The Indian, he don't believe in the God, white man's God," Willie often said. "He believed in the Great Spirit, that's what [Indians] called what they believed in, the Great Spirit, some kind of spirit."

One day Willie's trousers split from the crotch to the bottom of the pant leg. That was the end of St. George's Industrial School for him. "I'd go to the seamstress three times and she had no time to sew my pants. So, the third time I told some of the boys I was going to run away." "He had his family. He had the village on Muck Creek. He wanted to be home," Adams says.

Incensed and unafraid, Willie and two classmates struck out down a trail to the Puyallup Valley, on a journey that would take them forty miles. They hopped a fence in Hillhurst and slept under the cover of trees. "This other boy and I kept going," Willie explained. "I had an aunt that lived up this little creek. We stayed there overnight. At that time, my father had already gone up to St. George School to see me." But by the time Kluck-et-sah arrived, Willie and his classmates were long gone.

One night, Willie woke in a sleepy haze and saw his granduncle riding by, singing. "He had other Indians with him passing by on horseback. I woke up. I just had a dream."

As they neared home, Willie and his friend heard the roosters crow, and they took off running. "I stayed all winter. It must have been the fall of the year," Willie recalled. "The other boy stayed with us, Mike Leschi. His folks lived in Tenino. Later his father came and got him."

After a short-lived respite at home, Granduncle Henry took Willie to the Cushman Indian School on the Puyallup Indian Reservation. "This was not a Catholic school. This was where I used to get a licking for talking Indian. I couldn't talk English. I must have never learned nothing at St. George. When I got into this other school, I kept talking to the other boys in Indian and they'd go and tell on me. 'You're not allowed to talk Indian in this school! All boys get a whipping if they talk Indian!'"

Willie quickly learned to read a white newspaper. In fact, he learned English so well he started to forget his Native tongue.

School administrators sent the boys to bed at 9:00 in the evening. A few of them sneaked out at night. Willie went once. He and his buddies crept out of their rooms and crawled through a window to sneak from school grounds. A Japanese man owned a restaurant nearby where you could get a decent meal for a quarter. "The restaurant had a lot of little booths, and when you sat down they pulled a curtain around your table. It was really something," Willie recalled.

The growing Nisqually even took up the big horn in the school band. He was the spitting image of every other member. Their identical uniforms buttoned to the neck. Their traditionally long hair rested just above the ears. In pictures, they wore the same impassive look. The school band of Indian children routinely played the reservations, blaring, incredibly, America's national anthem.

During his last stretch at school, administrators made Willie Frank a cop. He pocketed twenty-five dollars a month carting meals to "inmates." "These were schoolboys and they had a jail there where they kept the bad boys who ran away to town or something like that. I was about twenty-two years old when I left school. I was a full grown man. I must have been there for eleven or twelve years."

"When they put my grandpa in that BIA school, what did it take from us?" asked Alison Bridges. "What did that do? . . . He was stripped of his culture. He was stripped of self-esteem. Coping skills, social skills. . . . And that's what happened to Indians."

Just after the turn of the twentieth century, Willie closed the doors on life at Cushman.

LIFE WENT ON while Willie was away. All of his parental figures and grandparents died during his time at Cushman—most notably Aunt Sally in 1895 and his father in 1896. Willie returned to Muck Creek to live with a granduncle. He picked hops. He tended to elders, the sick, and the homeless. On Sundays, the community held horse races. There were two racetracks on one side of the prairie and one racetrack on the other. The Indians played slahal, an ancient bluffing game in which teams try to identify marked deer bones hidden in players' hands. "*Slahal* went on and they had a card game they called monte," Willie recalled. "The men and women would play monte and slahal and the whole gang would have horse racing."

Mostly, Willie fished. He'd catch his salmon in the Nisqually River and haul his fish into town in one of Henry Ford's Model Ts that put

Gramps (Willie Frank Sr.) in the hop fields at Roy, Washington. His Aunt Sally Jackson and sister Lizzie Frank John appear at his side.

America on wheels. One day in 1916, however, authorities hauled Willie into town. They accused him of unlawful salmon fishing. For Willie, the event marked the first episode in a sixty-six-year struggle for treaty fishing rights.

AT THE CUSP of America's entrance into World War I, a couple of businessmen propositioned the U.S. War Department with plans for a military base across a swath of prairie land near Tacoma, Pierce County. By an eight-to-one margin, local voters approved the necessary two million dollars in bonds to gift the land to the U.S. and build Camp Lewis on roughly seventy thousand acres. A. V. Fawcett, then mayor of Tacoma, hyperbolically predicted, "Tacoma, the City of Destiny, is now ready to establish that destiny as a world power." Camp Lewis included private lands and two-thirds of the Nisqually Indian Reservation east of the river. It included the home of Willie Frank.

Because reservation land is held in trust with the federal government, it requires congressional approval to be condemned. Nevertheless, plans for nearly eight hundred buildings and sixty thousand men marched forward in the spirit of war. Non-Indians and Indians alike were uprooted from their homes. The whites came to see Willie and several dozen families who lived on allotments. They showed up out of nowhere one night on his family's 205 acres at Muck Creek, and then unloaded Indians into a shanty town: "Indian, he had to move out. . . . They brought the Army trucks from Fort Lewis and unloaded these old people and hauled them over on this side of the river, Thurston County side; unloaded them under the great big fir trees; got long limbs to stick out, and unloaded these old people under that tree."

The fast-paced condemnation of the Nisqually Reservation stirred up interest in Congress. Although a 1920 report urged the government to return acreage to the Nisqually Tribe, Indians never reclaimed their homeland. In 1921, the Committee on Indian Affairs revealed that Pierce County had begun condemnation proceedings without the express knowledge of the Department of the Interior: "The records show that, unknown to the department, proceedings were instituted early in 1918 by the authorities of Pierce County, Wash., to condemn approximately 3,300 acres of allotted Indian land on the Nisqually Reservation for the purpose of turning the same over to the U.S. government for the use of the War Department in enlarging its activities at Camp Lewis."

Further, the committee concluded, "The ambition of Tacoma to acquire one of the Army posts, and the war necessity, caused Pierce County, Washington, in April, 1918 to condemn the best two-thirds of the Nisqually Reservation, being the part east of the Nisqually [River] where most of the Nisqually homes were. The Indians were scattered to seek homes elsewhere. Such is the fate of the little band whose fathers fought against an unjust treaty to make secure their homes."

Allottees were paid only $75,840 for the land. The committee proposed a second payment of another $85,000 to twenty-five families on the Nisqually Reservation. The payment compensated for loss of land, treaty rights, and the removal of Indian bodies from five reservation graveyards that were located on the condemned land. The families received their money. "Congress appropriated more money," says George Walter, a longtime employee of the Nisqually Tribe. "Congress never really explicitly approved the condemnation, but they did implicitly approve a condemnation by saying that the compensation was inadequate and appropriating funds for compensation. So the Indian reservation still exists."

"When they condemned our reservation for Fort Lewis and sent us across the river to become farmers they didn't only condemn the land," explains Georgiana Kautz, a feisty Nisqually and former tribal chair who grew up in hard times on the reservation. "They condemned the people and the language and the ceremonies . . . and the Bureau [of Indian Affairs] stood there and didn't do a damn thing about it. No one did. We never got running water or electricity 'til '69."

THE CONDEMNATION left Willie with eight thousand dollars in his pocket. Eventually, he used some of the money to buy more than six acres of land on the lower Nisqually River, downstream from the reservation and near the Tacoma-Olympia paved highway. "Ah, this is only land I could buy in the valley," Willie recalled, ". . . got cheapest land; six acres cost me a thousand dollars. We got eight thousand dollars for our land; 205 acres we had." The investment became a legacy. Over time, Willie's six acres became one of the most talked-about places in Puget Sound. "Never have to pay any tax on it," Willie always said. "Just like the reservation . . . I built a nice little house."

FOR WILLIE, the hardships kept right on coming. He'd married twice already and shortly after moving to his enclave, he buried his third wife, Josephine Pope. Pneumonia killed her in 1923. Three years after Josephine's death, Willie lost his younger sister, forty-year-old Lizzie John.

WHITES CAME FOR WILLIE again in 1936. They caught him fishing off the reservation without a license. "You can't fish the river with a net, Willie Frank. It's against the law," whites had hollered at Willie. They routinely crept along the riverbank at dusk, pushing tree branches out of the way and peering through the brush for Indians who dared to fish.

"Well, maybe so, but I've got a treaty. . . . The Treaty of Medicine Creek in 1854 with my people. . . . I'm Willie Frank, Nisqually Allottee No. 89." Throughout his lifetime, Nisqually Allottee No. 89 watched as authorities arrested and interrogated his family. He later recalled a warden telling him, "Your treaty isn't worth the paper it's printed on." Each time officers dragged someone he loved up the river-bank in handcuffs, Willie knew why. The traditions of the American Indian collided with the whites. "They got beat up, locked up, berated and belittled physically and verbally, inside and out," says Hvalsoe Komori.

In 1937, Willie got his day in court. He secured an injunction to keep the state away from Indian fishermen. "That was the time that he started fighting for the river," says family. "And he got into federal court, and got an injunction." The injunction held through 1944.

Through the years, Willie kept right on fighting. "From the days of his adolescence when he fished, and worked in the woods and the hop fields, he labored for all Indian people, particularly young people. . . . People who come into Frank's Landing would gain strength to take into the world," Hank Adams says.

Eventually, rheumatism got the best of Willie's hands. In 1954, he caught his very last fish. His legs grew too stiff for the canoe, the water too cold for his hands. His eyes dimmed with age. "I don't see too good now," Willie explained. "I walked right off the end of my darn canoe. I knew it was time to quit."

He may have stopped pulling net, but Willie walked around with a cane tapping on the trees so they knew he was still there. He never did run out of steam. He never gave up on the Nisqually River that springs from the southern side of Tahoma. He never gave up on the salmon. He never gave up on the Treaty of Medicine Creek that protected his way of life. Deep down, underneath the skin of the Nisqually Indian, Willie Frank was a warrior. That's how the elder wound up on the witness stand at the age of 103. His history made him a legend, Gramps to all in his presence.

The case officially ended with Judge Grossman's termination order in 1993, ten years after Gramps's death. Grossman ruled in favor of the Indian people, observing the powerful link between Gramps and his son: "Mr. Frank recalled the river's former majesty and importance to the Nisqually Tribe and eloquently expressed his desire for restoration of that irreplaceable resource. . . . His spirit and vision, however, live on in his son, Billy Frank Jr."

By all accounts, Gramps's fight for the Indians of Puget Sound was in fact too intense and too long for a single lifetime. He bottled his passion for the Indian way and passed it on.

As the legend holds, every fifty years or so, a violent storm ravages Indian Country near the southernmost tip of Puget Sound, where the salmon run. Out of the ashes a Nisqually Indian appears, a baby boy bearing the name William Frank. If the tale has any truth, March 9, 1931, doubtlessly saw a record-breaker of immense proportions. The date marks the birth of an unparalleled warrior. His name is Kluck-et-sah, but most people just call him Billy.

Chapter 2

"I Live Here!"

Billy Frank Jr. took his first breath on March 9, 1931, six days after President Herbert Hoover signed "The Star-Spangled Banner" into law as the national anthem. One day, Billy would defend his country; then he'd spend a lifetime challenging the nation to rise to its ideals.

The Nisqually Indian grew up in a small house on the river, not far from the historic Medicine Creek Treaty council grounds. Most people wouldn't have called the Franks rich, but Billy's father often said they had everything and more outside their back window. "When the tide is out, the table is set." The Nisqually River meandered through Billy's backyard, fanning out over the land and flowing into Puget Sound. Nearby, fishermen landed canoes and loaded salmon onto scales, exchanging stories and laughs.

The town of Nisqually was small, "a couple of gas stations and a tavern," recalls Herman Dillon, a longtime family friend. The future chairman of the Puyallup Tribe of Indians met Billy sometime between sliding into first base and plunging into the river. "You'd think we were a couple of monkeys climbing trees," Dillon jokes. They played a lot of baseball. They spent even more time on the river. And they fished.

Most of Billy's indelible childhood memories are set in the natural world. He grew up a fisherman, like his ancestors. On the same river,

Billy (left) and Melvin Iyall with Willie Frank Sr.

in much the same manner, he made a clean incision straight down the belly of the salmon, removing its insides and slime. "We'd clean 'em and smoke 'em until they're dry," Billy remembers. "Mom and Dad, you know, they were smoking fish all the time. The salmon is an important part of us—who we are."

Billy never depended on a calendar. Nature tracked time. As surely as the rain poured down on Seattle, the salmon returned and proclaimed the coming of fall. In December, the late-running chum raced to spawning grounds after three or four years out at sea. You could always spot chum, known as dog salmon for their canine-like teeth.

Long before he walked to a one-room schoolhouse, Billy became a student of nature. He learned the life cycles of the different species of salmon. Salmon are resilient to be sure. But they depend on intricacies of nature to survive. The temperature and health of the water, the force of its flows, and the state of gravel beds all take part in creating the delicate habitat of the fish.

Billy learned the Nisqually River, the way it meanders across the heartland and changes course through the years. He swam every stretch of that river growing up. "The river moves. Our river isn't like the Puyallup River. . . . Our river moves across that valley and back and forth. One year you'll have a place to set net and the next you won't have a place to set." He learned the importance of medicinal plants like Oregon grapes, wild cherry, and prince's pine, an evergreen plant that relieves stomach pain when it's dried.

Early on, Tahoma (or Rainier), the great water source of the Nisqually watershed, mesmerized Billy. He relished the sight of the icicles that dangle like daggers inside the mountain's ice caves. "Oh, God almighty. You know, we pray to the mountain every day. We wake up and pray to the mountain. It was a wonder of the world. It's just this magical place that the Nisqually River comes from. And water is still coming out."

Billy caught his first salmon at age eleven and the nuances of fishing passed down another generation. "My dad always told me to prepare for the salmon coming back. Don't get caught in a hurry. Have it done in advance. He told me about a guy cutting a net in the dark and stabbing himself in the stomach. 'Don't be like that,' he told me."

A lifetime on the river taught him the techniques of an expert fisherman. "When you set a gillnet, you have got to have a backwater coming back up the river. . . . You can't just set a net out in swift water and expect to catch any fish." Billy's ancestors trapped fish in

From his birth, Angeline Tobin and Willie Frank Sr. taught son Billy the Indian ways.

weirs, underwater fences made of wooden stakes. They would remove the traps from time to time, sending schools of salmon off to spawn. Billy mostly caught salmon in gillnets. He engineered his own catch-and-release philosophy—catch what you need, and release what you don't. "I always tell my kids, 'If a salmon gets away from you, don't cuss. Don't say anything. That salmon, he's going up the river. He's producing more salmon for you and all of us. The salmon—he's coming home. And we've got to take care of his home. He journeys out there for six, seven years clear to the Arctic Ocean and then he comes back clear to the Nisqually River.'"

NATURE WAS NOT Billy's only teacher. "My parents lived a long time. Dad lived to 104 and Mom, I think, was 95. And they were with us for that long of time, teaching us."

"My dad would put us all in the boat," Billy recalls. "All he had was oars, never had no motor of any kind. We poled up and down the river. We poled clean up to the reservation. We poled all over. We went out with the tide and come in with the tide. It was a different life for us.

"He'd take us all down to the mouth of the river and we'd flounder fish, all the family. We'd walk up the river, and get into the log jam, and get logs and rafts, and come down the river, all of us. This was the playground of all of us, this whole river. Those were long days, those days in the summertime."

In the heat of summer, Billy slogged it out in berry fields and tree farms. When the leaves turned, he climbed back into a twenty-two-foot shovel-nose cedar canoe and set a net clean across the river. Billy took his cue from the sun or the tide and headed home to butcher fish.

WHEN WILLIE FRANK chaired the Nisqually Tribe and sat on the council, his son absorbed his gravitas and ethic. "My dad—he took me wherever he went," Billy says. "We'd walk to meetings, you know. We're packing a box. The secretary has a little box of papers that she keeps the minutes of everything. We never had no building like Nisqually has got up there now. We just had each other's home that we all just kind of went to and gathered in them homes and kept the business going. But, see, I walked with Dad, listening to him. We've got to keep the government going."

He learned the creation story from his father. Willie rejected the whites' religion and entire system of values. "Dad said the Catholic Church was full of B.S.," Billy recalls, "that most of all the Catholic Church was. It just comes out of him like that. They tried to make him pray all the time [in boarding school].

"The Creator is the one who brought us here. There's all kinds of creation stories and how we came here. The Creator gave us everything we have. That was his belief, and Mom and all of us. The Creator put that salmon there for us to survive. And all the shellfish,

Billy's maternal grandparents, James and Louisa Tobin. James appears more like a frontiersman in photographs. The great oyster baron lived at Mud Bay.

and this clean water, and our medicines, and all of our food, our animals. We respected all of them. We took their life because it was given to us for our life."

At home, Billy's mother, Angeline Tobin Frank, taught him to respect women. She was a disciplinarian. "That's the way them old folks grew up," says Billy's son, Sugar. "You had to show respect or the women would let you know."

"She always talked to me about women, how important women are," Billy says. "Women are the most important thing in our life, in our communities, because they survive."

Angeline's second husband, Andrew McCloud, died in 1927.
Gramps raised his friend's three surviving children, along with
Rose Frederick and Billy, at Frank's Landing.

ANGELINE WAS A SURVIVOR. She grew up at Mud Bay and was raised
by an oyster baron, James Tobin, and her mother, Louisa Kettle, a
renowned basket weaver. Her grandfather was Sitkum Kettle, leader
of the band that formed the Squaxin Island Tribe, and an appointed
minister known for his genial disposition. Angeline was widowed
young and had lost three children before Billy was born in 1931. Angie

endured a strained marriage with her first husband that never met her mother's approval. "... ew he liked to drink!" Angie recalled once to an oral historian. "He wasn't mean or anything, but you don't like a drunk person. You get sick of it. And so I left him." Angie's second husband was Andrew McCloud, a Puyallup Indian who used to go out fishing with Willie. "They were very close," says Billy's sister Maiselle. "They did everything together. They fished together here on the river, but they also were fish buyers for a white company. They went together down to the Columbia River and bought fish from the Indian fishermen there."

In the summer of 1927, cancer took McCloud's life and Willie saw to it that his friend's family would survive. "[Willie] thought he should take care of Mom, and her and my dad's kids—Rose, Andrew, Don, and me," Maiselle says. Willie was already separated from Angie's younger sister, Ida. He ended that relationship and married Angie.

WITH THE EXCEPTION OF boarding school, Billy's upbringing was not unlike his father's. He learned the old ways surrounded by several generations of family. Billy's childhood scrapbooks prominently feature oldest sister Rose Frederick and the McCloud children—Andrew, Maiselle, and Don. "They all raised me," Billy says. "But it was easy raising; it was a different time."

Billy called Rose "Fritz." She was twenty years his senior, with an open face and dark hair that fell to the base of her neck. He can still hear Rose speaking Lushootseed, the indigenous language of Salish tribes. When Billy was a kid, Rose raised six children at the Landing in hard times. Her daughter Mary often depended on Billy. "My Uncle Billy—he's the main one that always helps me," Mary used to say. On school mornings, Billy roused Mary and Rose's other kids out of bed. The small army passed the home of Mrs. Wallace, the delightful neighbor with delicious chocolate chip cookies. Mrs. Wallace also raised obnoxious geese, however, that waddled after the children, feathers flying. "Oh Jesus! Geese are crazy . . . they got their neck out after you. We're all hanging onto each other and we're little guys.

BILLY FRANK JR. PERSONAL COLLECTION

To supplement income, children often helped pick hops. Billy (center) in hop fields.

You know? We laugh about that now. But it was very serious," Billy recalls.

BILLY SMILES when he thinks of his late brother Andrew, whom everyone called Sonny. When he was seven or eight, Sonny marched off the family homestead at Mud Bay, where he had been living with his maternal grandparents. He hoofed it more than twenty miles to the Landing and made a bold announcement to Willie:

"I ran away! I ran away!"

"You don't ever have to go back there anymore," Willie told him. "This is your home, you stay here. You don't have to go back . . . if you don't like it."

Willie catapulted to stardom in Andrew's book as "the greatest thing on earth." Billy never forgot the story. "I always remember that because that was the kind of guy Dad was. He took care of those kids as if they were his own."

From the start, the smiley, chubby-cheeked boy adored his big sister Maiselle, who became a second mother. Maiselle too had spent time at Mud Bay. She lived there for seven years watching her grandmother, Louisa Tobin, weave cedar root baskets—masterpieces of beauty—and cook for religious conventions of the Shakers. Louisa died the year Billy was born, however, and Maiselle moved home to the Landing.

When Billy was eight, Maiselle boarded the bus for Chemawa Indian School, the nation's oldest continuously operating boarding school. The separation devastated Billy, and Maiselle never forgot their goodbye. "Billy just stood there screaming and crying at the top of his lungs," says Tom Keefe, a family friend. "Maiselle felt so guilty all the way down there and every day she was at that school. I remember her recalling that image frozen in her memory, all the way to Oregon. She couldn't stop crying, because she just saw Billy's face. . . . To this day, the dynamic between the two of them is very loving. Maiselle is definitely the big sister/surrogate mom in his life."

"We missed each other," Billy recalls. "She was going off to school at Chemawa, which in them days was a long ways away, clear in Salem. I never dreamed of even going to Salem, Oregon." But school has always meant something to Maiselle, Billy says.

In 1939, enrollment at Chemawa was down from its onetime peak of a thousand students in 1926, but it was a fully accredited high school. Like all Native American students, Maiselle was scrutinized upon her arrival from the top of her head to the soles of her feet. "I recommend enrollment and suggest the following: Home Management, Industrial Art, and Music," the administrators concluded at placement.

Maiselle's brothers, Andrew and Don, joined her. In fact, according to Don's daughter, Nancy Shippentower-Games, Maiselle and Don

Don, Maiselle, and Andrew McCloud all attended the sprawling Chemawa Indian School in Oregon. Later in life Maiselle said leaving Billy behind was excruciating. The memory of her teary-eyed brother stayed with her while she was away from home.

ran away. They dodged cars on the long trek home only to be promptly returned to Chemawa by their disapproving mother, Angie. "She wanted them to have an education," Shippentower-Games says.

One year, Maiselle brought a classmate to the Landing, and for brother Sonny the rest was history. "Edith came home with her on Christmas vacation and that's when her and my brother met. They've been married sixty or seventy years now," Billy says with a chuckle.

Despite the happy outcome for her brother and her friend, Maiselle hated Chemawa, says Carol Burns, a documentary filmmaker. "The girls were only trained to be domestic servants and they functioned as domestic servants."

For some Natives, boarding school was a positive experience and offered electricity, running water, and indoor plumbing for the first time. For others, however, like Willie and Maiselle, the boarding-school experience was miserable. Willie and Maiselle weren't alone in their bitterness.

On the 175th anniversary of the Bureau of Indian Affairs, Kevin Gover, assistant secretary, offered an apology for the BIA policy designed to "destroy all things Indian" at America's boarding schools. He apologized for "brutalizing them emotionally, psychologically, physically, and spiritually . . . never again will we seize your children. . . . Never again."

Despite Maiselle's unhappiness at Chemawa, the years in Oregon planted a seed. One day, she would dedicate the rest of her life to the education of Indian children.

BILLY WAS CLOSEST in age to his brother Don, the confident, loving, and youngest McCloud. Don had a heartfelt laugh and a signature sense of humor. Many Indians are well-known storytellers and Don was never without commentary. When he got older, Don would tell stories to his children as he poled canoes on the river. "When he checked his net, he would always throw a fish on the banks," says Shippentower-Games. "We would ask him why he was doing this and he said: 'If you don't feed the little people, they would play tricks on you!' He told us a story when he went one night and he forgot to throw the fish. Pretty soon, he seen little lights and his hair stood on end and rocks were flying at him so he didn't forget to feed the little people anymore."

Tragedy struck when Billy was twelve. Rose lost her husband and overnight became a single mother of six. Her husband, Herman Buck John, was a paratrooper who died with honor. He had slung his sea bag over his shoulder for war the last time Billy saw him alive. With his nieces and nephews in tow, Billy followed his uncle down a dirt road. "He turned to the right to go down to the highway and catch his bus. We never saw him again. He got killed over in Germany." Private Herman John of Nisqually died in the European Theater of Operations, 1945.

Rose depended a lot on Willie and Angie. She lived frugally, with

HANK ADAMS PERSONAL COLLECTION

Billy's sister, Rose Frederick John, with four of her children: Louise, Annie, Herman Jr., and Sandra.

kerosene lamps and a wood stove, and hauled water back and forth from the Nisqually River. She and her children picked hops to make ends meet. Eventually, Rose moved to the Salishan Housing Project in Tacoma. Her children split time between Salishan and the Landing.

Trouble didn't end there for the family. Billy's childhood home—"one of the best houses around at that time"—caught on fire in the 1940s. "Only the fish house survived," Angeline Frank told the newspaper man. The Franks had left town. They returned to find their home gone. Reports are mixed on just what happened—the work of an arsonist or a wood stove. The end result was the same. "We had a big house up front [on the property], a beautiful house with a bathroom and all. Then someone burned it down 20 years ago. We lost everything."

Out of the ashes, the Franks moved into their two-room fish house that sat on top of an old water break. "Both rooms were bedrooms" and one included the kitchen. There was a small porch and a narrow pantry. "You couldn't see land looking out the back window," recalls Billy's nephew Ray McCloud. The Frank home sat dangerously close to the Nisqually River.

ONE DAY IN THE WINTER of 1945, as the temperature hovered in the mid-forties, Billy Frank Jr. became a fighter. Along the Nisqually River, Billy pulled thrashing and squirming steelhead and dog salmon from his fifty-foot net. To avoid the keen eyes of game wardens, he'd set his net in the river the night before. The downed branches of a fallen maple covered his canoe perfectly. But in the stillness of those early-morning hours, as he diligently butchered the chum, a yell pierced the silence. For Billy, life would never be the same.

"You're under arrest!" state agents shouted with flashlights in hand.

"Leave me alone, goddamn it. I fish here. I live here!" Billy fired back.

"I fished in the daylight and they start taking my nets," recalls Billy. "And I'm fourteen years old. When they started arresting us, I'd go set my net at nighttime. I never used a motor. I'd pull my canoe. I'd go up there like four in the morning and pick [the fish up] and come home."

That morning, locked in a physical hold by game wardens, a warrior emerged. Billy knew he'd have to fight for his fishing right himself, the culture and heritage he knew. "I thought nobody protects us Indians," Billy says. "The state of Washington, they protect their sportsmen, their commercial fishermen and everybody. But nobody protects us Indians, not even our tribe. They weren't capable of the infrastructure to take care of us, take care of us in the political sense of legal and policy and technical. We never had no technical people. We never had no science people on the river. We had nothing. And I always thought, Jesus, we need somebody to be out there shaking their fist and saying, "Hey, we live here!"

EVEN WITH THE fishing struggle, ask Billy about his childhood, and it is other memories that stick. He remembers the scents and ceremonies of salmon bakes, placing the fish on skewers and laying them down alongside a fire where they'd bake for hours. He remembers scavenging the foothills for Indian medicine, "healing medicine that is still around the country. We go up to the mountain every year in the month of September and pick huckleberries on this side of Mount Adams." He can hear the sound of racing horse hooves reverberating across the prairie. He can see himself standing on the back of a galloping horse, clasping onto his father's shoulders as they charge over grassland around Puget Sound. The patriarch meant everything to the boy; the moment would prove a metaphor for life. By holding onto the beliefs of his ancestors, Billy learned to rise above an impossibly bumpy world.

Chapter 3

The Survivor

Dubbed the fabulous fifties, a new era dawned in America. World War II had ended. The Puget Sound area boomed. Parents flooded the suburbs. But for Billy, the 1950s brought ups and downs. He fulfilled a dream and became a U.S. Marine, but picked up a drinking problem that stole twenty years. He married and became a father, but watched as more than a hundred Indian tribes in the nation were terminated in the wake of aggressive changes to federal Indian policy.

Billy's number came up for the draft in 1952, in the middle of the Korean War. Peace had collapsed in 1950, when the North Korean Army crossed the thirty-eighth parallel that divides Korea. A military clash over communism broke out that took two million lives in three years.

Like many other Native Americans, Billy prepared to serve his country. He joined the U.S. Marine Corps and boarded the troop train for Camp Pendleton in California, one of the nation's largest marine installations. "Not everyone succeeds in the Marine Corps," points out friend George Walter. "It's not like being drafted into the army. You have to volunteer. You go through a lot. Billy is a patriot. He was ready to go to Korea and put his life on the line." After basic training, Billy was assigned to the military police where he achieved the status of an expert marksman. Billy learned police technique. He

BILLY FRANK JR. PERSONAL COLLECTION

Billy becomes a U.S. marine in 1952.

learned the kind of blind faith you place in teammates you implicitly trust. After his service, he shared an instant rapport with other men in uniform.

WHEN HE COMPLETED his training for the Marines, Billy married Norma McCloud. She took the bus to San Diego and they lived at Camp Pendleton for more than a year.

Norma was pretty, loving, and generous. "She took care of anybody and everybody," says Sugar Frank of his late mother. "She wasn't out for anything," says Georgiana Kautz, Norma's younger sister. "She just loved to be what she was, and loved to watch sports, and loved to take care of kids. They meant so much to her."

Norma had survived a rough childhood on the Nisqually Reservation. Like all but two of her ten siblings, she was born at home.

GEORGIANA KAUTZ PERSONAL COLLECTION

Married while Billy was a marine, Billy and Norma raised
three children and endured the struggles of the fish wars.

Norma's sister, Georgiana Kautz, remembers the family hitchhiking
to see the doctor. The McCloud home had no electricity or running
water, and they weren't alone. Most families on the reservation lived
without electricity until 1963 or 1964. Nonetheless, the McClouds
made the best of it. "You're out there doing things: baseball games,
dances, pow-wows, drinking. And Billy met Norma and they fell in
love. . . . Billy was just a young man that had a lot of good things
instilled in him by his father and by his mother," says Kautz. "And a

NORTHWEST INDIAN FISHERIES COMMISSION

*To put food on the table, Billy and his brother Don
McCloud work as linemen.*

lot of that was to fight what was happening to tribal people. It began
at an early age for him, and he never walked away from that part of
his life."

THE KOREAN WAR ENDED and the U.S. Marine Corps released Billy
from duty. He and Norma drove from Camp Pendleton to the Landing,
where they would start their lives together. The family compound
was home to Willie and Angie. Billy's sister Maiselle lived there with
her husband, Alvin Bridges. Herman John Jr., Billy's nephew, also
called the Landing home. Reporters described the family setting as
modest, with "dogs and cats and 30 pet chickens, part banty, part game
cock, which fly through the air and roost in the trees at night."

For extra money, Billy earned a living building power lines. He joined the International Brotherhood of Electrical Workers Local 77 in Seattle. "Both my brothers worked for the power companies. So, in my spare time that's what I'd do. I belonged to the union and I'd just hire out in the union when I wasn't down here fishing."

KNOWN AS A rags-to-riches story and an astute military leader, Dwight Eisenhower clinched the White House with the campaign slogan "I like Ike." But his policies as president unleashed a fury in Indian Country. Under Eisenhower's administration, the Termination Act of 1953 severed ties between the U.S. government and Indian tribes. The new policy created a storm of protest in Washington, D.C.

"They were terminating tribes throughout the nation," Billy says. "It was a big fight. We talk about treaties in 1854 . . . and all of a sudden we've got abrogation of the treaties right off the bat. And so he started that abrogation in 1950," Billy says. "[Eisenhower] turned jurisdiction over to the state of Washington and the other states throughout the country. . . . He allowed liquor on the reservation. Those were the three things he did to wipe us out, get rid of us."

More than seven decades after Indian children were forced into America's boarding schools came another wave of assimilation practices. The Termination Era plucked tribes from the landscape one after another. As author Garrett Epps summarizes, "Their approach was simple. Tribes who were considered 'ready' for assimilation were 'terminated.' The federal government closed their tribal rolls, sold off their tribal lands, and sent each tribal member a check for his or her share of the proceeds." The Termination Act included provisions to abolish the tribes' federally recognized treaty status, allot the remaining tribal land, and remove health care from the control of the Bureau of Indian Affairs.

Members of Congress backed this major policy shift as freedom for Native Americans—independence from the United States government. Many Native Americans, on the other hand, viewed termination as yet another attempt to strip them of their culture and make them white.

"People just thought these old treaties were past history," explains John Echohawk, head of the Native American Rights Fund. "The time of Indians was over. There was no future. They forced us to assimilate."

Although no Washington Indian tribes were terminated, Native tribes in Oregon were. In all, 109 tribes across the nation ceased to exist in the eyes of the federal government.

From 1949 until 1960, the Bureau of Indian Affairs relocated an estimated thirty-five thousand Indians to urban areas for which the men and women were grossly unprepared. The number of Indians living in urban centers doubled. Their wages were less than half of their Anglo counterparts. The new legislation legalized the sale of tribal land, and Indians lost two-thirds of their reservations in private sales. The relationship between tribes as sovereign nations and the U.S. government had collapsed.

At the same time, Congress passed Public Law 280, which gave five states exclusive jurisdiction over crimes committed in Indian Country. Other states, like Washington, opted in. As leading scholar Carol Goldberg-Ambrose puts it: "Tribes had not exactly thrived under the prior regime of federal authority and responsibility. But when the states took over, with their alternating antagonism and neglect of Native peoples, tribes had to struggle even harder to sustain their governing structures, economies, and cultures."

Henry Jackson, longtime Washington senator, originally championed termination, but later flipped his position.

It wasn't until December 22, 1973, that Nixon signed the Menominee Restoration Act, repealing the legislation that had authorized the termination of Indian tribes.

THE 1950S WERE indeed bittersweet for Billy. As Indian tribes faced termination and the unknown, he and and Norma braved a new world as parents. The couple could not have children naturally and decided to adopt from Mary Miles, Billy's niece, and Orland Paul, a Tulalip Indian. In both cases, Billy and Norma took the babies straight home from the hospital immediately after birth. They were the proud parents of Maureen and James Tobin (Sugar).

"We had a little shack that was just a frame with 2 x 6s, no insulation and one light in the middle, just a shell," recalls Sugar. "That's where me, Dad, Mom and my sister lived."

"I tell you, we just took care of them babies," Billy says. "We were always on the river. We would take them down clam digging and everything. We never had any big motors. We had little motors. . . . We'd come back in with the tide. We lived down here at tidal water."

"Dad got a good boat one year," Sugar remembers. "Grandma used to make him go down and take the whole family and go flounder hunting at the mouth of the river. They'd walk around. I was too young. I was scared by baby crabs and everything, but I remember it. They'd walk around waist deep, and step on the flounders."

"I was the smallest, the youngest, and actually I was the only boy," Sugar adds. "My toys were the river, snakes, and frogs."

Sugar spent most days waiting for a king to strike. "I'd untie [Dad's] little dinghy boat and I'd jump in and paddle out to the set and hang onto the cords and wait for the fish to hit. But there were very little kings."

Or, as he walked the riverbank hunting for hooks and string, he would break off a willow stick. "And I'd go get a periwinkle in the river, and I'd hook it on the hook, and tie a rock on there and just throw a hook in the water and wait for the fish on the shallow side." But usually, he'd catch only bullheads.

Maureen was a typical older sister, Sugar says. She didn't like chasing snakes much and the two sometimes bickered. One summer out on the boat, the kids were sleeping on a bench Billy made when Maureen rolled over and plunged straight into the river. "Dad shut the motor off, right?" Sugar recalls. "He jumped in the river, and it was only . . . about a little over his waist. He picked her up. The boat shut off and comes right back at him. He put her in, jumped in the boat, started it up and we took off."

Learning the heart of their Indian culture, Maureen and Sugar prepare fish for a buyer.

As BILLY RAISED his young family, personal demons interfered. It was illegal for him to drink, but a bootlegger around the corner gave preferential treatment to Indians in uniform. The disease lasted twenty-three years, "at least from the time in the Marines, from '51 to '74," says Hank Adams. "It wasn't lawful to serve Indians until 1953. . . . He drank and learned to drink in San Diego, Long Beach. He was addicted from that day until 1974, when he came out of Schick Shadel."

Billy is candid about the addiction. For many Native Americans, alcohol masqueraded as a friend, boosting courage and deadening the pain of a vanishing heritage. "Like a lot of our Indian people . . . he drank," recalls Ramona Bennett, a Puyallup Indian. "He drank. You know, we self-medicate. I was into drugs, too. We drank to ease the pain." Billy's wife, Norma, also suffered. Out of all eleven children in Norma's family, only Georgiana Kautz escaped sober. "It was what you did," Kautz explains of alcohol's hold on her family. "You grew up. You learned how to drink. You learned how to party. You learned how to dance."

The late Vine Deloria, a respected Indian scholar, explained the high rate of alcoholism in Indian Country as a reaction to the expectation that Natives conform to general society. "People are not allowed to be Indians and cannot become whites," he writes. They are, in effect, suspended between the culture they know and the culture society accepts. The consequences are steep.

"I would think a good deal of drinking is the absence of any ritualized culture for most Indian people in most areas, outside the Southwest where they weren't pressed as fully culturally as they were elsewhere," offers Adams. "It's hard not to drink when you're sort of held down and it's poured down you."

Time on the road for work didn't help. "Billy as a lineman . . . you go off in a crew," Adams says. "You travel to Southeast Alaska. You go to Montana. You go to Utah, Northern California, Oregon, and Washington. You're off in your crew and what do you do at night? You even sneak a little on the job too, if not lunch. Someone's got a bottle. And that's a high paying job. But there are some high costs on the road. And it's mostly in the hard liquor area. There's not as much beer as there is hard liquor on those kinds of activities because the hard liquor is easier to transport. Single men going off to the last frontier. . . . You think that's expected of you, to have a hard drinking life. But you find that it's hardly a difference for a married person."

Financially, Billy and Norma were strapped. "They would travel to Montana to pick up cigarettes, to pick up firecrackers," says Kautz. "We spent a lot of time together. They ran cigarettes. They ran firecrackers. They ran booze out of Nevada. The Indians couldn't fish, sell cigarettes, booze, or firecrackers . . . so they ran them under the law to survive."

Billy's niece Valerie tried to convince her uncle to stop drinking. "You could do so much for the Indian people if you would just become sober," she told him. "Valerie was very close to both Norma and Billy," recalls Adams. "She babysat for Sugar and Maureen throughout the '60s because Billy and Norma both drank. Valerie was there for their kids."

Like her daughter, Maiselle also attempted to get through to Billy. "She was always worried about us," Billy says. "We're on the river and we're raising hell and all that. We'd drink beer and different liquor."

Brutal epiphanies eventually helped Billy rise above the drinking. "You just think, 'God damn.' I'm looking at this tower sixty feet up in the air and I'm saying, 'Jesus, I've got to climb this thing today?' You've got a hangover. And your body is telling you, 'Quit drinking.' And it's telling you over and over, 'You used to be able to drink and the hangover didn't bother you.' I just got tired. I had a bottle of whiskey. It was the last drink I ever had. My body was telling me to straighten up. Now I look back at all the wasted time."

It was Maiselle, says Adams, who finally got through to Billy. She convinced him to walk through the doors of Schick Shadel, a fifty-bed treatment center for alcohol addiction in Burien, Washington.

Alcoholism had hit their small Frank's Landing Indian Community hard, but as usual they found humor in tough times. Tom Keefe, a close family friend, recalls an evening Billy and Al Bridges spent in treatment together.

"Al's great, great, great-grandfather was an Irishman who jumped ship and married a Puyallup woman," says Keefe. "Billy remembered when they got into Schick Shadel and they were sitting for the orientation meeting. There was this big chart on the wall that showed racial groups, and it was set up like a horserace. The first two ethnic groups, far ahead of the rest, that were alcoholics were Irish and Indian. Al looked at him and said, 'Billy, I think I'm a goner.'"

"[Billy] hasn't drank since," says Adams. "[Maiselle] had five people that she put in there, and he was the only one who never drank again.

She put her other brother Andy in there. She put their nephew Melvin Iyall in there, Al Bridges, her husband, and the fifth person she put in there was me."

Schick Shadel does not offer a twelve-step program for patients. It relies on aversion therapy, a technique that retrains the mind, memory and senses to be repelled by the taste and smell of the drug.

Billy winces at the memory: "What they do is they make you heave your guts out. You can't even smell alcohol. They get you to the point where you can't smell it. You just heave up. So, we got out of there and then I just quit. And my daughter died, and my granddaughter I just loved so dearly. And then they thought, 'Well, Billy will start drinking again.' Then Norma died and 'Billy will start drinking again.' Then [Sue] Crystal died. I'll never touch that stuff."

"It took that thirty days and it took that treatment," says Adams. "And it was part of learning about himself and that he could live without that constant recourse of alcohol."

In 1974, at the age of forty-three, Billy took his last sip of alcohol and, in turn, discovered a great confidence. "When you quit drinking you've got to get away from [the people who drink around you.] They're going to say, 'Oh god damn, take another drink.' You go into the tavern with them or the cocktail lounge, where the hell ever you go. And so I'm watching these guys, 'No, I don't drink anymore.'"

"Most all of my friends now, they've quit drinking. Nugie [Neugen] and all of my buddies on the river here, I'm watching these guys and nobody drinks anymore."

"We gained Billy's full contribution at his point of sobriety," Adams says. "At Capitol Lake [1968], when he was arrested, he wouldn't have been there except he was drunk. And at that point, you couldn't get him out there unless he was drinking and/or drunk. . . . He learned that he had greater courage without drink than with it."

Billy was coming of age when he first picked up the bottle, and twenty years older when he finally set it down. "A lot of people today, they just see Billy Frank the big shot, the success story, the

Billy Frank who gets his picture taken with presidents and senators and governors," a family member once said. "That's all real for who he is now, but that wasn't always him. That's not the full picture, and our young people would benefit from knowing the rest of his story."

Billy developed a sense of humor about his addiction. Years after he quit, at a summer concert in sweltering heat, diehard Bob Dylan and Tom Petty fans baked inside RFK stadium in Washington, D.C. Billy, Suzan Harjo and their partners sat amongst the crowd.

"It was packed and 105 degrees in Washington, which is just awful. We were burning up," Harjo says. The foursome decided water was too precious a commodity and began dousing themselves with beer. Even Billy, who'd sworn off alcohol years before, dumped one cold one after another over is head. "Even when I was drinking, I never smelled like this," he laughed.

Chapter 4

Surveillance

Years after a forty-two-year-old black seamstress refused to give up her bus seat to a white man in Alabama, Billy Frank Jr. refused to pull up his net in Washington. The civil rights movement accused a nation of calling one race better than another. The Northwest fishing struggle accused a country of breaking a treaty in its own backyard. Like the civil rights movement, the fishing struggle has deep roots. By the early 1960s, more than a hundred years had passed since the signing of the Medicine Creek Treaty secured off-reservation fishing rights for tribes.

"We ceded all this land to the United States. . . . We made the people of this country free," Billy told a Department of Commerce gathering in 2005. "They weren't free. You weren't free. The people that come out there in the state of Washington and our territory was not free. They didn't own nothing until we ceded the land to them. Now after that, they could go to the bank, start a bank. They could start a town. But then, they didn't honor that treaty. They didn't honor that treaty one bit."

When the 1960s brought diminishing fish runs, trouble stirred up on Washington riverbanks. Fisheries managers for the state called the runs "alarmingly depopulated" and "erased from the American scene."

"What this adds up to is a tremendous threat to the fishery resources of the state," announced John Biggs, director of the Washington Department of Game. "It's bad for Indians and whites alike." The feud over salmon and the sea-going steelhead trout was emotional. Fish remained critical to the tribes for ceremony and survival. Washington law prohibited them from netting steelhead, a state game fish, or from selling steelhead caught on their reservations, writes Al Ziontz in *A Lawyer in Indian Country*. Hook-and-line sports fishermen believed with fervor that their paid fishing license and landing fees guaranteed them first rights to the feisty steelhead trout, and they made a big and powerful voice in Washington.

NON-INDIANS and the state blamed the thinning runs on Indian fishermen who stretched their nets across the river mouths, where the take is especially heavy. Many Indians did not honor fishing restrictions or bag limits, believing the regulations infringed upon their treaty rights. "Indians are becoming super citizens," groused one non-Indian. "Indians may have a right to reservation land, but under the U.S. Constitution, all individuals are forced to obey the law of the land once off the reservation."

Billy and Native fishermen said they were taking less than 5 percent of the catch (a figure confirmed by later estimates), while non-Indians, whose boats dotted the migration path of the fish like signs on a freeway, scooped up the rest. Fishing licenses were issued liberally, and commercial fishermen aboard enormous vessels were deeply invested in the lucrative industry. "We don't go out chasing the salmon," Billy says. "When salmon come home . . . we have ceremonies. We have offerings. We have our religious and our cultural way of life.

"Everybody [else] was catching our fish. When they got to the Nisqually River, they'd close us down for conservation. The state of Washington would do that. They intercepted salmon as the migrations come home. By the time it got to the Nisqually River, there was no salmon left to catch. We said, 'The hell with them!' We started fighting to get our salmon back." The fight and rising emotions played out in the courtroom and on the riverbank.

IN 1960, JOE McCOY, a Swinomish Indian, was charged with fishing when the Skagit River was closed. One hundred people crowded into the courtroom to hear his case. "A few individual fishermen unregulated on the Skagit could definitely destroy its salmon runs," declared Edward Mains, assistant director of the Washington Fisheries Department. "By gillnet they could take up to 98 percent of a run." Mains considered unregulated Indian fisheries an "endless chain" and the "weakest link" in the state's salmon fisheries. McCoy's attorney argued and convinced the lower court that the 1855 Point Elliott Treaty trumped fishing regulations.

The Washington State Supreme Court, however, disagreed and ruled, "None of the signatories of the original treaty contemplated fishing with a 600-foot nylon gillnet which could prevent the escapement of any fish for spawning purposes." The state court decision authorized Washington State to regulate Indian fishing, provided its intent was to conserve fish runs. Thor Tollefson, head of Fisheries for the state and a former congressman, pushed to abrogate treaties and pay off tribes. "The treaty must be broken," he said. "That's what happens when progress pushes forward."

The McCoy decision touched off an uproar in the winter of 1963. At Frank's Landing, fishermen held an emergency meeting and then protested at the Capitol two days before Christmas. Janet McCloud, outspoken activist and wife of Don McCloud, led the "No Salmon, No Santa" campaign. As protestors waved their picket signs, McCloud accused the judge of kidnapping the holiday. "He's making law where he has no right to! Our aboriginal rights were granted to us under the treaties of the nineteenth century with the U.S. government. The only court that can change them is the United States Supreme Court. . . . There will be no Christmas for many of us."

The state's progressive chief executive, Albert Rosellini, welcomed the protestors for a face-to-face meeting, but quickly sent them off. "Nice to hear your problems, come back again," the governor said.

Billy recalls his frustration at the time. "'You could fish on the reservation,' they said. Piss on you. We're not fishing on the reservation. We don't live on the reservation. And so the Bureau of Indian Affairs, you name it, everybody was against us, even our own tribe. But that didn't stop us. We just kept on going."

THE FISHING STRUGGLE played out most dramatically on the riverbank. In the early 1960s, Washington State officers, in power boats and on foot, began surveillance of Native fishermen. Eventually the state confiscated Indian gear and won court orders prohibiting Indian net fishing in the Puyallup, Nisqually, and other rivers.

In the winter of 1962, as the late chum run darted upstream to Muck Creek, dozens of officers surrounded Frank's Landing in a major raid. A spotter plane swooped overhead. Authorities made a half-dozen arrests and bold accusations. The fishermen are not Nisqually Indians, the Game Department charged. Billy, then vice chairman of the tribe, attempted to prove the identity of Indian fishermen through a stack of affidavits.

Identifying treaty Indians proved difficult for state officers. John Biggs, director of the state Game Department, demanded clarification of treaty language and a definitive list of Indians enrolled in treaty tribes. "Anyone who thinks he is an Indian is taking the fish— not to eat, but to take down to Portland and sell," Biggs accused.

Meantime, angry whites were starting to take matters into their own hands, warned Walter Neubrech, head of enforcement at the Game Department. They tore down an Indian net in force. According to the *Seattle Times*, "Fist fights" broke out on the Puyallup River, and "some of them are now packing shotguns."

After the arrests at the Landing, the Nisqually Tribe passed resolutions to ban whites from fishing the stretch of the river that cuts a swath through the reservation. In March 1962, the tribes had attempted to form their own intertribal fish commission to work through the struggle, but it never got off the ground.

In 1963, the headline "Skagits on Warpath?" appeared in the *Seattle Times*. "They [the Indians] have been crowding us," Neubrech reported to the seven-member game commission. "They've threatened us and there has been some bodily contact with some of our people."

The crackdown pushed on and drove Indian fishing underground. What was once the open pride of the tribes was practiced in secret and in silence.

"I fished at night," Billy remembers. "I pulled my nets out at dark. I hid my canoes. "

"We'd go to this island just right above the Landing, probably a mile or so, and he'd drop me off there," recalls Sugar Frank. "They had a little coffee can full of gasoline and he'd light that on. I'd stand around that coffee can with all the other fishermen at nighttime. They'd make two or three drifts and fill up his canoe. He'd come pick me up and we'd head back down about eleven at night with a boatload of fish."

Peering through binoculars, officers prowled riverbanks for canoes, gillnets, and Indian fishermen. Often, they confiscated nets.

Sometimes, the Indian fishermen fought back. Billy was the self-proclaimed getting-arrested guy. "We were fighting for our life—our survival," he says. "We fished. We sold our fish. We ate fish. That was what we did. You go down there and there ain't no fish. There ain't no boats. There ain't nothing. So, that really pisses you off, you know? So you do whatever you got to do."

"Are we under arrest?" asked Al Bridges, Billy's fishing companion and brother-in-law during one encounter.

"This net is illegal gear and we are taking it at this time," a Fisheries officer yelled. "I'm telling you right now . . . you are under arrest."

"The Fisheries people were bad, but the Game Department was really awful, real thugs," remembers Tom Keefe. "They were always out there on behalf of the white steelhead fishermen, harassing Indian fishermen, cutting loose their nets. The Game Department people just

MARY RANDLETT

More than just the home of Billy and his family, Frank's Landing was a gathering place for tribal fishermen to sell their catch.

thought that it was basically blasphemous for anyone to be catching steelhead with nets and selling them. In their view, steelhead were supposed to be reserved for so-called sportsmen, who were non-Indian people who didn't want to mow their lawns on the weekends, and would rather leave their wives and kids at home and go stand testicle-deep in freezing water with a fishing pole trying to catch a steelhead as some iconic rite of passage. And they became a political force in our state."

One night after the sun set, Billy's father walked outside and discovered state officers hovering at the Landing. "They're pulling your nets—the game wardens!" Willie shouted to his son.

Billy chased after them as they rowed away with two of his nets inside their boat. He jumped in his car and intercepted the officers at

A patrol officer monitors the waters, pulling a net presumably set by an Indian fisherman.

a nearby landing. "I went down and had a fight with them. I pulled them nets out of their car. My dog salmon are all over the ground. I said, 'You sons of bitches! You guys are stealing my net and stealing my fish!' And they were hollering at me. And there was a MP standing there, a military police guy. And I said, 'Are you in this, son of a bitch?' He never said anything. I pulled them fish and put them in the back of my—I only had a coupe that I was in, a Chevrolet coupe, with a trunk. And I was throwing my fish and the net back in the car. They took one net and I got the other one. They didn't arrest me that time."

IN ADDITION to his personal encounters, Billy says the state followed, roughed up, and mistreated his family. One night after dark, his niece Alison Bridges woke as a spotlight cast shadows and crept across her bedroom wall. "I'd wake up at two in the morning and there would

HANK ADAMS COLLECTION

Willie and longtime wife Angeline stand on the porch at their Frank's Landing home.

be huge spotlights going up and down the river and they'd be looking for my dad," she said.

Her father, Al Bridges, went to jail so often that Alison and her two sisters started fishing in his absence. They would push off from the shore at night dressed in black clothing. Crouching inside a small boat, they drifted by wardens silently. Every time an officer puffed on a cigarette, the girls could make out his profile. They weren't the only women or children suffering. Many, like Billy's niece Nancy Shippentower-Games, lived in poverty: "We didn't have no food, and our dads were in jail. When I went to see [my father], I had shoes that were falling apart." The families hawked motors, sold pop cans, and tolerated a lot of bologna and bread. When food was especially scant, the women showered at dinner time; their hunger pains couldn't take the smell of food.

As the surveillance of Indian fishers continued for years, Willie and Angeline Frank showed their resilience. "Mom and Dad . . . they were our security," says Maiselle McCloud Bridges. "We'd sit down and talk about day's events at the courthouse. We were drained. We'd be able to forget. We were just home with them and we felt safe."

Chapter 5

Renegades

In January 1964, the threat of snow and rain loomed as Billy and treaty fishermen gathered on the banks of the Nisqually River at Frank's Landing. They dug in their heels and craned their necks, eyeing a white flag of truce at the top of a pole. It once signaled a brief respite in the fishing wars.

But on this winter day, peace eroded and battle lines were redrawn between the state of Washington and Indian fishermen at the Landing. The Native American activists returned to the river in a show of protest. Bolstered by a recent state Supreme Court decision, Pierce County prohibited nets in the Nisqually River. "We are certain the Indians will not continue fishing after receiving copies of the restraining order," Walter Neubrech of the Game Department said confidently, after the state secured the order.

But the fishers were not dissuaded. Still they would cast their nets and would risk personal freedom to fish. They lowered the white flag of truce and unfurled the American flag—a flag of pride they called it—and watched it snake its way up the pole. This particular flag was special. It once draped the coffin of Herman John Sr., Billy Frank's brother-in-law. "We're fishing under this flag and under the treaty signed in 1854 with the U.S. Government," activists declared on a sign fastened to the pole.

Raising the inverted flag, Frank's Landing. Fishermen protested in 1964 by lowering a white flag of truce and raising the American flag. The demonstration carried forward the next year, in 1965, when they raised the inverted flag shown above.

"Right out here by the fish house, right here where Wa He Lut School stands today, saying we're committed to this fight," Hank Adams recalls of the atmosphere. "Our cousin, our brother, gave his life in World War II. This flag draped his coffin. We're carrying on this fight."

The Native Americans pledged their allegiance to the United States that day—both to serve the country and to fish its rivers. "Our people have fought and died for the United States and we have an agreement with it to fish these grounds. We plan to do so . . . and this flag will give us courage," said Janet McCloud, a Tulalip Indian and activist. Then, in a gesture of their resolve, the fishermen cast their boats. Arrests followed.

"The court didn't say we had to stop, but only that the Game Department could control our fishing," Billy told the *Daily Olympian.* "We are catching mainly chum salmon, or dog salmon as some people call them, and a few steelhead. . . . We have no trouble with the Fisheries Department over catching chum salmon—only with sportsmen over the few steelhead we take. We're not depleting the salmon!"

"They must think the steelhead swam over behind the *Mayflower.* With or without the Indians' help, the white man is going to deplete the salmon runs just like the buffalo," quipped McCloud.

Emotions ratcheted up. "We had the power and force to exterminate these people from the face of the earth, instead of making treaties with them. Perhaps we should have!" snapped an assistant Pierce County prosecutor at the time. "We certainly wouldn't be having all this trouble with them today."

BY MARCH, the fishermen reached a tipping point. They organized, pulled together, and pooled minimal resources. "We just said we're not moving no more," recalls Maiselle, Billy's older sister.

With a mission to renew their treaty rights, the fishermen and their families founded the Survival of the American Indian Association. Survival was the kind of organization that strategized from the kitchen table and scraped up every dime. It began with more heart than money, more energy than people, more will than public support. Fred Haley, a prominent candymaker from Tacoma, donated a Xerox machine. The activists raised fifty dollars at a fish bake and retained Jack Tanner as their attorney. Regional director of the NAACP, Tanner was lead attorney for African Americans in their own pursuit of justice. Tanner, himself African American, hoped to spur on the fight for Indians. "Now is the time for those who believe in Indian treaty rights to join them," Tanner announced.

What Survival lacked in resources, it made up for in a media strategy decades ahead of its time. A primary orchestrator was Hank Adams, a twenty-year-old "skinny Indian kid with black-rimmed glasses," who called Survival a "Chronicle of Courage." The skinny kid turned out to be one of the most pivotal people in Billy's life. Adams, an Assiniboine-Sioux, came originally from Fort Peck, Montana, a place they call Poverty Flats. His mother married a Quinault Indian and Adams grew up on the reservation of the Quinault Nation, the largest in Western Washington. Adams sailed through Moclips High School as editor of the paper, student body president, and a star athlete. After two years at the University of Washington, however, he traded college for a calling, dedicating the rest of his life to the wellbeing of Indian people.

"Adams was hooked to all the professors of our country, the good ones and the bad ones, people who are out there talking about the law and the protection of treaty rights," says Billy. "Adams is too smart to go to law school. Law school would tie him down. He can shoot for the stars and that's what he's been doing in his lifetime. We're just tagging along."

Adams's mark is everywhere in Indian Country, from its seminal events to its most obscure. He is as elusive as he is intelligent and loyal. Next to his immediate family, Adams is among the closest to Billy, a brother he talks with every day. For his part, Adams knows Billy's life backward and forward. He's a family historian who spews

SURVIVAL NEWS...

THE RENEGADE

Official Publication - Survival of American Indian Association

FRANKS LANDING, LACEY, WASHINGTON 98501   June 1972   THE RENEGADE

from treaty to treachery

"The right of taking fish at all usual and accustomed grounds and stations is further secured to said Indians in common with all citizens of the Territory..."

There has been no modification of the treaty since its ratification. It now stands as a contract between the original tribal groups and the United States with its more than 220,000,000 people, rather than the lesser numbers represented 117 years ago. The right itself, however, has remained constant in its character and in its limitations.

In transmitting the treaty to Washington, D.C., on Dec. 30, 1854, Territorial Governor Isaac I. Stevens wrote of its purpose and terms:

Beyond that point in time, the treaty right entered a state of uncertainty. Scarcely before there was enough time for dust to accumulate and justify a question of the treaty's antiquity, federal troops had to be stationed at various Indian fishing sites in Washington State to protect the Indian fishermen and their curing houses from the vandalism and violence of marauding white citizens in 1806.

By 1905 the United States Supreme Court was called upon to decide an issue involving the Indian fishing right. Reversing all inferior courts and contrary rulings, the court decided that treaty Indians could not be denied access nor easement to their

HANK ADAMS RESIGNS SAIA POSITION

TACOMA NEWS TRIBUNE   SAT., JUNE 24, 1972

Adams Suit One of 4 Dismissed by Judge

By WIN ANDERSON

A civil suit brought by Indian activist Henry "Hank" Adams against Tacoma Police Chief Lyle Smith and others was one of four Indian-initiated civil suits dismissed this week by U.S. District Court Judge William Goodwin on motions by the plaintiffs.

that military conscription for service in the armed forces was a violation of the terms of the Treaty of Medicine Creek.

In his petition for dismissal, William Frank Jr., writing for the plaintiffs, said the "color of law" under which the defendants have acted in these areas is "nothing more

Hank with his father, Louie Adams, in Montana. Before moving to Tahola, Washington, Hank lived on the Fort Peck Indian Reservation, one of the largest in the country.

dates, court cases, and the complex family tree like a machine gun firing away.

"Hank Adams, early on, was the one who got your attention because he was right in your face," recalls Dan Evans, governor of Washington when tribal leaders resisted state law. "He was doing things out on the river. He was making sure you understood that there was a problem. And Billy was the guy who very quickly started to say, 'This isn't working. We've got to find a better answer.'"

Adams's role in Billy's life came by happenstance in 1963. He stood inside tribal offices of the Quinault Nation. A flier in a wastepaper basket piqued his interest. The National Indian Youth Council (NIYC), an activist group founded in New Mexico in 1961, planned to meet in Roosevelt, Utah, to launch a national awareness campaign. The mission of the NIYC, "to provide and ensure that every Native American person has an equal opportunity to participate, excel and become a viable member and asset to his/her community," struck a chord. Adams had already developed a strong interest in tribal fishing rights and state jurisdiction over Indian affairs. On a whim, he opted to go. Like a scene straight from Hollywood, Adams hitchhiked, caught a bus, and hopped in a tribal car to reach Roosevelt, some thousand miles away.

"You'd have to be crazy to hitchhike out of Quinault!" Billy jokes, because of the isolated surroundings of the reservation village at Taholah. Adams found luck, however. Biologist Jim Heckman picked him up, along with Guy McMinds, a Quinault Indian. The three headed for the meeting on the Uintah and Ouray Reservation at Fort Duchesne. It was hot, dry, and the third weekend of August.

Luck did not end there. Marlon Brando, the actor, brought Kent Mackenzie, a filmmaker, to Utah for the same meeting. Mackenzie had recently finished the 1961 film *The Exiles*, a project that chronicled life for Native Americans at Bunker Hill, a forgotten corner of Los Angeles. Best known for his legendary acting ability and broodingly handsome looks, Brando possessed a deep passion for civil rights. He characterized white society's treatment of blacks as "rage" and bowed out of a movie production to devote more time to the struggle for racial equality. Of the country's relations with the Indians, Brando once seethed: "Christ Almighty, look at what we did in the name of democracy to the American Indian. We just excised him from the human race. We had 400 treaties with the Indians and we broke every one of them."

When the conversation at the NIYC meeting turned to civil rights, Brando urged the group to get involved in the movement "and break through the pervasive larger indifference of the American people by getting their attention. The greater force against you was indifference rather than the people who were hitting you all the time. Then if you could break that indifference you could get the mass of non-Indian people on your side."

Months later, after Brando marched with Dr. Martin Luther King Jr., the group reconvened in Denver and decided Brando would go to Washington State, where tribes were already actively resisting the crackdown on treaty fishing rights. "Ever since I helped raise funds for Israel as a young man and learned about the Holocaust," writes Brando in his memoirs, *Songs My Mother Taught Me*, "I developed an interest in how societies treat one another; it is one of the enduring interests of my life.

"In the early 1960s, several members of the Indian Youth Council from the Pacific Northwest told me that they had decided to challenge government limits on salmon fishing by Indians in western Washington and along the Columbia River. Century-old treaties guaranteed their tribes the right to fish at their accustomed places in perpetuity—'as long as the mountains stand, the grass grows and the sun shines.'"

Word spread that Brando might fly to Washington. "If they [Indian fishermen] feel there is an encroachment on their rights, Indians should confer with proper authorities. If this fails, they should turn to litigation," Sebastian Williams, a Tulalip Indian, told a crowd gathered in Seattle.

The public started to weigh in. One citizen called the Indians' fight for treaty rights shaky because it reflected a lifestyle long gone: "He [an Indian fisherman], probably is going to drive to the fishing spot, use some store bought materials in his gear, land a hatchery fish and take it home to a refrigerator."

AT 2:00 A.M. on March 2, Adams roused reporters to catch Brando fishing the Puyallup River in one of the biggest local news stories of the year.

"Marlon Brando is coming and we're going to have a fish-in, just like the black people had sit-ins," Bruce Wilkie, a Makah Indian, told his attorney, Al Ziontz. "Meet us at the Puyallup River bridge where Highway 99 crosses the river, just outside Tacoma, Monday morning at eight o'clock."

Brando's presence drew big-name journalists and stirred emotions across the country. The fishing struggle bumped from the sports page to the front page, and into the American living room. Throngs of journalists showed up toting the large television cameras of that era. Charles Kuralt, a CBS anchor, met Hank Adams for scrambled eggs and bacon.

"One of the things that Marlon did was bring the news media, and I mean, boy, big time. . . ," Billy recalls. "And that was part of our tools of telling the story. Oh, he was great, Marlon Brando was a great person, and he took a lot of Indian causes."

Accompanied by Bob Satiacum, a Puyallup Indian arrested for fishing violations in the 1950s, and the Reverend Canon John Yaryan of San Francisco, Brando took a very public stand in support of treaty rights but never caught a single fish. The catch came from Johnny's Seafood Company. "I got in a boat with a Native American and a . . . priest. Someone gave us a big salmon we were supposed to have taken out of the river illegally and, sure enough, a game warden soon arrived and arrested us."

"We knew the game wardens would make arrests," confirmed Mel Thom. The NIYC wanted to catch the state hassling Indians on tape, and further its campaign.

HANK ADAMS PERSONAL COLLECTION

Holding a couple of steelhead, world-famous actor Marlon Brando lends support to Northwest Indians in 1964. "One of the things that Marlon did was bring the news media, and I mean, boy, big time . . ." Billy says.

The scene played out in local newspapers.

"YOUR PURPOSE is to openly defy the state law?" charged a Game officer as they landed.

"My purpose is to help these Indians," smarted Brando, wearing a lumber jacket and surrounded by a reported five hundred Indians. The movie star told the crowd, "We made treaties as a young, weak nation when the Iroquois Confederation could have wiped us out.

When we got stronger, we broke them. . . . The government has been trying to divide and conquer the Indians. Their rights must be protected."

The officer put a quick end to the hostile banter and the show for the crowd: "I won't argue with you. You should have your day in court. I think that's what you're looking for."

Brando tossed his fish to an Indian in response as a woman yelled: "You can't do this to us. We have a treaty!"

"What are you going to do with the fish, give them to some white man?" snapped another with a baby strapped to her back.

"This is all they have left," Brando said. "Everything has been taken from them. They intend to hang on to these fishing rights."

The state said it had no intention of making arrests, but Norm Mattson pulled Brando into custody for catching a couple of eight-pound steelhead. Reputedly, Suzan Satiacum, Bob Satiacum's wife, scratched Mattson and even spat in his face.

A prosecutor from Pierce County, John McCutcheon, called the whole affair window dressing. "Brando's no fisherman!" he grumbled. Eight days later, the court dismissed the case against Bob Satiacum; charges against Brando and the Reverend Yaryan were never filed.

PROMISING A violence-free protest, tribes from across the country converged on the Capitol the next day. Indians from other areas, such as the Seminoles of Florida and the Nez Perce of Coeur d'Alene, took part in the "largest intertribal demonstration" ever held there, organized by Hank Adams. Many were the great-great-great-great grandchildren of the treaty signers. Tribal leaders danced. They delivered impassioned speeches. Accompanied by Brando, they roamed the halls of the legislative building in full regalia. "We were ending the government's divide-and-rule system among Indians," announced Thom.

The tribes issued a Proclamation of Protest, calling for the creation of a Native advisory committee and scientific research of tribes and commercial fishing, as well as an end to fishing arrests in "usual and accustomed places." Adams and other organizers issued a public statement: "The past and present history of treaties between the federal government and their captive Indian nations exemplify a treaty as a 'convenient way of license to steal' for the government . . . the seeds you sow are the crops you reap." Despite a four-hour meeting, most Indians left dissatisfied.

"Until the laws of the state or court decisions of the state indicate otherwise, I must ask all citizens to abide by the conservation regulations established by the state," Governor Rosellini announced. "Without regulation, the Pacific Salmon would be as rare as the Dodo Bird."

Nonetheless, a giddy Wilkie walked on air. "This has been the greatest Indian victory of the modern day."

INDIAN ACTIVISTS and Brando had more to do. After a late-night skull session at an Olympia hotel, the group targeted La Push, near the tip of Washington's Olympic Peninsula. Brando spent the night in a drafty cabin, a far cry from his accustomed Hollywood lifestyle, awaiting a fishing trip the next morning. The wind howled as it tore through thin walls and chilled Brando to the bone. He arose with a high fever, weary and coughing. Brando feared he was suffering from pneumonia or, at best, the "chest cold of all chest colds."

"But the Indians looked at me expectantly, and I knew I had to go," he writes in his autobiography:

> I wrapped myself in a blanket and got in the boat while icy waves whipped up by the wind sprayed everyone, and as we left shore I thought, "I'm not going to leave this boat alive." I suspected that I had pneumonia, that I was going to die and that my body would be dumped into the river. Hunched over, I told one of my Indian friends, Hank Adams, how awful I felt, and he said, "You know what my grandmother used to say?"
>
> And I thought, "My God. Finally some words of wisdom . . ."
>
> "If you smile, you'll feel better."

I just looked at him and thought, "What in this poor, pissed-on world are you talking about? I'm dying, and you're asking me to smile?"

We traveled up and down the river for an hour waiting to be arrested, but no game wardens showed up. "I don't mind dying," I thought, but to die so senselessly on a freezing river without being arrested seems absurd. Only later did we learn that we'd been on the wrong river. Patrol boats were looking for us somewhere else; I'd faced death—or so my melodrama let me convince myself—for nothing. One of the Indians' lawyers got me to an airport, and I flew home and entered the hospital with pneumonia, where I swore that someday I would repay Hank Adams. . . .

One reason I liked being with the Indians was that they didn't give anyone movie-star treatment. They didn't give a damn about my movies. Everyone's the same; everyone shares and shares alike. Indians are usually depicted as grumpy people with monochrome moods, but I learned that they have a sardonic sense of humor and love to tease. They laugh at everything, especially themselves.

Nine years later, the actor refused an Oscar for his role in *The Godfather*, citing the movie industry's treatment of Indian people.

THE ARRESTS OF BILLY and five other fishermen in March 1964 became the origin of a famous legal dispute that climbed to the U.S. Supreme Court three times—in 1968, 1973, and 1977. The Puyallup Trilogy, as the court case came to be known, includes legal challenges against the Nisqually and Puyallup Indians.

The state of Washington sued the fishermen hoping for a declaratory judgment that would deem state fishing regulations necessary for conservation. Such a judgment would lead to an injunction and criminal penalties for any Indian fisher who violated the order. At the time, the state argued that the Indians "were and are a conquered people without right or title of anything."

The six fishermen faced criticism from the tribes. Nisqually leaders chastised them as renegades for violating laws to assert their treaty

Shunned by their own tribes, fishermen were dubbed renegades for exercising their treaty rights on the banks of Washington rivers. Pictured are Jack McCloud, Don McCloud, Billy Frank Jr., Neugen Kautz, Herman John Jr., and Al Bridges.

rights, and the theater played out all over the front page. "We got some of our own people calling our family renegades for standing up for their rights. I never could get that," says Billy's son, Willie Frank III.

Meantime, George Boldt, a bright, tough federal district judge, rejected petitions for the "renegades" writs of habeas corpus and sent them to jail for a month. "We'd Rather Fish Than Be on Welfare," activists declared on picket signs as they protested the fishers' hearing.

"There was six of us that actually kept going back to jail," Billy relates. "We kept defying the state of Washington and the state judges. These sportsmen were shooting at us down at the mouth of the river. You could hear them spraying the boat. . . . When we started first going to jail, they put us in with all of the other people that was in jail, you know, bank robbers and everybody. They'd always ask us: 'What are you guys in for?' 'We're in for fishing.' 'Fishing?! What the hell are they doing? We're here for robbing a bank and killing somebody.'"

The renegades lost ground with their tribes, but gained ground with sympathizers. Their struggle remained front-page news. "First, at the beginning, nobody saw what we were doing," says Billy. "We were getting raided, and then finally they were beating on all of us, up and down the river. Finally, we got connected with the churches and all of the kind of fathers of Seattle. They come out here to witness what was going on. And that was a big time, a big change."

Although the struggle of Indian fishermen hit the papers, they remained an undisputed underdog. White society "didn't think we were smart enough, educated enough, or organized enough" to pull off the uprisings, says Joe Kalama, archivist for the Nisqually Tribe.

THE FISHING STRUGGLE worked its way from the riverbank to the floor of the U.S. Senate. Billy and the tribes could have lost their treaty rights in a buyout. In an attempt to resolve the fishing crisis, Warren Magnuson, Washington's longtime U.S. senator, proposed the government buy the tribes' treaty rights or allow the state to regulate off-reservation Indian fishing. "These [Indian] treaties are still on the books today," Magnuson attested. "They are supreme law of the land and they must be respected and honored. . . . The only concession reserved to the Indians was the right of taking fish at all usual and accustomed grounds and if they are to be deprived of any part of this they should be properly compensated. . . . I believe these treaties are part of our heritage—but solely, in support of fish conservation, I believe that these treaties should fit present day conditions in the overall consideration for maintaining our fishery resources."

Magnuson told the U.S. Senate that his request for an estimate of the Indian fishery from the Department of Interior remained unanswered; such a figure could not be estimated "since this includes commercial as well as subsistence fishing." The Interior Department did note that the Corps of Engineers paid more than $26 million for the loss of Indian fishery rights when The Dalles Dam was built.

Magnuson's proposals died in committee, but the Sportsmen's Council, an organization founded in 1934 to protect wildlife and promote sportsmanlike hunting practices, was girded for battle: "Your rivers are being destroyed. The most dangerous force at this time is the Indian fishery that exists in our rivers with total disregard for all accepted conservation principles. . . . The people of Washington and the other 49 states think of the Indian as the 'Poor ignorant Redman who has been deprived of all of his rights.'" The council continued in a letter to members: "Since 1924, he has had all of the rights you have, plus many more. . . . Help eliminate ignorance by informing the public of the truth."

Chapter 6

Canoes and Clashes

It is next to impossible to say with certainty how many times Billy Frank Jr. has been arrested. But this much is clear: by the time the fish wars ended, Billy had been pushed out of his canoe, hauled up the riverbank, bashed, and threatened.

"I was all alone down here fishing," Billy recalls. "I'm the only Indian that lived on the Nisqually River. There were some shacks up the river that the fishermen would come down and stay in, but I lived on the river and I fished on the river. So, they'd take me to jail and nobody would know I went to jail.

"First they took us over to Spanaway court, a little kangaroo court I called it. I don't know who was the judge, but they'd just make their case and the judge would find us guilty. And then we'd go to jail. Now that was in Tacoma. They never brought me to Olympia because I know everybody here. So they took us to Pierce County where the Superior Court was more against Indian fishing. You know, they were all elected people. And so they would haul us that way."

In jail next to criminals of every kind, Billy usually stood accused of poaching—fishing with the wrong gear, or in the wrong place. Judgment day came and went. Cycling through the court system took Billy away from his family and livelihood. It required hard-earned money when he was usually just scraping by.

Then, in 1965, the fishing struggle took his canoe. Canoes are a source of great pride in Indian Country. They're made from cedar trees that can grow for a thousand years. Billy's canoe told a story, like a window into the past. It traveled the river that cuts across his homeland. It held the fish that fed his family. And for years, it witnessed the growing tension with the state. And Billy's canoe was special. The Nisqually Indian had traded Johnny Bob, a master carver, some dog salmon for it years before. Johnny Bob could carve a canoe with only six or eight inches of draft. By 1965, the canoe was even better. "I had just bought me a new motor, a 20-horse Merc," Billy recalls. "I was so proud of that canoe. I could pole the canoe Johnny Bob made me eight miles upstream. It didn't matter how shallow the riffles were."

The year 1965 had already been tough on Billy. In the fall, a tug-of-war between fishermen and the state ensued until one of Billy's nets snapped. Unfortunately, he'd borrowed $150 for the net and had been saving every dime for Sugar and Maureen's school clothes.

"This is just plain stealing," Billy complained to Jim Land, a deputy sheriff for Thurston County. Billy argued to Land that his family's six acres maintained reservation status. The United States held the land in trust for the Franks and had allotted it to his father in lieu of his lost acreage at Muck Creek. The state disagreed. "We've tried to get our day in court, but the state's got lots of money. How can you fight them?" he asked.

"We're going to shoot 'em next time," Billy told Land. "This is just one big merry-go-round. It's making us sick."

IN THE FALL of 1965, Al Bridges set a net in the Nisqually River, near Frank's Landing. "He was so happy being on this river fishing," Billy remembers. "And that was his life, and the life of all of our brothers and nieces, and all of them. They give their life to this river."

Bridges was a real mentor to Billy, his closest fishing companion and brother-in-law. He was kind and serious, once characterized by the *Seattle Times* as a man without a country. Bridges was rejected by his tribe and "hounded" by the state. He spent as much time as Billy

Willie Frank Sr. stands with son-in-law Alvin Bridges.

exercising his treaty rights early on, if not more. "The Indian is more free when he's fishing on the river," Bridges said in the documentary *Treaties Made, Treaties Broken.* "He's apart from the whole country. I mean, you're way up here all alone, you're not punching a clock in the city to go to work at 8 in the morning and get off at 4:30 and somebody's riding you all day. But the white man is trying to get all of us to leave the reservation and go to the city. And I can go to the city of Seattle right now and I can find you Indians by the thousands on skid row up there. And now they don't own nothing. Nobody wants them. They're nothing but bums."

"Al, you want to go down and set your net?" Billy called out from his dugout canoe on that October day.

"Yeah, just wait till I get this anchored." The fishermen climbed into Billy's twenty-two-foot cedar canoe.

The expert fishermen approached the mouth of the Nisqually River. As they set Bridges's net, Billy spotted a wealth of silvers in his own. That's when he heard a motor in the distance.

"God damn! These guys are after us. Run to the front of the boat, Bridges," Billy yelled.

The tactic was called boat ramming. A patrol boat slammed into his canoe, spilling Billy and Bridges headfirst into the water. "Those bastards rammed us at full speed, and knocked us clean over. We had our hip boots on and it was harder'n hell to swim. I honestly thought I was going to drown," Billy said.

Billy had grown up on the river and respected its force and swiftness. Each year, the river dragged down some unlucky fisherman after water filled his boots. Even experienced fishermen lost their energy. Billy, swathed in heavy raingear and hip boots, knew for all his time on the river he was not above an accident.

Officers caught up to Billy and Al. They handcuffed the soaking-wet fishermen and carted them off to Pierce County jail. Billy sat for hours on a concrete bunk. His clothes dripped. The water in his hip boots chilled his feet.

One of the most historic canoes in Puget Sound Indian Country has a story of its own.

The state confiscated Billy's canoe that day and carted it to a warehouse where it sat for years.

"Now the canoe was a rather large craft made of a log," recalls Frank Haw, a former manager with the Department of Fisheries. "We've got this place where the patrol officers would store confiscated equipment. And I don't think I've ever been in there, but I know it was filled with all sorts of things: nets, and guns, and gaff hooks, fishing rods and everything."

Upon his release, Billy sent a telegram to Steward Udall, acting secretary of the Interior. The conflicts with the state were out of hand. In a plea for federal help, Billy recounted a 2:00 a.m. raid by the state's "riot squad:" "Leonard Squally, Nisqually Indian, and Hattie Iyall, vice chairman's wife, were wounded and hospitalized. Young children were thrown into barbed wire; many more were injured."

Years later, after the dust settled, Billy reminded the fisheries managers about his missing canoe: "You guys got my canoe!"

Frank Haw went looking for it, and discovered the canoe in the Seattle warehouse in 1980. "So by golly, it was Billy's birthday as I recall," Haw says. "We had some kind of a little get together. And that was during the Ray Administration and Gordon Sandison was there. And I mentioned this to Gordon, 'I heard that Billy's canoe is in our storage shed some place. Let's give it back to him.' And Gordon thought that was a great idea. So, it took a big truck because of the size and weight of this thing, and we hauled it to the place where we had this little get together and presented it to Billy."

The canoe had dry rotted over sixteen years. Its original carver, Johnny Bob, then ninety years old, restored it, and Billy's historic canoe now hangs from the ceiling of Wa He Lut Indian School looking out on the Nisqually River.

BILLY'S MOTHER was aghast at the array of brawls unfolding on her doorstep. "Oh boy, they had a fight! They were stopping the Indians from fishing, and this is Indian *land*," Angeline cried in utter dismay.

Witnesses provide varying accounts of the uproar on October 13, 1965 like bystanders reconstructing the scene of a fatal car crash. The Indians' take is documented in affidavits and a special report, *The Last Indian War*. The state's perspective is articulated in a subsequent investigation and report sent to the governor.

From the Game Department's perspective, its enforcers showed remarkable restraint. They knew about the planned fish-in. According to the rumor mill, Indians planned to use firearms against state officers "if need be to protect their rights."

As officers huddled at an Olympia warehouse that morning, Bob Josephson, chief of Patrol, gave orders to observe, warn, and arrest quickly. Two four-man crews crouched in nearby powered patrol boats. Roughly thirty additional officers scattered across Nisqually Hill.

Around 4:00 p.m., fishermen threw in their nets. Officers approached and chaos erupted. Officers claim they were booed, jeered, and even spat upon: "They picked up rocks and sticks and let them have it when they hit the shore." Officer Monte Seigner was "beaten with an oar" so badly blood dripped to his chin. "Blood was flowing freely from wound and down the right side of his face," fellow agent Armon Koeneman told investigators. One officer said Indians pounced on him so hard they broke his ribs.

"These people aren't Nisquallys," criticized Reuben Wells, chairman of the Nisqually Tribe. "We think we should be able to fish anywhere on the Nisqually. But we're willing to abide by the law."

There were multiple arrests, according to the state, for fishing violations, assault, and interference with officers.

Indian fishermen tell a far different story, calling the episode a vicious and unwarranted attack on nineteen women and children. The Native Americans had announced the fish-in at Frank's Landing to keep up their fight for treaty fishing rights at ancestral fishing sites off of their reservations. Fishers, children, reporters, and the family dog—a dachshund with one blue eye and one brown—sat in a boat out on the river. As the late Janet McCloud recounted, shouts filled the air: "Get 'em! Get the dirty S.O.B.'s!"

"They had billy clubs made out of lead pipe," Willie Frank recalled.

Indian activists accused the state of "carrying nightsticks" to "snuff out" a fish-in. When officers tried to arrest fishermen, the Indians pelted them with rocks and sticks, screaming: "You're on federal land."

Decades after the attack, Billy's niece Alison remembered her confrontation with a state officer: "There was a huge log that came out of the river. And, my sister and I were standing there and this game warden, he grabbed me by the hair and he started to slam my head into the log. . . . So my sister was fighting with him . . . and we got up to the cars and they were arresting my mom. . . . They were hitting my dad in the back with those brass knuckles. . . . They were clubbing him and hitting him. . . . One of the game wardens turned around

Alison Bridges saw violence first hand at the so-called Battle of Frank's Landing on October 13, 1965.

and he just punched my sister in the face . . . the blood was just spurting out. I was thirteen."

Don Hannula, a much-admired beat reporter for the *News Tribune* and later the *Seattle Times,* recalled no drinking of any kind, and "if there was any brutality, it was by shoving the children," he observed. Hannula "criticized the state quite strongly for playing into the hands of the Indians."

He wasn't alone. The state took more lashings from Representative Hal Wolf of Yelm. A box boy at Wolf's grocery store got a phone call from a relative back east "concerned about the Indian uprising."

Wolf accused the state of giving Washington a bad name and hung news clippings of the skirmish on his office walls. Wolf said he was assured that fishermen would be observed only and arrested later to avoid the very outcome that occurred.

Jim Siburg witnessed the incident with his wife and children: "The thing that upset me so about it was the way the state people came in there and the guys were around with billy clubs and they would gang up on these poor little Indians. The guy they hustled off first couldn't have weighed more than 125 pounds. They must have had four or five guys. The guy hustling him to the car had a sap hanging out of his pocket. The state people should have maintained a cooler atmosphere.

"I saw one of the state people pick up a little girl, who couldn't have been more than ten years old, by the hair. She had probably been throwing rocks at him."

The observations, though conflicting, were starting to sway public opinion toward the Indians. "We have received letters of support and donations from all over the world," Janet McCloud told Hannula.

"Regarding the state's treatment of Indians . . . I think it was intentionally vicious and racist, probably from the time Washington became a state," says Susan Hvalsoe Komori, a former attorney for the Nisqually Tribe. "The Game Department really wanted to eradicate Indians in the years I lived out there. They regarded the fishery resource as their own—especially steelhead."

J. Johnson, publisher and editor of the *Auburn Citizen*, boarded a plane for Washington, D.C., and warned the Interior Department: "If something isn't done somebody is going to get killed." Johnson was taken seriously but turned away and told, "Only the state had authority."

THE STATE'S NEW chief executive, Dan Evans, had taken the helm that January. "Your first impression of this is we've got to stop the violence. We've got to stop this kind of unlawful behavior. It was the

Game Department Police really—the game agents—that were engaged in this uproar and war on the river."

In his early days as Governor, Evans says he backed the state in its regulations of off-reservation net fishing. He recalls telling Billy, a young activist at the time, "You've got to follow the law. And the law is that this [steelhead] is a game fish and you shouldn't be fishing it."

After October 13, on-duty officers with the departments of Game and Fisheries faced serious charges. A doctor accused one officer of hitting him in the stomach with a nightstick and drinking on the job. Evans demanded a full report.

"I didn't like what was going on, didn't like the violence and talked to the Game people and they said thank you very much but the Game Commission is telling us this is what we want to do," he recalls. "I tried to talk with them and to see if there wasn't a way out. And they were determined to break this thing. They were determined that steelhead were game fish, they were being supported by the sport fishermen and the sportsmen's organization. The hunting organizations all joined in. They were all on the side of the Game Department. I do remember going to the head of the Game Department and saying this can't go on. We look terrible."

THROWN STICKS, rocks, and clubs outside Billy's home did enough damage in twenty minutes to result in stinging accusations against the state. Allegations of excessive force on the part of state officers were turned over to the Bureau of Indian Affairs and the Federal Bureau of Investigation. The case went to trial.

A jury in Thurston County Superior Court deliberated for two hours and cleared seven Indians charged in the "Battle of Frank's Landing." Attorney Al Ziontz argued that the fish-in was a staged demonstration, a show, and the net they used was "virtually incapable of catching fish." Therefore, the officers used excessive force, Ziontz said persuasively. Officers testified that "no nightsticks, long flashlights, or blackjacks were used." However, Ziontz brandished "a blackjack confiscated by Indians at the time with name of a game warden on it" and entered pictures of officers with "nightsticks and flashlights" as evidence.

That particular court case ended, but the feud was far from over. According to Hank Adams, the state led some thirty attacks against fishermen on the lower Nisqually from 1962 through 1970; it made more than a hundred arrests of Native people on the Nisqually and Puyallup Rivers and at the Landing. The state continued its crackdown, and sports anglers weren't about to give up. "The Indians and the sportsmen have been fighting on these rivers forever," Billy's brother, Andrew McCloud, once said. "We've gotten so fond of them as enemies, I guess we'll never be able to think of them as friends."

Chapter 7

As Long as the Rivers Run

More than a fisherman and the face of the struggle for treaty rights, Billy lived at its nerve center, on six acres, fast becoming a landmark in one of the most tumultuous decades in modern American history as a tide of opposition rose in the 1960s. After the Battle of Frank's Landing in 1965, Billy's family enclave continued to bear witness to the Indians' battle for sovereignty.

Take the year 1966. Talk of a rally percolated through the rumor mill that January. Northwest Indians planned to burn the sitting governor, Dan Evans, in effigy at Frank's Landing. "I don't think up to now I've been burned in effigy," the governor quipped. Still, Evans held firm, "If we allow people to determine which court injunctions and directives they choose to follow and which they choose to break, we descend to the rule of the jungle."

Two hundred Indians from more than fifteen tribes arrived at the Landing. Some, like the Walla Walla and Nez Perce, crossed snowy mountain passes to air their grievances, to rally and to dance. They lit a teepee-shaped bonfire in a drizzling rain.

Janet McCloud, Billy's sister-in-law, lashed out at Evans: "He unleashed his Game Department to come down upon us like a bunch of mad dogs!"

WASHINGTON STATE ARCHIVES

At Frank's Landing in 1965, a crowd and network news cameras look on at fisherman Al Bridges with several chinook.

Yakama Indians led the war dance as drums sounded and "two maidens threw a life-sized effigy of Governor Dan Evans on the fire, while the Indians cheered and emitted war whoops in approval in a two-hour rally."

"I think our ancestors were fools to sign the treaty," shouted one Indian woman. "What have we got to lose? What are you fighting for?"

In the court of public opinion, the symbolic hanging did not reflect well on the tribes. Evans was picked on "because he happens to be the state's chief executive, who is required by the Constitution

to enforce laws as they are written and interpreted by the courts—not as he might wish to apply the laws," criticized the *Seattle Times*. "It is apt to do the cause more harm than good. It certainly will not damage the governor's image any more than will the flames of the 'burning in absentia' singe his jacket," the newspaper opined.

Dan Evans is hardly a stranger to the pitfalls of public office. The moderate Republican is a legend in Washington politics, with forty volumes of scrapbooks documenting his trials and triumphs. He is a three-term governor, a one-term U.S. senator, and a one-time serious contender for the vice presidency.

When Evans took over the governor's office in 1965, you could have tripped over the disgruntled citizens climbing the Capitol steps.

"We were just on the eve of the fish wars," Evans remembers. "I ran into all of this almost immediately, not what I expected. I first met his dad, Bill Frank, who lived to be a hundred. He was still pretty active at that time, and his son, Billy, was kind of a firebrand. The whole thing started on the Nisqually with the Game Department. The Game Department was run by the Game Commission, a seven-member commission, all of whom had been appointed by my predecessor. So I had no real power over the Game Commission until I started appointing my own members."

"The sportsmen and just the 'good old boys' of this network of white people—they had their own way so long," Billy recalls. "They fished whenever they wanted. The Washington Department of Game was a private sports enforcement agency put up by the state of Washington, and it was to protect the sportsmen."

Evans's knowledge of Indian issues garnered during eight years in the state house of representatives—four of which he spent as Republican leader—paid off. But Evans says he still had a lot to learn.

YOU COULD HAVE heard a pin drop when the governor walked into one of his first meetings with the tribal leaders in the mid-1960s. The governor's conference room was usually the setting for press conferences and meetings with dignitaries, and it looked the part. Velvet window treatments framed campus views. Grand chandeliers hung above a long table, with Evans's chair—the tallest of fourteen—sitting prominently at one end. On this day, not a single smile greeted the governor. No one spoke a word. Evans noted a large number of tribal members—many in full regalia—flanking the table.

"When you have meetings like this, even with groups that are antagonistic or that have problems, there is usually a little banter before you get started," Evans says. "This was pretty grim. I realized that they had been through many meetings like this going way, way back and in every one they'd come away empty-handed."

Evans, in 1998, testified before the U.S. Senate about those early years as governor and the Washington State Indian Affairs Commission he appointed by executive authority in 1967: "Tribal leaders of the many tribes in Washington State gathered and listened solemnly and without expression to my initial proposals for closer cooperation and respect. They brought with them the century of broken promises and lies which represented their previous experience with governmental leaders."

"Over the years, I grew to really admire and respect the tribes and got really very close to an awful lot of the tribal leaders as time went on," Evans says today. "That initial skepticism began to diminish as we began to make some progress. It took years."

The head of the Game Department, John Biggs, was pulled in every direction. "I was pounding on him on one side," Evans says. "The Game Commission were some of the Good Old Boys and they were all hunters and fishermen. The Game Department, obviously, represented the sport hunters and the sport fisherman."

THE MID-SIXTIES brought more celebrities to Frank's Landing. Known for his "biting brand of comedy that attacked racial prejudice," Dick Gregory played a nightclub in Seattle when the invitation arrived from Billy and other activists to join them at a Washington powwow in February 1966. The African American had sympathized with the Indian all of his life. He fished in Washington to correct an injustice, he says. "America had gone all over the world dropping bombs and upholding treaties. . . . Now we turn our backs on the Indian in America, who is the oldest resident American, and say, '*Your* treaty was no good.' . . . The day must come when America shows the same concern for her treaties with the Indians, as she does for her treaties with other countries." Gregory also knew something about hard knocks and fighting for what you've got. "When there was no fatback to go with the beans, no socks to go with the shoes, no hope to go with tomorrow, [Momma would] smile and say: 'We ain't poor, we're just broke.'"

At the powwow, a fishing activist was hooked. Calling it a campaign of dignity for all men, Gregory headed to Olympia with his wife, Lillian.

"I deplore these self-appointed guardians of the Indians' fishing rights when they have little knowledge of what the situation is all

HANK ADAMS PERSONAL COLLECTION

To honor Lillian Gregory and her activism during the fish wars, the Frank's Landing Indian Community will dedicate its boat launch to the wife of the famous comedian.

about," Evans lamented in response. Unless there was a threat to the resource, the governor discouraged the state from arresting "celebrities," especially noting Gregory's run for mayor of Chicago at the time.

"This is going to be about as much a publicity stunt as the Boston Tea Party," Gregory snapped.

From the other side of the river, Game officers watched the Gregory fish-in, but heeded the governor's warning and never apprehended him. "I fail to get very excited about this sort of thing," said Biggs. "I can't see where a comedian can play any important role in the problem of off-reservation Indian fishing." Days later, however, authorities arrested both Dick and Lillian Gregory. At the Thurston County jail, the celebrity inmates received telegrams from Dr. Martin

Luther King Jr., British philosopher Bertrand Russell, and James Farmer, national director of the Congress of Racial Equality.

With wife Lillian still in jail, Gregory posted five hundred dollars bail to slip on a suit and take part in a college panel discussion on Indian fishing rights at St. Martin's College in Lacey. After the forum, the activist returned to the riverbank. That's where he found Billy, wearing hip boots and poling a canoe. "This is for Evans," Billy shouted as he and three other fishermen pulled a handful of steelhead from their net. Gregory and a rousing crowd yelled in approval from the shore. In its sweep of the river the night before, the Game Department had missed a submerged net, hidden by the bridge on Old Highway 99.

Both sides took a beating in the press for Gregory's involvement in the fish-ins. Elmer Kalama, a Nisqually Indian, said Gregory's presence was hurting their cause. "We are not fighting for civil rights," Kalama said. "We have our civil rights. We can vote and do anything any other citizen can do. We just want our fishing rights."

Characterizing the jailing as the latest shenanigan, the *Times*'s Herb Robinson castigated the state. "Officials performed a preposterous flip-flop by arresting Gregory for illegal net-fishing only four days after they had indicated action would not be taken if the violation clearly was part of a fish-in and not a threat to conservation of the state's fisheries resource." Robinson continued, "The Indians, meantime, have undercut the dignity of their own position by resorting to the importation in the past of controversial figures such as Marlon Brando and Melvin Bell to generate additional publicity for their fish-ins. Even some Indians themselves were dismayed at the antics on the banks of the Nisqually where men and children joined Indian fishermen in brawling with the state game agents and where Gov. Dan Evans was burned in effigy."

At first, Gregory acknowledges, his involvement was met with some skepticism. But his name drew interest in Northwest fish-ins across the country, and the tribes appreciated his droll sense of humor. Once asked by a reporter if the tribes would welcome him as a new member, Gregory retorted, "No thanks, I've got enough problems."

Gregory caught more fish in Washington, and later served more time in jail. He fasted behind bars. When his weight plummeted to 135 pounds, authorities approved him for house arrest. "They sure as hell didn't want a black man dying in their jail," Billy says.

IN EARLY APRIL 1968, seventy-two hours before Martin Luther King Jr. was assassinated, he sat in Atlanta next to Hank Adams at Paschal's Motor Hotel and Restaurant, a gathering place for the civil rights movement. King had just missed his daughter's birthday and the group agreed to keep the meeting brief. Adams was named to the steering committee of King's latest undertaking, the Poor People's Campaign, a crusade to end poverty. King had threatened sit-ins in the halls of Congress if lawmakers did not meet demands of the President's Commission on Civil Disorders:

> The Reverend Martin Luther King, Jr. and the Southern Christian Leadership Conference have announced a Poor People's Campaign in Washington to arouse the conscience of America to reconstruct our society in consonance with the democratic process. We join with Dr. King in renouncing violence as an instrument of change, and support his plan for a dramatization of the desperate conditions of the poor in rural areas and city ghettoes as expressed through the current Poor People's Campaign.
>
> In the present climate of tension, citizens should be given every opportunity to petition for redress of their grievances. Society must recognize that non-violent demonstrations are a salutary alternative to self-defeating violence.

By 1968, King had professed his dream and won the Nobel Peace Prize. Lyndon Johnson had just announced he would not seek reelection to the presidency. King summarized Johnson's contributions to the civil rights movement and the standing of Indians in the country held the group's attention.

King was a hero of Billy's. The elder remembers the synergy of that period in history. "He was looking for what he was looking for in civil rights. We were looking for protecting our treaties, and our natural resources, and natural world. We gathered up together and we marched with him. We did a lot of things together back in D.C. Them things are direct action things. All of that in that time was direct action." At the end of the meeting, the group stood, clasped hands and sang, "We Shall Overcome." Within seventy-two hours of the Atlanta gathering, an assassin targeted King. The way Billy puts it, hope for Indians went out the door.

King's dream for the Poor People's Campaign lived on at the U.S. Capitol, precisely as the leader had planned. Participants demanded "more money and dignity for the needy and hinting disorder if the demands aren't met." After the funeral, Adams and the steering committee met to plan a May 1 schedule for the Committee of One Hundred.

In May, twenty-four Indians met at Frank's Landing, where they were urged by Wallace Anderson, a Tuscarora tribal chief who goes by Mad Bear, to join the cause. "The Indians and other races in this country cannot be kicked around any longer," Mad Bear told them.

Billy's family caravanned to Washington, D.C. Maiselle Bridges and Edith McCloud recruited marchers. Billy arrived to join the cause when he wasn't on the job as a highline electrical worker.

IN THE MIDST of the campaign, the U.S. Supreme Court dealt a mighty blow. Together with a case involving Puyallup Indians, the high court considered off-reservation treaty rights of Billy and five other "renegades" to fish with nets on the Nisqually River in 1964. It examined the Treaty of Medicine Creek and considered the constitutionality of state fishing laws. The major case known as *Puyallup I*, of the Puyallup Trilogy, upheld the state of Washington's rights to restrict off-reservation fishing, provided that regulations conserved the resource and did not discriminate against the tribes. Whether a total ban was necessary and whether regulations were discriminatory remained unanswered by the court. "The manner of fishing, the size of the take, the restriction of commercial fishing and the like may be regulated by the state in the interests of conservation, provided the regulation does not discriminate against the Indians," the court held.

"The Supreme Court ruled that they have a treaty right to fish there with rod and line but not with the forbidden nets. In granting them the right to fish at the 'usual and accustomed places,' the treaty did not grant the right to fish in the usual and accustomed manner," reported the *Washington Post*.

"The decision reflects nothing more than a political compromise and a surrender to industries of the Northwest," Hank Adams told reporters. Marchers pounding the pavement to bring justice to the poor protested on behalf of Indian fishermen. They attempted to pry open the doors of the court and broke at least four windows. Adams led the charge and persuaded police to allow protestors to personally request the court to amend its decision. "We expected the doors to be shut because the doors of justice have been closed to American Indians for many years, for centuries. We came here to open them and we opened them."

"We want Justice!" cried George Crows Fly High.

"We had not been able to get the support of all the other Indians in the Poor People's Campaign to support that decision to protest," Adams says. "But we did secure the support of all the Hispanic, Chicano, Puerto Rican, and Mexican-Americans that were involved. We had about five hundred Indians and Hispanics make this major demonstration at the U.S. Supreme Court protesting. We were there all day protesting. We were going by the U.S. Supreme Court building single file. There were all these court personnel, clerks, everyone out standing up on the top of the steps looking down.

"When we got the full length past the Supreme Court, we stopped and turned. Primarily female personnel, clerks, secretaries, so forth—

Signs warn state officers to stay away from Frank's Landing.

they started screaming. 'Ah, they're coming in here!' and they all ran back through the doors.'"

One of the most important outcomes of the Poor People's Campaign was the commitment of the Justice Department to "bring lawsuits if necessary against the states of Oregon and Washington to protect treaty fishing."

DAYS AFTER THE U.S. Supreme Court loss, the tribes lost a powerful advocate. Fresh off a huge California primary victory for the presidential nomination, Robert Kennedy was moving toward a press room when Sirhan Sirhan fired a pistol within an inch of the candidate's head. Kennedy was pronounced dead within twenty-six hours.

"Robert Kennedy we met in Portland, Oregon, and then they killed him in Los Angeles, so another hope went out the door," says Billy. "Martin Luther King got killed. All of that . . . our hope kind of drowned out."

"Those losses impacted Indian people," says Adams, who had served as a consultant to Senator Kennedy's staff. "Made the fights that I've had to make more difficult, made them more necessary, perhaps."

TIME MAGAZINE called 1968 "the year that changed the world." At Frank's Landing, change blew in with the fall rains. The youth who arrived from all over the country—they called them hippies—lived in plastics tents and cooked on portable stoves. They wrapped themselves in army blankets and huddled around a crude sign nailed to a tree. A newspaperman asked how long they planned to stay. Until the Indians' fishing rights are restored, they'd answered. At that encampment alone, they stayed more than forty-six days.

At the time, the Seattle Times noted that you could have compared the Indian population of Washington to a "disappointing turnout for a Husky football game." Still, the movement for treaty rights grew. "They came from everywhere to join our fight," Billy says. "The kids came and stayed with us and went to jail with us."

Noting the recent U.S. Supreme Court decision, the state banned net fishing on the Nisqually River. Supporters arrived from as far away as Nevada, Wyoming, Montana, and California to guard the tribal fishermen's nets. They belonged to activist groups like the Peace and Freedom Party, Students for a Democratic Society, the Socialist Workers Party, and the Black Panther Party.

Officers made a string of arrests, mostly for interfering with authorities. They accused some supporters of being "bent on civil disorder." Indian fishermen reported at least two instances of tear gas near the encampment. When two sympathizers of the Native cause were arrested and given haircuts minutes before they posted bail, Hank Adams announced that certain tribal members would bear arms. "We are not seeking a confrontation," Adams clarified. "We just want to protect this property from trespass."

"These were tense moments," recalls Suzan Harjo, a Cheyenne and Muscogee woman appointed by Jimmy Carter in 1978 as congressional liaison of Indian Affairs. Harjo sees the six acres at Frank's Landing as a real world classroom. "[The] community got it early on that the way you develop a lot of support was to give people tasks. It's the oldest way of delegation in the world. You give a knight a quest. They were giving famous people a task, calling attention to the people who were trying to uphold their treaties, not just citizen vigilantes. They had a big story to tell. . . . These treaties aren't just for the Indians. These treaties are for everyone."

"Right up through the Boldt Decision, we had two or three hundred people living here," Alison Gottfriedson recalled years later. "To protect the nets, they stayed in tents. During the winter, it would snow. But they stayed in the tents even though it was cold."

MEANTIME, tribal fishermen took their case to the public—unfiltered. Cameras rolled for the making of *As Long As the Rivers Run*, an inside look at the struggle for treaty rights shot between 1968 and 1970. Carol Burns, a non-Indian filmmaker, characterizes herself as a "hippie who rejected the white man's dog-eat-dog world." The Indians were "roughed up and stomped on," Burns says. The documentary shows the impact of the fishing struggle on families at the Landing. When male fishermen were in jail, the women put on hip boots and fished. Footage shows officers dragging Billy's wife, Norma, and his sister, Maiselle, up the riverbank and across rocky terrain. "A lot of people have asked us how long have I been involved in this, or my family and I go back to when my little girl was two and a half years old, my

CAROL BURNS, *AS LONG AS THE RIVERS RUN*

State officers haul Billy from rocks during a fish-in at Capitol Lake in 1968.

youngest girl, and she'll be nineteen next month," Maiselle says in the documentary. "When she was two and a half years old was the very first time her dad was arrested and did thirty days in jail. This was her first experience in going into a judge's courtroom. If you call a J.P. a courtroom."

As Long As the Rivers Run captured the fallout from the fishing feud as it unfolded at Frank's Landing and at the Capitol in Olympia. On one occasion, in the fall of 1968, crowds lined the Fifth Avenue

Bridge. Indians and their supporters stood shoulder-to-shoulder in front of Kentucky Fried Chicken. Adams, running for Congress at the time as a Republican, revved up the crowd behind a bullhorn. Billy is shown sitting on a rock when police appear.

"They packed me up the bank and threw me in the sheriff's car," Billy recalls, before breaking into a grin. "Adams, the Fearless Fos, comes flying into the police car," he adds. Billy calls Adams "Fearless Fos" often and everywhere. The nickname stuck years ago, taken from a character in the immortal *Dick Tracy* cartoons. He's "pure, underpaid and purposeful" the creator said of his character.

"What the hell are you doing here?" Billy asked Adams that day in the police car. Adams was the organizer in charge of the demonstration.

"We're going to jail."

Billy tells how officers then tossed "some white kid" into the police car for asking them too many questions about Indians. "What the hell are *you* doing here?" Billy quipped.

IN 1968, FRANK'S LANDING activists and supporters staged emotional demonstrations at the Temple of Justice and the Thurston County courthouse. "Now another beautiful young red sister, Suzette Bridges," a woman said as she introduced Billy's niece to the crowd. Bridges, a young enrolled Puyallup Indian, delivered an impassioned speech:

"When we go out and talk to all these citizens of America, we tell them, 'You'd better do something about your government, because your government is awfully sick. And it's trying to make my people sick.' I keep trying to explain to these people that we're never, never, never going to be like them."

Tears streamed down her cheeks as she cried to the crowd, "I don't know what's wrong with Dan Evans! And I don't know what's wrong with Thor Tollefsen! Why is it that they keep practicing genocide on my people?" That day, activists dropped a parting gift for the governor on his doorstep. The mansion cook didn't know what happened to the "mystery" fish, but gibed that "there'd be no salmon cooking in her kitchen" that night.

IN OCTOBER 1968, a force of state officers raided the continuing encampment at Frank's Landing. "This thing is clear out of perspective," fired R. D. Robison, a Fisheries assistant director. "They're not concerned with Indian fishing rights. They're trying to incite riots."

The community at Frank's Landing viewed the encampment as direct action, a tool to protect their treaty rights. State officers were ordered to leave the Frank trust property and informed they were trespassing. Adams said the officers insisted they "have a right to go anywhere," and brandished clubs. They directed a boat on the other side of the river to take a net that belonged to Billy, his wife, and his niece," Adams wrote in an open letter to Governor Evans. Adams warned the state's chief executive that Willie Frank's fear of the whites had since grown, and the state would not be permitted on the property. The letter noted the recent court order "prescribing haircuts for prisoners immediately upon entry into the Thurston County jail— citing sanitation as the basis. It seemed clearly evident, however, that the order was secured primarily to carry out the threats against Al Bridges and other Indians, as well as non-Indians now involved in the fight over fishing rights." The situation grew so intense, Adams told Evans in the same communication, that sessions took place in which Fisheries Department officers planned to "create an incident wherein they could 'justify' homicides premeditated."

By October's end, fishermen secured a guarantee from the Justice Department that it would protect their civil rights. They removed armed guards from the property. Money came in from benefit performances by the Grateful Dead, Redbone, and James Taylor. Canadian Indian Buffy St. Marie arrived and wrote a song about the fishermen.

For his part, the governor had established a special fact-finding group on Indian Affairs which interviewed fishermen. A couple of months into 1969, staff members talked with Billy. In the governor's papers at the State Archives, interviewers note: "Billy did not once speak with malice, but was as friendly 'as an old shoe' and appreciative of any assistance that could be given. He did wonder why the state has kept the nets of the acquitted and asked for assistance in that area."

Among the conclusions of Evans's committee: fishing is a matter of "great emotional importance" to the Indian people, the Nisqually Tribe does support its members fishing off reservations, and attitudes of the state and county authorities toward Indians and their treaty rights are "excessively arbitrary and punitive."

When December arrived, Walter Neubrech, head of enforcement at the Department of Game, placed a call to the Bureau of Indian Affairs, expressing the state's interest in purchasing Frank's Landing. "He indicated that at the present time there were about 20 Hippies getting really entrenched in the area and this would be one way of getting them off the property."

The state never acquired the land.

Chapter 8

Takeovers

Like the regal bald eagle that soars above the trees and a distressing past that nearly left it extinct, Billy Frank and fellow Indians at the Landing see themselves as survivors, indefatigable soldiers of sovereignty. They are extensions of each other who used to trade personal effects, such as necklaces, when they traveled.

"They really have a collective knowledge, a collective wisdom, a collective history and they have expanded each other beyond human size," says Suzan Harjo, a congressional liaison of Indian Affairs appointed by Jimmy Carter. "It's that kind of spirit that has made non-Indians fear us and some still do. That's what they mean by tribalism. . . . What they don't understand is that the power comes from uniting over the good and to have this day and this life. It's generational and it's timeless." The Frank's Landing family united with tribes across the country in a sweeping movement. Its catalyst was the much publicized takeover of Alcatraz. For their ancestors who, a century before, brokered treaties with the United States and surrendered their homeland, Native Americans climbed into boats on San Francisco Bay in November 1969. They hauled water up jagged cliffs of Alcatraz Island armed with twenty-four dollars' worth of glass beads, a "precedent set by the white man's purchase of [Manhattan] Island about 300 years ago," note activists in the proclamation, "To the Great White Father and All His People." An 1868 treaty with the Sioux Nation gave Indians "exclusive reversionary title" to any unclaimed federal property, the new occupiers said. Alcatraz may have once locked up the likes of gangster Al Capone, but soon after it deteriorated in salty air and shut down, Indians from thirty tribes mobilized. They united on Alcatraz as they came together on Washington riverbanks. What they wanted was recognition of their treaty rights and a way of life. They wanted an end to poverty and a chance to preserve their heritage. When they took over Alcatraz, every American with a newspaper read the news.

"We're taking back Indian land," organizer Dean Chavers told Willie, Billy's father, on the eve of the takeover.

"Good for you!" Willie replied from Frank's Landing, informing Chavers that supporters were headed to San Francisco Bay and "the rock." The occupation of Alcatraz, which lasted nearly nineteen months, is considered a turning point, triggering a wave of seventy-four takeovers across the country that helped shift public policy toward Native Americans.

UPRISINGS CONTINUED in the Pacific Northwest. Billy's son Sugar had just turned nine when they arrested him at Fort Lawton, a decommissioned military base on the west end of Seattle. "He was only about that big," Billy says laughing and extending his arm. "We were all there, my boys and everybody." The plan to take Fort Lawton came in the midst of pending legislation that approved a no-cost transfer of the post to local government for parks and recreational use. Bernie Whitebear, a Colville Indian, led the effort to reclaim the installation as Indian land.

On a wind-whipped day in March 1970, Whitebear confronted Henry "Scoop" Jackson, a longtime and popular U.S. senator from Washington State:

"We believe the time has now arrived for the Indian to use his own initiative, take charge of his own destiny and at the same time make a contribution to greater society," Whitebear told the senator.

FORT LAWTON!

MADE IN OKLAHOMA BY INDIANS AT ALCO PRINTING 1612 N.W. 41h. OKLAHOMA CITY CK-5-9901

INDIAN LAND

In March 1970, Native Americans unite in a campaign to take over Fort Lawton, a decommissioned military base in Seattle.

"You will have to go through the Department of the Interior. . . . I can only emphasize the need to follow the law on that because otherwise you wouldn't be eligible," Jackson warned. Early in his career, Jackson pushed for the termination of Indian tribes. He later changed his mind and authored key legislation to promote Indian self-determination.

"He wasn't even paying attention," said Sid Mills in disgust. "That's how they all are." Mills, a Yakama Indian, had withdrawn from the U.S. Army to remain in Washington and fight for treaty rights. He married Billy's niece, Suzette. On the morning of the invasion, hundreds of Indians walked the beaches, scaled bluffs, and stormed the compound. Bob Satiacum, a Puyallup Indian, read the proclamation: "We, the Native Americans, reclaim the land known as Fort Lawton, in the name of all American Indians by right of discovery."

In no time, the 392nd Military Police Company arrived. "Move in and take them away!" hollered an M.P. sergeant.

"The army closed in on scattered groups of Indians," Billy says. "Women were knocked to the ground. Men were clubbed. Cameras were smashed. Movie film and tapes were destroyed. Sixty-four people, the youngest of them three years old, were held all day in two cells."

Once again, tribal fishermen drew Hollywood. Just the night before, actress Jane Fonda announced to Johnny Carson and late night television that she would use her celebrity to help coastal fishermen reassert their treaty rights.

After a visit to Frank's Landing, Fonda was whisked off first to Fort Lawton and then to Fort Lewis, the site of a second invasion. In the aftermath of the occupations, Indians leveled stinging accusations against military police, describing beatings that took place behind bars. The U.S. Army insisted the only time any "military person touched anyone was to help them off the post." But a newsman witnessed one young Indian who was shoved against a desk. Fonda and eighty-four Indians received letters from the army expelling them from the post.

One week later demonstrators returned to Fort Lawton. Again, they walked the beaches, climbed the bluffs, and lit a fire as the sun rose. "If you read me, listen," Whitebear ordered over his walkie-talkie. "We are in position on the Fort Lawton Indian Reservation. We have erected a teepee, started a fire and about 50 of us are waiting for the MPs to arrive."

A handkerchief rose in the air as a flag of truce. "The colonel says he has 30,000 troops at his disposal and he will call them if necessary," Gary Bray told the crowd.

"Let him!" someone shouted in return.

"It was a little terrifying when I saw them white helmets come," Sugar says. "I kind of got scared. And then after I realized they were just going to arrest us, not actually beat us, I kind of calmed down and just listened to Alison [Bridges]."

"Just lay down and make them pack you!" Alison urged.

"We just hugged each other and laid down so we made them work," says Sugar. "They didn't even handcuff us. They just put us on a bus and they took us to their jail."

"The Indians were defeated once again by the United States Army," Billy says.

The invasions at Fort Lawton and Fort Lewis intrigued journalists across the world. One call came from the Italian News Agency: "'Is it true that you have twelve thousand Indians living in your city?'" asked a journalist in bewilderment. "'How do they get along with everybody else?' They are everybody else," he was told.

Protests continued at the fort until the government agreed to negotiate a land deal. Days before Halloween in 1973, Jackson dedicated Discovery Park to the British sloop HMS *Discovery* that explored Puget Sound in the eighteenth century. "The whole country owes you a debt of gratitude," Jackson told the crowd. The city of Seattle, Native Americans, and the federal government signed a ninety-nine-year lease to construct a center to promote Indian culture, heritage, and education. In May 1977, the Daybreak Star Indian Cultural Center at Discovery Park opened its doors.

AS TAKEOVERS CONTINUED in 1970, tragedy struck the family, with the death of Valerie Bridges, Billy's niece. Billy and Valerie shared a passion for the Nisqually River. She had grown up at Frank's Landing—swimming, fishing, and watching Billy's children—and was considered an expert swimmer. One May afternoon she lingered after a swim with her sister Alison, following a long day planting bare-root seedlings for an industrial tree farm.

Willie, Billy's father, organized an all-out search when Valerie failed to return from the river. Georgiana Kautz remembers a dog continually plunging into the river and returning to shore. Eventually, the canine led the search party to Valerie's shampoo bottle, glasses, and comb; her body was discovered nearby. Most likely, Valerie had suffered a seizure or a leg cramp. She had been taking medication for periodic blackouts.

Indians came together 150-strong to bury Billy's niece. Semu Huaute, a Chumash medicine man, directed in the production of a funeral wheel. "These people that I loved so much . . . all of a sudden are gone . . . Valerie, my niece . . .," Billy says, reflecting on the time period. Until she died, Valerie fought for Frank's Landing and the right of Indians to fish there. Days before the river claimed Valerie's life, she and Alison swam out in the channel to "determine by string measure, how much land across the river should belong to their grandfather. The hope was to resolve the status of Frank's Landing that by her death had been embroiled in debate."

Valerie and her family had recently pored over documents at the BIA, hunting for information on the condemnation of the Nisqually Reservation that could shed light on the status of Willie's six acres. "In her lifetime, the state of Washington did not enact or promulgate one statute or one regulation that would have allowed Valerie to fish for salmon as a Nisqually or Puyallup Indian," Hank Adams says.

At the time of her death, Valerie was awaiting sentencing for a third-degree assault conviction stemming from a September 1969 tussle with a Fisheries officer and a two-foot-long vine maple club. "I was going to protect my property," Valerie told the court. In Valerie's defense, Billy's daughter Maureen Frank testified that officers treated her cousins like "men" and burst into tears on the witness stand. Valerie was named a codefendant in an upcoming trial on the jurisdiction of Frank's Landing and whether the land should be treated as a reservation. "The trial meant so much to her," said Adams. "Now the best memorial to her would be a free Frank's Landing."

THE SIGNS WARNED intruders to stay off Indian land. Puget Sound Indians established a camp in August 1970 on the banks of the Puyallup River, a glacier-chilled waterway that springs from the west side of Mount Rainier. Every September, the salmon run the Puyallup. For thousands of years, Indian fishermen caught a bountiful catch there as silvers and kings headed home to spawn in the Pacific Northwest.

But trouble was in the air on September 9, 1970. Campers, a mix of tribal fishermen and supporters, guarded nets to protect them from state raids.

"The camp was set up . . . because the pigs down there . . . beat up Indian people for fishing and just for being there," said Sid Mills, a Frank's Landing activist.

Billy headed for the Landing to wait out the storm. "What Billy did was take the children. His own daughter, Maureen, spent some time at the camp. Billy and Norma and probably Maureen babysat Powhattan at their home at Frank's Landing," recalls Burns, a documentary filmmaker who participated in the encampment that day.

Another group of children, including Billy's son, Sugar, sought refuge at the home of Ramona Bennett, the Puyallup woman in charge of the encampment. "I just seen the panic in the guys' faces," Sugar says, "that they're getting ready to come in and we need to get the kids out of here. So I got escorted out before they even got there."

The departments of Game and Fisheries, supported by the city of Tacoma, descended on Indian land to "enforce fishing and health laws."

"We are fishing! We're armed and prepared to defend our rights with our lives," Billy's sister Maiselle shouted.

"Lay down your arms! Peacefully leave the area," authorities shouted.

"There was a net strung from the Railroad Bridge downstream for some 100 feet," the Game Department's Walter Neubrech recalled from the witness stand years later. "As the two officers launched a boat to seize this net, four shots were fired at them from the opposite bank on which we stood. We did not actually see anyone tending those nets, but our job was to remove them from the Puyallup River. At that time the Indians and their sympathizers attempted to burn the Railroad Bridge with fire bombs.

"The Indians challenged the Department of Fisheries making it known that they would defend these nets from confiscation with guns . . . a good number of them did discharge weapons. The bullets came dangerously close to some of the officers involved. They used fire bombs and large knives and clubs. They exploded at least three fire bombs."

Many Dog Hides, head of encampment security, said an Indian activist threw a fire bomb on the railroad bridge to hold back the state as authorities moved across the bridge. "It's a sad thing we have

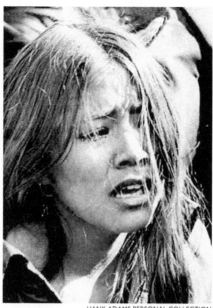

HANK ADAMS PERSONAL COLLECTION

Alison Bridges, in one of the most published photo-
graphs of the fish wars. September 9, 1970.

to bring guns out. But we are a dying people and have to fight for our survival, as we have been doing for 500 years," he said.

"They were all up on the [Highway] 99 bridge, with rifles, and we could see their rifles kicking, and you could feel the bullets going by; there is nowhere you can go," said Bennett.

"Your face burned," remembered Alison Bridges, recalling the tear gas. "It felt like someone put a lighter up to your face. It burned the inside of the mouth [and] the inside of my nose. Once they realized they were able to come in, they came in, and started clubbing everybody."

"If anyone lays a hand on that net they're going to get shot," yelled Bennett.

By the confrontation's end, roughly sixty people had been arrested.

A bridge was charred black. A number of Indians and supporters were recovering from tear gas and beatings. Demonstrators from New York, New Mexico, Arizona, California, and British Columbia were apprehended, but the charges against them were ultimately dropped. Questions of jurisdiction and the size of the Puyallup Reservation remained until a federal court decision in 1974 "fully settled the reservation existence question in favor of the Tribe."

Nine days after the dramatic raid, Stan Pitkin, U.S. Attorney for Western Washington, filed a complaint at the U.S. courthouse. The federal government, on behalf of Billy and Indians from various tribes, was suing the state of Washington for violating treaties.

THE VIOLENCE on the Puyallup did not cease. In the winter of 1971, vigilantes approached Hank Adams and Mike Hunt, a fisherman, as they tended net near a railroad trestle that crosses the Puyallup River. Adams told police that one assailant shot him at point-blank range. The bullet struck his abdomen at an angle and exited without piercing the stomach cavity. "You . . . Indians think you own everything," the perpetrator growled.

Hunt, a short distance away, heard the blast from a small caliber rifle. As he ran toward Adams, he saw two white men escaping the scene on foot. "I can't identify him," Adams said of the gunman, "but hell, I've seen him before. In a thousand taverns, in a thousand churches, on a thousand juries." Adams eventually sued, accusing authorities of depriving him of his civil rights, failing to aggressively investigate, and spreading false rumors about the crime. Police never arrested Adams's attackers. Adams moved to dismiss the case, seeking other remedies.

ACROSS THE COUNTRY, tribes continued to unite. In 1972, the newly minted American Indian Movement issued a twenty-point proposal, authored by Adams in Minneapolis. The list of demands called for a new life and a new future for Indian people: "If America has maintained faith with its original spirit, or may recognize it now, we should not be denied." The demands included "restoration of constitutional treaty-making authority and establishment of a treaty commission to make new treaties."

Soon afterward, on October 6, 1972, hundreds of Indians left reservations mired in poverty and other problems, in search of solutions and government accountability. They called their cross-country trek to Washington, D.C., the Trail of Broken Treaties.

The idea for the Trail of Broken Treaties was born at the funeral of Richard Oakes, a Mohawk Indian who had occupied Alcatraz Island. Demonstrators pushed for increased funding and more effective Indian programs that would keep pace with the times. The BIA, in their view, had become a "dumping ground for incompetent government workers" and was insensitive to the very Indian affairs it promised to protect and serve.

The trek was timed with the last leg of the presidential campaign, the race between Richard Nixon, Republican, and George McGovern, Democrat, which ended in a landslide victory for Nixon. The journey originated in Seattle, Los Angeles, and San Francisco with support from churches—primarily Lutherans, Episcopalians, and Methodists.

At the end of the journey, November 1972, activists chose to occupy the Bureau of Indian Affairs. Adams, organizer and lead negotiator, says the decision to invade was actually made by elders—women living in rat-infested quarters that were offered to the Native Americans. Emotions had ratcheted up among the demonstrators. Adams relates the story: "'What should we do? What should we do?'—rejecting everything until they said, 'Let's take over the Bureau.' 'Oh yeah!'"

"First," Ramona Bennett agrees, "there was never any intent for us to occupy anything [early on]. We were actually told to wait at the bureau building. The Department of Commerce was clearing an auditorium and a gymnasium for us, bringing in military kitchens, shower units and all of that . . . We were told to wait at the BIA building and we were attacked by GSA [General Service Administration] guards while we were waiting. We were attacked and then barricaded ourselves in."

Calling the BIA the Native American Embassy of Washington, demonstrators broke into the building, inverted American flags and destroyed computers. They posted signs—"Aim for Unity. Custer died for your sins."

They refused to leave, even though two-thirds of the occupants were women and children. "The worst thing the police can tell you is send out the women and children," Adams says. "The women particularly feel that they can't go out. If they leave, all these guys will be slaughtered. That's the best way to assure a standoff, to send out the women and children. The women won't leave, I'll tell you that. They wouldn't leave Wounded Knee, and they wouldn't leave the BIA building."

"Them things are direct action things," Billy says of the occupation. "All of that in that time was direct action. But it was for a cause that got us to where we want to be."

Adams relates the story from inside the occupation. As he negotiated living arrangements for activists, and a possible exit from the bureau, Indians "prepared the second floor for burning." A court decision came down that allowed occupants to be removed from the BIA by force, unleashing mayhem.

"The moment that the judge at the lower level issued that order, Dennis Banks said to George Mitchell [a leader of the American Indian Movement] from Minneapolis, 'Well, let's go back and tear that place apart,' or 'let's go back and destroy it,' or something like that. And they did. They broke the toilets all up and did all the plumbing damage. As one of the [news] writers said, 'What level of rage would involve someone to sit down and twist each key of a typewriter?'"

Billy remembers crawling out windows. "That was the big-time takeover. We got surrounded by all the park people. And Nixon wouldn't let them come in on us, until we finally negotiated out of that."

During the occupation, Billy got lost on the streets of Washington, D.C.—first on foot, and then in a car.

"I never knew D.C. for Christ's sake. I really was lost. But I'd find my way back."

Bureau occupants had threatened to burn the entire building unless the Nixon administration met their demands that included, among other things, ousting Harrison Loesch, assistant Interior secretary. "I really believe there would have been up to hundreds of people killed if they had tried to force us out," Adams said.

The takeover ended after a week when the Nixon administration promised to protect activists from prosecution and provided travel money home for those taking part. Damage was estimated at two million dollars.

DURING THEIR STAY, Indians discovered "incriminating evidence" against the bureau. They packaged the documents in question at night, and then transported them out of the building—straight under the nose of authorities—during a forty-car Indian caravan escorted by police.

Adams was later arrested while attempting to return documents to the BIA. His soft-spoken negotiations earned accolades from the media and Native Americans who took exception to the backlash against him. "For nearly a month Hank Adams called, begged and pleaded with the scattered groups of Indians to return the records that are of vital importance to the tribes. For his concern he was vilified by the elected tribal officials and cursed by White House assistants," wrote Vine Deloria Jr. "Arrest the man. But arrest him for the crime of responsible citizenship of which he is surely guilty. Or for the crime of humanity in which he has surely participated."

The case against Adams and seven other Indians was ultimately tossed out. The U.S. Commissioner of Indian Affairs, Louis Bruce, resigned. The department ousted Assistant Secretary Harrison Loesch and Deputy Commissioner John O. Crowe. Native Americans still criticized the BIA for failing to address their issues and for its paternalistic nature.

While in Washington, D.C., Adams planned a meeting with a

retired judge from Washington State named Judge George Boldt, who would become one of the most important players in the fishing rights struggle. At the time, Boldt headed President Nixon's Pay Board. "I want to get his feelings on changes to the federal structure," Adams told reporters, referring to "a number of matters affecting the Indians."

MID-AFTERNOON in January 1973, the window pane of a door at the Department of Game in Olympia shattered. Filing cabinets blocked back entrances. A stuffed pheasant lost its tail feathers. The intruders, a hundred or so of whom seized the building, festered with anger. The day before, three men were arrested on fishing charges, and two women were taken in for obstructing an officer. The state advanced on them in speedboats, armed, they charged, with rifles and pistols. More of their gear was confiscated. The fishermen had had enough. "You fish, and wait—wait and worry," explained one fed-up angler. During the next day's occupation, the anglers opened the office door of Director Carl Crouse, and picked up the phone.

"First, we called Hank Adams," Billy recalls. "But Adams was back in Washington [D.C.]." So Sid Mills dialed Crouse at home.

"You stole all of our boats and we want a meeting with you," Mills accused.

"If you all want to talk to me, come down to my office Monday morning," Crouse replied.

"Well, maybe you ought to come down to your office now, because that's where we're at," Mills retorted.

"So then we heard the sirens and they surrounded us again," Billy says. After two hours, as authorities surrounded the building, the protesters evacuated peacefully, once the Game Department agreed to meet with them. But they had discovered notebooks filled with files on Puyallup and Nisqually Indians, including Billy.

Also taken—charged attorney Larry Coniff later—were files on a court case involving the Puyallup Tribe's right to fish exclusively a seven-mile stretch of the Puyallup River.

Billy was there when the demonstrators gathered the next day,

After occupying the Washington Department of Game to demonstrate for treaty rights, tribal leaders sit down with their foes to bridge the divide in January 1973.

weary and frustrated, to meet with the Game Department: "When Judge Goodwin was a U.S. attorney, I begged him for help; when Representative Brock Adams was a U.S. attorney, I begged him for help; I've begged U.S. Attorney Stan Pitkin for help. None of them have helped us. All they've done is kept us going in circles." Billy also complained to the Game Department about the missing gear: "You bastards never take any old stuff, just the new gear." Crouse confirmed he would disclose a list of confiscated gear and pull authorities off the river until Friday.

The respite didn't last. Even in the wake of projections that there would be "blood on the river," the Game Department refused to pull back, arguing that many of the fishermen arrested were not enrolled members of treaty tribes. Billy rebuffed the charges, calling the fishermen family and Puyallup-Nisqually Indians who had every right to fish in usual and accustomed places: "There are Indians from all over the country fishing the river with nets within the reservation."

Adams accused the state of spying on Indians, in particular the Nisqually and Puyallup tribes. He called on Congress to investigate. As it turned out, the dossiers discovered at the Game Department included personal information, gossip, and criminal records related to nearly one hundred Nisqually Indians and more than fifty members of the Puyallup Tribe. The Puyallup dossiers, as reported in the *Washington Post*, included "accounts on their marital problems, high school grades, cash purchases of such items as birthday presents and fuel oil, and the amount of food in household cupboards." According to Adams, they "seized an uncompleted arrest report from the typewriter of Chief Neubrech. It disparagingly stated: 'The Indians down at Franks Landing are trying a new tactic to get press attention. They got a bunch of horses trying to make out like their [sic] fierce Plains Indians. We think our arrest actions should take the fire out of them now.'" Adams says Nisqually Indians were likened in an office memo to "wild animals in the jungle."

In mid-February 1973, two days after a major raid at the Landing, a group of Indians and Governor Evans privately agreed to suspend arrests and drop weapons.

As NATIVE ACTIVISTS reclaimed land and buildings, the Nisqually River claimed portions of Willie's six acres, chipping away at his shoreline. Land, and the fishing rights that came with it, were all that remained of treaty negotiations with Stevens, Superintendent of Indian Affairs. And the acreage suitable for a residence was eroding. Six acres became five; five became four; four became three. The Nisqually carved a hundred feet out of the riverbank in 1972 and swept away 1.5 acres. A tree tumbled to the ground and crushed a small fish-processing house. "He would go off by himself and into another room

Willie Frank Sr. watches as floodwaters take more of his shoreline in 1976.

and lie down on his back with his arms outstretched and his eyes closed," says Maiselle, Willie's daughter. "He would be very still for quite awhile, almost like he had left his body." It helps relax the mind, he told her when she finally asked.

The erosion also weighed heavily on Billy. It could sink his fish business. Worse yet, it could harm the families who made their homes there. It could weaken security at the Landing used by so many treaty fishermen. The Frank's Landing Indian Trade Center sold fresh and smoked fish and had served as a general store since 1971. Its proceeds paid for court costs accrued during the fish wars, funded the Wa He

Lut Indian School founded by Billy's sister Maiselle, and supported Willie and Angeline. Soon, flooding threatened all.

High waters were not an overnight problem. The military owned the property across the Nisqually River, and it was "adding gravel bar and dry land as fast as Frank's Landing was losing it." After the Army land was riprapped with rock and cement in the early 1960s, it altered the course of the Nisqually River, causing Frank's Landing to flood. The floods had persisted for years, yet generated little or no help from anyone, despite the land's trust status with the U.S. government. The south corner of Frank's Landing started to erode in 1965. Floodwaters crept underneath Willie's home, which sat on pilings, and dug a six-foot hole. The house began to pull apart, creating inch-wide gaps between the floor and walls. "I told them, and they agreed, that the river would eventually make a new channel through their property, and that the two houses and cabins were not on safe grounds," a property manager reported to the BIA. By 1968, the channel next to Frank's Landing was thirty feet deep.

By the mid-1970s, the families were just trying to survive. Flood-waters regularly overtook the property. Sometimes sandbags arrived but, more often than not, families jerry-rigged their own blockade, strewing together car parts on cables and buttoning them down on each end in an attempt to repulse the river.

In December 1975 came the declaration of a disaster area. Water levels rose four or five feet above the bankline. Three families evacuated. Wells and septic tanks were washed out. As described in a letter to the BIA, the floodwaters "undermined several trailer homes which were moved to higher ground." In 1976, floods destroyed a building and a dock and took more of the shoreline. Billy was frustrated that the U.S. Army Corps of Engineers and the BIA had done nothing to solve the problem. "I've stood on these banks with Corps officials and talked about the problem," Billy complained. "The[y] blame someone else, that someone else blames another. But passing the blame doesn't solve the problem." The Corps responded that its hands were tied—Frank's Landing was private property. The BIA said it wasn't "geared for disasters and we don't get any money for disasters." Billy accused the bureau of negligence. "We demand affirmative action immediately from those agencies responsible and liable."

The Frank's Landing family ultimately made a formal request of Congress for emergency funding to pay for a protective, temporary barrier and replacement land for the lost acreage: "Frank's Landing is Indian Land held in restricted trust status by the United States, and the United States is obligated by treaty to protect such lands." The request came after more than a decade of appeals to the BIA and various government entities.

Rechanneling the river would be too costly, Billy concluded, and with his father settled on the notion of replacement lands from the federal government. They targeted nearby land that could accommodate their homes, school, and a fisherman's life. The notion won the endorsement of the hydraulic engineer who studied the problem, U.S. senators Warren Magnuson and Henry Jackson, and several other members of Congress.

The Frank's Landing family proposed U.S. Army land tucked between the I-5 bridge and the North Pacific Railroad Bridge as a suitable replacement. The area had been the scene of various crimes— rapes, shootings, and stolen cars. "Target practice" transpired on the land that unfortunately relied on moving objects at Frank's Landing. Several animals had been killed. But homes and schools could sit safely on the replacement land while allowing the river to meander as nature directs it. In 1976, Billy applied for a permit with the U.S. Army to build structures that control erosion, open a pre-existing channel of the river, and recover acres that had washed away.

Finally, federal funding paid for riprap in 1977 to hold the river back. The riprap washed out in the 1996 flood and was replaced later that year.

Chapter 9

The Shelf Life of Treaties

T he battle over Indian fishing rights appeared interminable in 1973, an assembly line of expensive court cases that had cycled through the American justice system for decades. The state sued Indians. Indians sued the state. A lot of Native fishermen went to jail. The United States Supreme Court had first taken up treaty fishing rights nearly seventy years earlier, in 1905, before most Indians were American citizens. Theodore Roosevelt sat in the White House then, and Albert Einstein had proposed the theory of relativity.

In 1973, treaties brought the U.S., Indian tribes, and the state of Washington back to court, yet again. The judge would decide what Indian ancestors understood when they ceded land to the nation in the 1850s.

U.S. v. Washington brought immediate and long-term ramifications. Washington Indian tribes had everything to lose, and everything to gain. A tribal victory would peacefully return an Indian to the river and put salmon back on the table. Native Americans could practice their heritage. A tribal loss would threaten livelihoods and eventually customs. To Billy, no court damages awarded to the tribes could make up for the loss of the salmon. While no one would catch the last fish in Billy's lifetime, he worried about future generations, when a

great-great-great-grandchild learned how tribal fishermen had fought
for a species of salmon gone extinct.

THE STATE CONCLUDED it was carrying out the laws, and spent more
time arresting Indian fishermen and managing court documents
than protecting fish. Arguing that Indians should share the same off-
reservation rights, privileges, and restrictions as their fellow citizens,
Washington maintained controls were necessary to preserve the
Pacific salmon for the future.

As attorney Stan Pitkin put it, tribal fishermen were in dire need of
a "case to end all cases." On the face of it, *U.S. v. Washington* was that
case. In February 1971, Stuart Pierson, an assistant U.S. attorney,
arrived in Washington to take the case: "Bob Satiacum had done his
thing and continued to do his thing. A lot of people were getting shot
at and Stan Pitkin [U.S. attorney] said, 'We need to do something to
stop this.'"

"The Nisquallys didn't have to go in and say this is Nisqually Tribe
against Washington," points out Charles Wilkinson, an attorney and
scholar of Indian law. "This is the goddamn United States of America."

Concerned about a lack of communication between the tribes and
their counsel, however, the Survival of the American Indian Association sent a letter to the U.S. attorney general arguing that the federal
government could not adequately "represent the rights and legitimate
interests of the affected tribes." Instead of establishing special regulations for tribes in "usual and accustomed places," Survival contested, the state should be prohibited from regulating them at all.
Hank Adams raised concerns that federal lawyers were marching
ahead in their representation without meeting face-to-face with
Indian tribes: "If this lawsuit proceeds with the United States adhering
to the positions that it presently maintains, unwarranted and grievous
injury shall be done to these valuable treaty rights."

The judge signed the pre-trial order, and "the case to end all cases"
moved forward after all.

Judge George Hugo Boldt.

The judge had neither Indian blood nor a deep background in Indian law. The presiding judge in *U.S. v. Washington* was George Hugo Boldt, a Caucasian notable for spectacles with thick dark frames, a bow tie, and a distinguished, judge-like face. Boldt was an Eisenhower appointee to the bench. Earlier in his career, as deputy attorney general, he had represented the state when the Tacoma Narrows Bridge collapsed and tumbled into Puget Sound on November 7, 1940. As a federal judge, he put away imposing figures like tax evaders Mickey Cohen and Dave Beck. It was Boldt who tried the case of the infamous "Seattle Seven" in November 1970. When the defendants, charged with conspiring to damage a federal courthouse, caused a scene and stormed out of Boldt's courtroom, the judge declared a mistrial and held them in contempt of court. Boldt refused to grant bail.

"Judge Boldt was a judge with a lot of prestige," assesses Wilkinson.

"He was a conservative judge. The tribal attorneys, as a strategy matter at the beginning of that litigation, spent a lot of time talking about whether they wanted to disqualify him."

In 1971, President Nixon had other plans for Boldt. He appointed him head of the Pay Board, a part of the New Economic Plan that put the deep freeze on American wages and prices. *U.S. v. Washington* was reassigned to Judge William Nelson Goodwin.

"Judge Boldt moved to Washington, D.C.," explains Billy. "He turned the case over to another judge who was from McKenna up here, up the river. And then when he come back home, this is years now, all of a sudden Boldt come back and he said, 'I want my case back.' So, he got his case back."

"Put on that table every single case from the beginning of the country that pertains to the rights of Indians," the judge told his law clerk. One by one, the two pored over every case, coming in on Sundays.

The tribes welcomed Boldt's return. At an early conference with roughly a dozen lawyers and the judge, Stuart Pierson noted Boldt's copy of *Custer Died for Your Sins*, a work by Vine Deloria, nationally recognized Indian activist and lawyer.

"The hardest part of this case was making sense of it," says Pierson in hindsight. "And frankly, making peace among all of the entities. . . . The Justice Department was interested in what we were doing, but did not get deeply involved. They really let us do the case ourselves."

The complaint focused on off-reservation treaty fishing rights secured in five treaties brokered between the U.S. government and Indians. For all its complexity, *U.S. v. Washington* hinged on the nineteenth-century Native interpretation of the phrase, "The right of taking fish, at all usual and accustomed grounds and stations, is further secured to said Indians in common with all citizens of the Territory."

Among the lawyers charged with relating the thoughts and intent of Indians long passed were Stan Pitkin, U.S. attorney for Western Washington, George Dysart, assistant regional solicitor with the

Department of the Interior, and Pierson, as well as Al Ziontz and Mason Morisset, lawyers in private practice. They were writing a clean slate, Pierson says. "All of the other decisions were myopic or factually incorrect. The facts were wrong; the approach was wrong. We had very little precedent to work with."

The relevant federal court case originated at Cook's Landing on the Columbia River. The defendant was Yakama Indian David Sohappy, once called the Martin Luther King Jr. of fishing rights. Sohappy built a longhouse out of scrap wood and defied state laws to fish. In 1969, federal charges against Sohappy saddled the State of Oregon with an injunction and affirmed treaty rights of Indian people.

Traditionally, Oregon law prohibited net fishing on stretches of the Columbia River and did not distinguish between Indian and non-Indian fishermen. However, in Sohappy, the court held that the state's fishing regulations discriminated against Indians by failing to acknowledge the treaties. Indians were a recognized group, the court ordered, and entitled to a "fair share" of the catch. A win for the tribes, but not good enough, Pierson says.

"We had strong disagreements," remembers Ziontz, "but the disagreements were mainly between the government attorneys and the tribal attorneys. The government attorneys started out feeling that the best they could come up with was a treaty right to take fish for personal consumption, but not for sale. And it took some persuading and some anthropological evidence to convince them that historically the Indians had always sold fish."

Plaintiffs in *U.S. v. Washington* identified two central objectives. The first was to establish the meaning of the treaties at the time they were brokered—how the Indian people would have understood treaty terms. History of the tribes was, therefore, a crucial component. For anthropological background of the tribes, plaintiffs relied on Barbara Lane, an anthropologist from British Columbia who believed the treaties did not apply any restrictions on Indians fishing at ancestral grounds. "In my opinion," she said, "the 'in common language' was intended to allow non-Indians to fish subject to prior Indians rights specifically assured by treaty."

"She was an extremely careful researcher," says Ziontz. "She had a superb memory and a huge trove of documents, so that whenever she said anything, if you challenged her she could immediately tell you exactly where this came from."

The second task was to demonstrate a better way to manage the fishery altogether. The fishery "had a history of poor management," says Pierson. The state was not only violating the Indians' treaty rights, in his view. It furthered the insult by wrongfully blaming the depleting runs on tribes. The fishery should be managed closer to the mouths of the rivers or in the rivers, he concluded, with the work of fish biologist Jim Heckman. According to Heckman, Native Americans could take all they want of the run, while applying common sense and escapement goals. Pierson recalls an early meeting with the biologist: "We want you to sit down and, forget about who's asking you, tell us the best way to manage fish."

"I don't have to sit down," Heckman retorted. "You get closer to the actual harvesting of the runs. . . . There's nothing wrong with nets. There's nothing wrong with gillnets."

Heckman "put together a report and a plan." He believed Indians could fish for steelhead in the Nisqually River without damaging the resource. In fact, Heckman said, between 1965 and 1970, chum had the best escapement record and the run was fished commercially by Indians only.

AFTER THREE YEARS of trial preparation that included depositions from both Billy and his father, nine attorneys graced the courtroom stage in August 1973. Billy stood in the back of the room worried the case was rigged.

"This is no mere contract dispute," argued Ziontz. The polished and witty native of the Windy City represented a handful of the tribes. "[It] involves human rights and the national honor of the United States."

"Good men and good countries keep their word," added attorney James Hovis. He called his legal strategy the "God and Country doctrine."

"Give us a decision . . . end the need for endless litigation . . . allow both Indians and non-Indians to get on with their fishing," pleaded an attorney for the state.

According to the state, if left to their own devices Indians could modernize their fishing techniques and overfish salmon runs. They should be treated the same as all citizens and not granted a superior status: "The U.S. Supreme Court always has drawn the line at the reservation boundaries and that Indian rights beyond that are in common with the rest of the citizens."

But even parties within the state disagreed on the answer. The Game Department pushed to ban Indians outright from steelhead in off-reservation waters; the Department of Fisheries proposed allotting a percentage of salmon for the tribes.

On the witness stand the Game Department's Carl Crouse defended the total ban. The resource simply couldn't survive Indian commercial fishing, he told the court.

Meantime, Walter Neubrech, now retired from the Department of Game, was asked point-blank if "his enforcement agents ever joined sportsmen groups as vigilantes." Neubrech said he knew nothing of the practice and blamed the riverbank flare-ups on a few "dissident Indians." Moreover, Neubrech said it was extremely difficult to identify Indians of treaty tribes: "It is almost impossible to acquire an official roll of tribal membership except for the Yakama Tribe. We know of no guidelines that have come down from the courts defining when an Indian is an Indian and when he isn't an Indian and what degree of ancestry he must have. It is difficult to decide whether a person you found on a stream with a net is, in fact, an Indian of the United States and a member of a treaty tribe."

According to Neubrech, numerous arrests had been made and most resulted in convictions. He gave specific examples to the court: "There was one Indian from a non-treaty group over in Eastern

"This is how I make my living," Billy told the court during U.S. v. Washington. *Above, Billy loads dog salmon on the Nisqually River.*

Washington. There was a defendant that was of Canadian Indian ancestry. One was from Mexico. One defendant did not appear to have any degree of Indian ancestry. One or two defendants were of Mexican American ancestry."

For the state's own protection, Neubrech said, wardens eventually carried guns. "From the time I started to work until the last five or six years, our agents were unarmed. Because of the necessity of self-protection, the decision was made that certain agents could bear firearms. Certain agents were authorized to carry night sticks in the case of mob gatherings and riots. . . .They have helmets and special tactical uniforms. The special tactical gear and defensive equipment have been issued to 15 wildlife agents. These picked men have received special training in how to handle mob and riot situations."

On September 10, 1973, Billy became one of roughly a half-dozen Indians to take the witness stand in *U.S. v. Washington*. He told state attorneys Earl McGimpsey and Larry Coniff that any fish that returned to the Nisqually River was fair game for the tribe. "This is how I make my living, is off Mr. McGimpsey's salmon and Mr. Coniff's steelhead . . . so, I don't want to break them down. Now, when I said I would like to take 100 percent of the salmon, I meant that them are the salmon that originated in the Nisqually River . . . and come back. . . . Now, I am not talking about the 8 million salmon that are caught out of the Nisqually River and the Puget Sound and other rivers."

Billy told the court the state had confiscated his gear for years. Often, he found his nets shredded or dry rotting in gunnysacks. His boats were taken. His motors vanished. Further, he argued, enrollment records for treaty tribes were unreliable and the Bureau of Indian Affairs had ignored repeated requests to expand the Nisqually Indian rolls and affiliate new members. At the time, the rolls did not include Billy's own children. "It looks like they want to terminate us," Billy charged. "It has got to go through the tribe and then the Bureau of Indian Affairs. I think they say they are going to open up the rolls but just like this fishing right . . . I'm going to be six feet under by the time all that stuff comes up."

Billy described changes in his lifetime and his father's—tracing the impact of humans on fish runs: "There is so many different things on the river now, like the dams, the lowering of the water, the timber . . . . You would be thinking of 50 or 100 years from now. You don't know the whole change of everything, what it would be in this fishery resource."

"I watched his expression as Indians paraded before him up to the witness stand and spoke," says Ziontz of the judge. "When Indians speak you listen. Because they speak gravely and from the heart and with very little folderol and curlicues. It's very blunt. It's very factual and Judge Boldt watched the Indian witnesses below him, listened and absorbed what they had to say.

"What they told him was a story of state oppression—oppression by our lovely state of Washington, the state I had fallen in love with and thought was so progressive and non-prejudicial. . . .The Indians had something. The whites wanted it. The whites took it," Ziontz says of the culture clash.

In the courtroom, Boldt grew frustrated with Dr. Carroll Riley, the state's anthropologist. "I don't know why you hesitate in answering simple questions," the judge said. "It disturbs me. If you persist in dodging the questions, it will bear heavily on my appraisal of your credibility and I might as well say so now." Under cross examination, Riley admitted he had no evidence to disprove the testimony of the anthropologist testifying for the federal government.

Boldt laughed when another witness, an angler, compared catching a steelhead to making love. "If you've ever made love—that's the nearest I can express it," he said in court. After reading a long list of favorite fishing holes, Boldt retorted: "That doesn't leave you much time for making love, does it?"

Judge Boldt "sat up there day after day after day listening to this laboriously delivered testimony sometimes from old Indians that couldn't even speak the English language," recalls Tom Keefe. "And if you sat and listened long enough you would get a sense for the historical injustice that was going on, and that's what he came to."

Billy remembers eighty-three-year-old Lena Hillaire on the stand with great fondness. She wore moccasins, traditional regalia, and a feather proudly fixed to her headpiece.

"Will you state your name, please?" the clerk requested.

"Oh, my name. It is Lena Cultee Hillaire, H-I-L-L-A-I-R-E."

"And [the state] asked her a question," Billy recalls. "I don't remember what it was, but she didn't understand what it was. And so

Judge George Boldt visits reservations after his historic ruling. Above, with Dorian Sanchez, Billy, and George Kalama.

she looked at Grandpa [Billy's father] right there, and she started to talk in Indian to Grandpa from the stands.

"And Grandpa answered her. The assistant attorney general stood up and objected to all of this, arguing that the witness shouldn't be allowed to talk 'Indian' in the court, and that he couldn't understand what the witness was saying. He was overruled by the judge. Judge Boldt said if Grandma don't understand what you're saying she can ask Grandpa, and Grandpa is answering her.

"Judge Boldt . . . you seen him thinking out a long ways about this whole mess we're in. . . . And he said that you got to get your fish back home, but then the fish has got to have a home. And there's dams on the river, and you've got to have in stream flows, the habitats got to be protected and all of that. It's not today."

On February 12, 1974, Boldt handed down a landmark 203-page opinion. During the trial, Billy had had his doubts about the verdict.

"We looked around, it was standing-room only, and it was all rednecks, sports fishermen. These guys got there and took all the seats. They wanted to show their power. I remember thinking, 'I hope this place isn't rigged.'"

The judge upheld treaty rights in usual and accustomed places, and defined the key phrase "in common with" as "sharing equally." He abolished regulations that discriminated against Indian fishermen.

"That for me is one of the biggest decisions of our time—in U.S. history, in world history," recalls Billy. "We didn't have any money. We didn't have any expensive attorneys. We didn't have any infrastructure to work with the state . . . or the federal government or the neighbors of anybody or the utilities that put the dams on the river."

Restrictive laws against treaty tribes in their usual and accustomed places were unlawful, Boldt said. The state's role is in preserving the runs, not regulating the tribes' share. Further, the treaty did not distinguish between salmon and steelhead. Boldt also clarified that no fisherman, Indian or otherwise, could destroy the fishery. Finally, he found that the Indians were allowed to self-regulate, co-manage the resource, and have the opportunity to catch up to half the harvestable catch. It was tribal attorney David Getchas who consulted a dictionary of the time period and concluded that the treaty phrase "in common with other citizens" meant sharing equally.

"And what [Boldt] said was the twenty tribes will all be self regulatory tribes at the end of this time," Billy recalls. "And you'll have your infrastructure. All your tribes will be together from Lummi to the ocean, from South Sound to North Sound and the Pacific Ocean. You guys will all have your infrastructure, you'll have your science, your technical people, your collecting data, your policy people, and your lawyers. . . . And the United States government said you guys will go back to Congress and you'll get the money. We'll get the money for the infrastructure of what we're doing, the Northwest Indian Fish Commission, to coordinate all of this. And so that's how this place was born. . . . Oh god. It was just great."

"This is American justice at its absolute highest: where you have established, wealthy, vested interests, and poor people—dispossessed people who have nothing to hang their hat on other than a treaty 120 years earlier that many are saying is outmoded," Wilkinson says. "You can't understand American justice fully without understanding the Boldt Decision. It is that paramount. It holds that high a place in our legal system and in our history and in our collective national consciousness."

THOUGH SOME TRIBES have pigeonholed Slade Gorton as a racist, the Republican, who would become a target of Northwest Indian tribes, says as attorney general he examined the case as a matter of law. It was special treatment of the Indians, not the color of skin, that concerned Gorton: "The state's view, which I still think is absolutely correct as a matter of law, was that it meant that they have the same rights that the citizens did because Indians weren't citizens at the time when the treaties were signed in 1853," Gorton says today. "And what Governor Stevens and everyone meant was that there'd be no distinction between Indians and non-Indians. The Indians would have rights 'in common with' the citizens, which of course meant that fifty or sixty years later when fish began to get scarce and you began to have some kind of conservation laws, the same laws applied to everyone."

"I know Slade personally," says Ziontz. "He's a very principled guy. He's not a racist. But his principles don't include a society in which Indians have a separate existence. He was very aggressive, leading the attorney general's office in resisting the Indians."

Pierson does not buy Gorton's argument that the Boldt decision made Native Americans super citizens: "It's a politically-charged and absolutely incorrect statement. . . . If you have a group of people who have a special relationship with the federal government, they're going to be different. That doesn't make them super." Says Pierson: "It prompted the state fisheries and game fisheries to recognize number one that they were not regulating for one group; they were part of a much larger ecological system affecting fish coming to spawn. To the people who were watching, it puts a lie to the statement that Native Americans were harming fisheries. They had developed a very effective way of managing."

"Everyone basically centers on the 50 percent but the more valuable consideration was the right for self-regulation and co-management of the overall resources," Hank Adams says.

"I think he [Boldt] resolved many of the fundamental questions," says Mike Grayum, executive director of the Northwest Indian Fisheries Commission (NWIFC). "One of the fundamental issues that he addressed was, what's the definition of conservation? Because the state used that word to justify stopping the Indians. It's a conservation issue. We need those fish to spawn. The judge wisely said, 'That's not how I define conservation. What you were doing, state, was making a wise-use decision. You would rather have the fish caught out there in the ocean than caught at the mouth of the river.'"

During their celebratory feast after the decision came down, Brando returned to the Northwest. "I remember Marlon Brando," Grayum says. "He was scruffy, wearing old dirty clothes, and had about two weeks worth of beard—he was kind of a nasty old man."

"I didn't come here to talk to any white people, I came here to see Indians," Brando groused.

Grayum retorted, "OK, well I don't much like you either."

As they dined on oysters and salmon, attorney Stu Pierson warned, "Don't think the fight's over; it's just started now."

Indeed. The state flat out refused to accept defeat.

Chapter 10

Storm

The backlash to the Boldt Decision reached far and wide, pitting fisherman against fisherman and judge against judge. Sportsmen and commercial fishermen were enraged. Within weeks of the opinion, they chartered buses from as far away as Wenatchee. Seven hundred strong, they marched in front of the U.S. Courthouse in Tacoma. They parked trailered boats there, hung an effigy of the judge from a tree, and flashed bumper stickers that read: "Sportsmen's rights torn to a shred, screwed by a Boldt without any head."

"Does anyone here agree with this decision?" a protester barked from behind a bullhorn.

"No!" the crowd shouted.

"Are you going to pay for the fish for someone else to catch?"

"No!" fishermen roared.

As written, Boldt's ruling called for dramatic changes in a large and lucrative industry. Fishing was a multi-million-dollar business in Washington. The courts found that existing regulations allowed the majority of fish to be intercepted by non-Indians, long before the salmon reached tribal fishers stationed at the end of their migration path.

Non-Indian fishing organizations filed lawsuits in response. Commercial fishermen called themselves "the forgotten majority" and

A U.S. marshal removes an effigy of the man at the center of the storm.

complained of reverse discrimination, drowning in debt, and having to sell off their boats. "I've never heard of such a thing— that one judge could rule against an entire industry," griped Robert Christensen, then president of the Puget Sound Gillnetters Association. "They would have shot Judge Boldt," Billy says without a trace of exaggeration. "They would have killed him they were so angry. . . . They were killing each other. They went crazy because Slade Gorton was telling them: I'm going to overturn this when it gets to the United States Supreme Court. . . . The non-Indian community didn't want to have nothing to do with Boldt anymore. They did everything to destroy this career of this judge."

Over the years, the judge himself described the attacks: "I was burned in effigy and they still do that. The fishermen have a champion and he maligns me continually and steadily, and he's spurred on by the attorney general here. He's got to be with the fishermen, don't you see? You just can't be honest in this state and get anywhere because of the enormous amount of condemnation heaped on me since I wrote that decision.

"Sometimes I get bales and bales of mail. Loathsome material. Sometimes they say, and put it in the paper, that my wife is an Indian. Well, she wouldn't mind that at all, but she happens to be a Scotch Presbyterian." Asked if the backlash gets to him, the judge replied, "I took an oath of office. It's right up there on the wall, and I look at it every day, have for twenty-five years."

An impetuous spirit filled the water. Boats rammed other boats in retaliation. At marinas, Indians were denied ice and gas.

Non-Indians were not unlike their Indian counterparts when fishing rights were on the table. Both groups publicly lashed out at their target. Both groups were labeled renegades. Both groups were cautioned that a few illegal catches could destroy future runs. While the Indians claimed Washington State was converting Puget Sound into a "Sportsman's Paradise," non-Indian gillnetters saw a fish farm "under the guise of conservation and special rights for the Indians."

"Prior to the Boldt Decision, the non-Indians were dependent on the state authorities and state policemen, game wardens and fisheries enforcement officers . . . to go after the Indians," Hank Adams says. "After the Boldt Decision, it was a call to the citizens to come out and oppose the non-Indian fishermen, the non-Indian canneries. . . . You had non-Indian commercial businesses and canners and so forth deny ice to the Lummis and the Tulalips. No one would sell them ice so they couldn't maintain their fish after harvesting them."

"It was complete anarchy and chaos," says Mike Grayum, executive director of the NWIFC. "Nobody was abiding by the rules of the court. The state Fish and Game agencies were not. The attorney general's office was not. They were being encouraged to break the law, if you will, and to fish as much as they want, wherever they want." Despite the Interim Plan approved shortly after the decision to see through its implementation, unrest remained.

"The trouble was that usually the tribal fishermen were at the end of the line," says Dan Evans. "The salmon runs would come in the

Strait of Juan de Fuca. Then they'd come in closer, toward the Puget Sound commercial guys, and then finally the Indian. And then they'd gripe about the Indians. They'd say, 'They're putting their nets clear across the river so no salmon are getting up to spawn.' So that's when we really had to get into it. A legal decision is one thing. They sit up there in those robes and they say a profound solution. But carrying it out is quite something else again."

In the summer that followed the Boldt Decision, the state of Washington slashed the bag limit for sports anglers from three salmon to two, and prohibited fishing within three miles of the Pacific Coast. Further, it restricted fishing within Puget Sound and the Strait of Juan de Fuca for commercial anglers and sportsmen. The fishermen sought injunctions in state court against the new fishing regulations and got them. Boldt, however, overruled the state court judge and declared six days per week the maximum number of commercial fishing days.

For Indians, the landmark decision ended a hundred-year wait for treaty rights and ushered in a new day. Indian fishermen invested in new boats and gear. They started catching more fish. As the end of 1974 approached, state authorities estimated that Indian fishermen would take some 160,000 salmon, non-Indian 110,000, and the hook-and-line anglers 90,000.

"It was kind of a shock to realize we were going to have to share this with somebody else," admits Jon Westerhome, a lifelong gillnetter on the Columbia River who, at the industry's prime, brought in two or three tons of fish per season. Even with so much at stake, Westerhome says eventually many fishermen came around and accepted the split. "The Native Americans were deserving," Westerhome says. "They were here first."

THE BOLDT DECISION leveled the playing field between tribes and government. Boldt held that existing law was unconstitutional when applied to treaty fishermen. The decision gave the tribes authority to manage their own fishery and to hold jurisdiction over Indians fishing away from reservations, in ancestral fishing grounds. "Judge Boldt made a decision that we are going to protect ourselves," Billy says. "There's laws written and there's a lot of principles come out of that decision. We're self-regulators. Now, we have to manage to get our salmon back. We are part of the system."

As A PART OF the system, the tribes established a new organization to represent all Western Washington treaty tribes. With no comparable organization in existence, Billy and Hank Adams arrived in Portland on May 1, 1974, where a think tank was underway to form the Northwest Indian Fisheries Commission, which would be charged with protecting treaty rights, managing resources, and educating the public. Charts and blueprints were scattered about. "I went up there and I spoke that day," says Adams, "and looked at their charts . . . and the only interest I heard discussed and the only interest I see up on these charts was who is going to arrest the Indian fishermen now. And I said, 'I'm tired of the Indian fishermen, of your tribes being treated as a criminal class! This isn't good enough! You're going to have to start over!'"

Adams slammed his hand down on a partition with such force it caused a thundering jolt. The partition crashed to the ground with a startling thud. Adams jumped. "It almost frightened me because I didn't realize that it was going to sound like an explosion. I went and tore all the rest down and said, 'You're going to have to start over!'"

Adds Billy with a laugh, "And they started over."

Guy McMinds, a Quinault, rose in support of Adams. "Maybe he's right," he told the room. "Maybe we've gone about this the wrong way." After what Adams calls the "gong" of the partition, a charter committee was appointed and put together a plan the tribes endorsed.

DURING THE CHAOS, longtime friendships formed in surprising places. Few moments can top the day Mike Grayum met Billy. His boss, the respected biologist Jim Heckman, sent him to the Nisqually River to "figure out what they're catching."

It was nine o'clock in the morning, a couple of days before Christmas. An Indian fisherman stood on a gravel bar in the middle of the Nisqually River as the chum run returned to spawn. With his hip boots on, Grayum navigated his way down the riverbank. He waded out to the bar and tapped the stranger on the shoulder. "And it was Billy," Grayum says. "He had a half-gallon of whiskey in his hand and hands it over."

As a young man learning the ropes, Grayum decided he'd better accept the gesture. "I don't know how long we were down there, but I was passing the bottle back and forth. I was getting my first real lesson, after I left school, on the fisheries. And he was telling me what I needed to know, and I've been working with him ever since."

Grayum had first become involved with implementing the Boldt Decision while working for the U.S. Fish and Wildlife Service. He describes his assignment of tracking who was fishing and where, after hours: "I was going to use this night scope and write down boat numbers—how many, who they were, where they were fishing. I get out there and there was so much ambient light from all these boats that blinded me with the night scope, so I had to put that away. . . . There were so many boats and so many nets in the water, and it was dark. You ran the risk of colliding with something. It was a city out there. And they were all illegally fishing. And 90 percent of them or more were non-Indian fishermen."

It wasn't just the tribes feuding with government; government was feuding within itself. Instead of freely exchanging information, the state and federal governments duplicated efforts. As Grayum flew over the Nisqually River scouting for fish nests once, he nearly met disaster. "I'm flying up the river in a chartered airplane and I'm counting redds. And we meet a state plane coming downstream doing the same thing I was doing. We damn near collided in mid-air. It was really a close call. I thought this is nuts, on the same day, we're doing the same thing, and we're duplicating the costs. It's crazy."

In another instance revealing the complex dynamic the Boldt

Decision created within government, Grayum recalls traveling to Portland to meet with his regional director at the U.S. Fish and Wildlife. By this time, he had devoted years to *U.S. v. Washington*. With the major legal questions answered, he wondered about his own future.

"My god, we've got to appeal!" the director told him.

"Wait a minute, you can't appeal. You won!" Grayum retorted. "They [U.S.] are so closely aligned with the state they were chagrined that they won a case," Grayum says today. "It wasn't just the state. There was a big faction of the federal government that was trying to find a way around this decision."

"Stay out of trouble," his boss told him that day. "Don't anger the state and you'll be just fine."

"But I'm supposed to be assisting tribes. By that very act, I'm not going to be making a lot of friends in the state."

"Well, just don't do that."

"Well, then I can't do my job."

Grayum made the decision then and there to leave U.S. Fish and Wildlife and take Heckman up on an earlier offer to join him at the Northwest Indian Fisheries Commission. Thirty-five years later, in 2012, he's still there.

IN A LETTER TO the Civil Rights Division of the U.S. Attorney's Office in 1975, Survival of the American Indian Association leveled serious accusations against the Department of Game. Allegedly, some fifteen patrolmen "brandishing clubs and handguns and using chemical mace attacked Frank's Landing—without any apparent reason, apart from their total lack of legal authority and jurisdiction. . . . The delicate state of health of the elderly Indian grandparents [and owners] of Franks Landing places their lives in jeopardy, even though weapons might not actually be used. Generally, at least a score of Indian children are present at Franks Landing—where an independent Indian school is operating and was in session Monday during the state raid." Survival argued that the Landing sits on reservation land and is therefore outside the state's jurisdiction.

At the time, Judge Boldt had shut down the Nisqually River to net fishing, both on and off the reservation. The state maintained that the fifteen patrol officers were protecting a Game patrol boat while officers confiscated a net from a closed section of the river. According to Carl Crouse, Game director, Indians threw large rocks at his employees as they confiscated nets. Crouse did concede that one officer sitting in a car used "fog Mace" to protect himself when an Indian approached.

The allegations grew more serious. Adams, on behalf of Survival, also claimed in the letter to have documentation "that the Washington Game and Fisheries Patrols have acted to set up confrontations with Indian people in order to seriously injure or kill particular Indian persons." Adams accused the attorney general's office of compelling "a number of these enforcement officers to knowingly execute false affidavits and to swear false testimony in both civil and criminal cases." Nothing came of the charges.

Meanwhile, *U.S. v. Washington* climbed its way through courts, further polarizing the tribes, non-Indian fishermen, and the state. Washington State appealed the Boldt Decision to the Ninth Circuit Court of Appeals. It lost in 1975 under sharp criticism from the court: "It it has been recalcitrance of Washington State officials (and their vocal non-Indian commercial and sports fishing allies) which produced the denial of Indian rights requiring intervention by the district court. This responsibility should neither escape notice or be forgotten," the court ordered.

In 1976, the U.S. Supreme Court refused to review the case, fueling the fire within the non-Indian commercial fishing industry. "We're totally disgusted!" a fisherman snapped. "The Court just upheld the white fishermen's status as second class citizens." Governor Dan Evans urged the state to enforce Boldt's decision despite the high pitch of rancor from the water.

IN THE SUMMER OF 1976, Jim Waldo, an assistant U.S. attorney, met Billy for the very first time. Waldo was assigned to help implement the Indian treaty decisions. Billy was blunt.

"You came in and met with Stan Pitkin and myself," Waldo reminds Billy years later, "and you were introduced to me as someone who spent more time in jail than out in the last two years. Your reply: 'If you guys would just do your job, I wouldn't have to go to jail.'

"His view was that the U.S. had up until the time, basically until Pitkin came in as U.S. attorney and got the backing from the administration, had never acted to really protect their rights and protect them," Waldo continues."So, the demonstration and the going to jail and everything around that was sort of the only option that was open to them. And I think they were right. I think the federal government just looked the other way on those treaties for the better part of the century."

Between May and November of 1976, Waldo appeared in court some twenty-six times on treaty fishing rights. One day he went in to see Pitkin: "We're treating this solely as a legal issue, if the law is clear, that everything is going to be OK. We've got economic issues, a feud with non-Indian fishermen—this is for many of them as much a way of life as it is for the tribes. And we've got racism, and we've got history. If the conflict between the state and federal courts proceeds . . . the federal government will end up having to take over management of the fisheries in court." Waldo was right.

THE BACKLASH to the court ruling escalated at Foulweather Bluff in October 1976. The entrance to Puget Sound, at the north end of Hood Canal, had witnessed illegal fishing, damaged boats, and clashes between angry gillnetters and patrol officers.

Most officers within the Fisheries Department viewed the Boldt Decision as patently unfair, says Frank Haw, a former Fisheries director. To put more fish in the hands of Indians, non-Indians had to give up theirs. Morale was down and the department was grossly unprepared for the anarchy that followed, Haw says. One of Haw's officers, Jim Tuggle, recalled a frightening scene:

Initiated by a few hotheaded gillnetters, multiple assaults against officers occurred as small patrol boats were rammed repeatedly by much larger and heavier gillnet boats. Shouts from enraged fishermen could be heard on the radio urging their cohorts to sink the patrol boats and kill the officers. Patrol boats were maneuvered quickly to avoid sinking and certain disaster. Despite attempts to avoid collisions, gillnet boats still managed to ram the much smaller patrol vessels. The confrontation became so violent that the U.S. Coast Guard dispatched a cutter and the commander of that vessel, Chief Bob LaFrancis, ordered the bow-mounted 50-caliber machine gun uncovered, loaded and manned. No closed season gillnet fishing arrests took place that night, but if it were not for Chief LaFrancis' decisive actions, several Fisheries Patrol Officers might have died that night—and perhaps some gill-netters as well.

One night in late October, the *Alaskan Revenge*, a large vessel, nearly rammed the *Roberts*, a patrol boat, intentionally, says Haw. Tuggle remembered the turn of events:

Here came the *Alaskan Revenge* on a certain collision course with a boatload of Fisheries Patrol Officers. Others aboard the *Roberts* had also focused their attention to the approaching disaster. Frightened shouts of the impending crash were acted on by Glen Corliss as he quickly put the engine of our vessel into gear in an attempt to avoid disaster. The *Alaskan Revenge* never wavered from its course as the other gillnetters had, and as I screamed, "lookout!" and as I dove for the opposite side of the deck away from the impact area, I heard two quick gunshots. As I scrambled to my feet, Glen maneuvered our boat so that the *Alaskan Revenge* seemed to pass through the would-be watery grave where our aft deck had been two seconds before, narrowly missing our boat. The *Alaskan Revenge* had missed us!

The engine of the *Alaskan Revenge* could be heard to drop in RPMS as I stood and looked around at my fellow officers to see what exactly had happened. Officer Howard Oliver had been the one to fire the two quick buckshot blasts that had saved our lives. Now the *Alaskan Revenge* was in reverse, backing away from our position, and apparently not under command or control.

The gillnetters accused the officer of an "unwarranted shooting." The injured skipper of the *Alaskan Revenge*, twenty-four-year-old William Carlson, had to be airlifted by helicopter to Harborview Medical Center in Seattle. As reported in the *Seattle Times*, he suffered paralysis of the left arm and leg after the shooting, "brain damage, blunted mental and psychological processes, disfigurement, pain, amnesia and fatigue." The scene was played in the media as though the injured Carlson were a martyr, seriously injured while trying to protect his livelihood. But Haw says Carlson was not a licensed gillnet fisherman.

The shooting led to a march in Olympia and a speech by Jim Johnson, an assistant attorney general and lead lawyer for the state, "to tumultuous cheers regarding the immorality of Judge Boldt's ruling" and what Johnson characterized as "morally reprehensible" law. Candidates for governor weighed in: "I would have done a lot before this even happened [if I had been governor]," said Republican candidate John Spellman. "I would have gotten the fishermen and the [State] Department of Fisheries together for negotiations."

The behavior of the state caught the attention of national media. "Washington State legal officials refused to enforce Boldt's order," noted the *Washington Post*. "They instead denounced the judge, and encouraged fishermen to believe his decision upholding treaty rights was capricious and unlikely to stand up on appeal."

To make matters worse, the fisheries management system was out of control, says Haw, with an excess of commercial fishing licenses and a "lack of authority" on the part of the state "to control mixed stock fishing off its own coast." Washington fish that originated in the state were being harvested in Canada.

The tribes remained determined to hold their ground, whatever the consequence. "I don't think a fish is worth the life of anybody," said Forest Kinley, a Lummi Indian at the time, "but if one of our people is drowned by those redneck gillnetters, there will be shooting."

Billy says the anger was rooted in a network of white people that had had its way for a long time: "You go back and read the laws. They were put here against the Indians when they became a state. . . . all of this land . . . from here to the Columbia River to Canada was ceded to the non-Indian in a treaty. So they built Seattle, they built all these towns and cities, they built the highways, the I-5 corridor, they built everything, they built the banks. . . . So they forgot about us, they went about their business and they had their own land . . . until that Boldt Decision come along."

Congress in 1976 enacted the Two Hundred Mile Fishery Conservation Zone. The act restricted foreign fleets from fishing within two hundred miles of the U.S. coast. Regional councils were established to recommend regulations to the Department of Commerce. As Billy recalls, "After the Boldt Decision there was the Magnuson Act. Now Senator Magnuson was one of our great senators in the state of Washington, along with Senator Jackson who he worked with. And so Magnuson put this act together, the 200 mile act we call it, the Magnuson Act. It's now the Stevens-Magnuson Act.

"Our tribes made sure that we wrote in that act along with the senator, that we had language that we the tribes would be at the table whenever there was a decision made on our resource and our salmon."

"The Pacific Regional Council has been resistant to full implementation of the treaty rights," concluded a report by the NWIFC. Some Indian tribes fished at sea. Federal authority could result in fewer salmon returning to their home rivers and streams.

IN 1976, AS THE NATION celebrated its two hundredth birthday, racism took on a whole different meaning for Sugar, Billy's son. A group of activists departed Frank's Landing on a Trail of Self-Determination. The cross-country caravan to Washington, D.C., intended to show the U.S. government the trials facing Indian people. "We will be trying to bring about serious negotiation," announced Native Sid Mills of plans for the peaceful demonstration on Indian affairs. "You can't do that with violence."

Billy, Sugar, Hank Adams, Curly Kid, and others recruited activists. In Jackson Hole, Wyoming, they awoke to the sliding door of a van nearby and a gun sitting on top of a tripod. "Because the Cavalry was coming through," Sugar explains, "and they thought we were there to cause trouble. They realized we were just kids, women and a few men and no weapons so they let us finish camping there." At Fort Laramie, Wyoming, police gathered in riot gear because word spread of an "Indian scare." In Ohio, where the caravan stopped to "hustle up money and gas," the city kicked them out. "It was too much trouble with the Natives and the community, so we moved on," Sugar remembers. In Pittsburgh, the Indians were greeted like a circus attraction. "All the people over there thought Natives were gone. They couldn't believe there were Natives still living. They even actually come up and told us that: 'We thought you guys were extinct!'"

Plains, Georgia, the small home town of Jimmy Carter, was the most shocking of all to Sugar, then just fifteen years old. The one-zip-code town was segregated and left a mighty impression on the teenager. "We stayed with the blacks in that town because it's divided, the whites on one side and the blacks on [the other] side. I didn't like the State of Georgia *at all*. They talk to you, but to have that separation with mankind . . . it was unreal. . . . It wasn't like that here in Washington State. There is racism, but nothing too extreme to where they're dividing the town."

The group arrived in Washington, D.C., and camped in a soccer

NORTHWEST INDIAN FISHERIES COMMISSION

After the landmark court decision, U.S. v. Washington, *Billy rose to power as head of the Northwest Indian Fisheries Commission. For decades, he has represented treaty tribes of Western Washington.*

field. The end of the week marked the celebration of America's Bicentennial and a parade that drew half a million people. Indians sat in front of the White House thumping drums.

A few days later, police arrested more than fifty Native Americans as they entered the Bureau of Indian Affairs Building and called for its abolition. "I went to jail, well juvenile hall," says Sugar, "Trespassing, I guess, on the BIA Building. But they didn't read us no rights, so the next day they just cut us all loose.

"I would never take it back. It was worth it. Without that war we wouldn't have what we got today. We'd be extinct. . . . That's the reason why we joined that Trail. We were trying to show the government what they were doing to the Indian people. It was self-determination."

THE YEAR 1977 was punctuated by a changing of the guard at the Northwest Indian Fisheries Commission (NWIFC), a major power shift in the Nisqually Tribe, and a family tragedy.

At the time, NWIFC leadership included five commissioners, each of whom represented a particular treaty area and its respective tribes. In 1977, the commissioners' terms were expiring, and Chairman Dutch Kinley was leaving the top post.

Billy and Hank Adams attended commission meetings and got a resolution passed that named Billy as commissioner of the Medicine Creek Treaty area, which included members of the Nisqually, Squaxin, and Puyallup tribes. "The fighting, that is, the fish-ins and demonstrations, is over now, I hope," Billy reflected to a reporter. "My past is in the past; I'm looking forward to what will happen in the next ten years as far as the development of the resource is concerned. Now we have to sit down and be reasonable. The State is a reality we must deal with for the sake of the people and the resource. I hope that the Governor of this state will appoint a Director of Fisheries who can and will work with Indian people."

Two months later, it was time for NWIFC commissioners to elect a chairman. The deciding vote rested with John Ides, a Makah tribal member. "John Ides just retired from the Air Force and had become involved in tribal politics and quickly became chairman of the Makah Tribe," Adams explains. "So, he was the undecided vote and he really didn't know. He hadn't been involved with these other tribes. . . . [He called back to Makah to see if they had any instructions, but they told him to use his own best judgment."

Ides knew Adams's brother and trusted his judgment. Adams advocated for Billy and sweetened the deal with a promise to limit Billy's chairmanship to two years. The strategy worked. Billy was named chairman of the NWIFC by a 3-to-2 vote.

Maiselle and Ramona Bennett, a Puyallup Indian, pushed hard for Billy to take the helm: "He has a great love of his Indian people," Bennett explains. "He has lived the deprivation and humiliation that the government put on us. He has survived that with great humor and no anger toward any specific grouping of people. . . . Even when these white people were shaking their fists at us and screaming obscenities—they'd be saying you *&%$@ Indians—he'd be listening to what they were saying about what could be done about the dams, the fertilizer and the pesticides."

It was a new beginning for Billy, as he entered a very visible leadership role in both the Indian and non-Indian worlds. "They started to know him personally in their own sphere of activity or in their boardrooms, as in the cases of banks, or in the cases of Rayonier or Weyerhaeuser, and in the government offices at the higher levels in the Congress," Adams explains. "And knowing him on a personal, face-to-face level, they discovered they liked him."

BEFORE THE CRUCIAL ELECTION, Billy was a party to a court case that dramatically impacted tribal politics for the Nisqually. *Frank v. Morton*, a case Billy won, opened enrollment at the tribe, significantly increasing participation in tribal elections.

"People became enrolled and there were more voters," says George Walter, a longtime non-Indian employee of the Nisqually Tribe. "Tribal elections at Nisqually, and every place in Indian Country, rise and fall on multiple issues. So, anybody who tries to explain something as one issue is just wrong. There were new voters in January 1977. There was a new set of people elected to offices."

Tired of tribal opposition to the movement for the renewal of treaty rights, Adams and Billy hoped to usher in a new era of leadership. "We did a letter in Billy's name to all the Nisquallys and ousted the Nisqually [Chair], Zelma McCloud, and her controller," Adams says, "the two people who had gone to the Commission and asked that I be prohibited from having anything to do with Frank's Landing. We took over the Nisqually government in the early election of '77. . . . They were spending all these years opposing off-reservation fishing and all this time opposing Frank's Landing, and more or less being run by the [Washington] Fisheries Department and their policy positions." Georgiana Kautz and Frankie Mccloud took over

"It's the worst thing that ever happened to him," says Hank Adams of the death of Billy's daughter Maureen.

as chairman and vice chairman. Billy was named fifth member and Indian Fisheries manager.

WHILE BILLY'S STAR rose in Indian Country, he suffered personally. The year 1977 was devastating for Billy, as his sister-in-law, Georgiana Kautz recalls. Kautz is an outspoken Nisqually Indian better known as Porgy. For years, Porgy went few places without a note tucked in her bag from Maureen Frank, Billy's daughter: "Ha ha, Porgy! I'm out in the sunshine, and you're in there working hard." At the time, Kautz had just won chairmanship of the Nisqually Tribe, a job that promised endless working hours indoors.

"I went to a tribal meeting and Maureen was with me," Porgy recalls. "But Zelma McCloud said to Maureen, 'You can't come in the meeting, you're not a Nisqually.' So, Maureen sat out in the car.

Billy, Willie Sr., and Maureen's daughter, Ca-ba-qhud.

Finally, I told them, 'I have to go home; I've got Maureen.' I came home. An hour later they called me and said, 'You're on council now; we voted you in.' That's when Maureen sent me the letter with Ca-ba-qhud. That's the one I carried forever."

Porgy also carried a photograph. Pictured were Maureen, a young, angelic-like mother, and her daughter, Ca-ba-qhud, a striking young girl with black hair and black eyes. "Billy and Norma—they'd come over to the house and Ca-ba-qhud would be there," Porgy remembers. "Billy would go down the road bouncing her on his arm. When it was time to go, she would just *scream* and want to be with Billy and Norma. They loved that kid so much."

"She was a beautiful girl," Billy says of Maureen, "and her baby and I talked on the telephone all the time."

Maureen Frank studied at The Evergreen State College and played softball in tournaments in the Northwest and Canada. She developed a passion for treaty fishing rights. In her father's shadow, Maureen learned the daily struggle for salmon and sovereignty. "All those things were instilled in her," Porgy says. "I mean, the Trail of Tears, she was there. She loved that battle. It was inside of her. Her and Valerie, Alison, Suzette and Sugar, they loved the fight. . . . Norma and Billy would take [Ca-ba-qhud] and they would kind of want to go out and do things so I would take care of [Ca-ba-qhud] for a lot." Maureen experienced many turning points in the Native American movement, including the occupation of Alcatraz, the encampments on the Puyallup River, and Wounded Knee.

A week before Maureen's nineteenth birthday, Billy bought her a Dodge. He called his daughter in Canada, where she was staying with relatives, to tell her that her new vehicle was ready.

On September 14, 1977, at 8:35 p.m., Maureen, three-year-old Ca-ba-qhud, and Yvonne Owens, a friend, were heading southbound on State Highway 97, just outside Omak in Okanogan County. Ca-ba-qhud slept soundly in the backseat. When an oncoming car struck their vehicle, the back seat flew forward.

"That woman was drunk, and hit her head-on," Porgy explains. "It killed Maureen and it killed Ca-ba-qhud, instantly. And Yvonne made it out of it somehow, someway."

"The lady was going to see her husband somewhere," Billy says. "It was the evening time. Right at Omak, they run into her—killed my daughter and my granddaughter. The other girl was thrown out of the car." "She lived," Billy says of the driver. "And I don't even know where she lives now or what. But that destroyed a big part of our family." The driver was hospitalized with head injuries, broken ankles, cuts, and bruises, while Owens suffered a head injury, broke her arm, and fractured her ribs.

"I remember they came back to the Landing, and we were all there," Porgy says. "So many people come, the Shakers, all of them come. Norma didn't know what to do. I said, 'Norma, you've got to do what you've got to do. You've got to be what your parents brought

GEORGIANA KAUTZ PERSONAL COLLECTION

Tanu with Dad.

you up to be. You can't be all of these things that people want you to be, and then deal with the hurt too.' So many people come in—it's fine to have a religion and a belief, but don't push it down somebody else." The accident "shattered our family," Billy says.

"That was his life. That girl loved him . . . and Norma," Porgy says. "It was like they tore their hearts out."

"It's the worst thing that ever happened to him," says Adams.

IF A SILVER LINING followed Maureen's passing, it was undoubtedly Tanu, a bright-eyed toddler with an infectious smile. Billy and Norma adopted the young boy through the Puyallup Tribe and Billy's father named him. With no tribal office at the time, few adoption records existed. But there was new life in the home at Frank's Landing.

Chapter 11

The Politics of Salmon

Indian tribes had long made a villain out of Slade Gorton. The intellectual Dartmouth graduate, who earned his law degree at Columbia University Law School, first jumped into Washington State politics as a legislator in 1958, and was elected attorney general ten years later. By the 1970s, Gorton was savvy, competitive, and tough. He believed Indians should be treated like other Washingtonians. "I find racism appalling," Gorton states. "But I do have a profound difference with the tribes. I don't think they should be treated differently than anybody else. I think the same laws ought to apply to everyone."

In 1976, Indians who already opposed Gorton found fresh meat. The attorney general contended that Indian treaties were breakable contracts, provided the federal government paid damages. He made his case to fellow Republicans. Gorton urged the party to demand that the government buy treaty rights: "If the Indians were paid for the right, I can assure you they would be among the richest class of citizens."

Tribes accused the attorney general of reneging on a state promise to let the federal courts settle the issue once and for all. "Now that Judge Boldt has rendered his decision, we find the state is backtracking and is unwilling to accept the United States Supreme Court

The upwardly mobile Slade Gorton as attorney general.

decision," stated Leo LaClaire, director of the Small Tribes Organization of Western Washington. "Not only have we been given double talk and a fast shuffle by Slade Gorton," he pressed, "but other state officials—notably Fisheries Director Don Moos—have been talking to us with forked tongues."

It wasn't just the tribes pressuring Gorton. Non-Indians made up a strong, vocal constituency, and in 1976 they nearly ousted Congressman Lloyd Meeds from office because of his stance on the Boldt Decision. "The fishing issue was to Washington State what busing was to the East," Meeds once declared of the contentious spirit. "It was frightening, very, very emotional."

The centrist from Everett sailed into office in the Democratic landslide of 1964. In 1976, Meeds found himself embroiled in a tough campaign against his anti-Boldt opponent, John Garner: "If you want to right the wrongs of the Boldt Decision, throw Lloyd Meeds out of Congress," Garner attacked.

Voters nearly did. At one point election night, Meeds clung to a 127-vote lead. By the time election results were certified, the margin of victory stood at a mere 526 votes. "He was a lawyer," explains Jim

Waldo, a former assistant U.S. attorney and facilitator of the post-Boldt era, "and he had come out and basically said, 'I don't necessarily like this decision, but it's a final federal court decision after the Ninth Circuit and we have to respect that.' Well, he came within a whisker of being defeated, because of taking that position. The commercial fishing industry and sports fishermen in his district, at that time, were a big political force. They weren't at all interested in hearing that, or hearing their congressman say that. So, the delegation was very antsy about what to do about this."

President Jimmy Carter agreed to establish a federal task force to work through the contentious fisheries dispute. The hunt was on for a settlement, a legislative solution to ease implementation of the Boldt Decision or soften the 50/50 division of fish. "Somewhere in the sea of my paperwork, there's a memo that was circulated in the Magnuson/Jackson operations to try to talk about what a legislative solution ought to look like," says Tom Keefe, a legislative director for Warren Magnuson at the time. "What people decided was 50/50 is way too much for the Indians; there's not that many of them. They don't deserve that much. We [the Department of Fisheries and its allies] think a legislative solution ought to be 80/20."

THE BOLDT DECISION had caused a clash within the court systems. The state supreme court held that the Department of Fisheries would violate equal protection rights of non-Indian fishermen and exceed its authority if it followed the Boldt Decision.

"The Supreme Court came out with a decision that took the view that this was impermissible, discriminatory policy by the State Department [of] Fish and Department of Game and, in essence, that they couldn't implement federal court orders. Since no federal court had ever enjoined a State Supreme Court, we weren't going to be the first," says Jim Waldo. The state and non-Indian fishermen, Waldo was convinced, were trying to "frustrate the implementation of the federal decision while they looked for a new case that would go to the [U.S.] Supreme Court." Meanwhile, the Department of Fisheries stood at a crossroads: implement the order and violate a state supreme court opinion; or ignore it in defiance of the federal district court.

Billy, the newly minted chairman of the Northwest Indian Fisheries Commission, sharply criticized the state: "Yesterday's NWIFC decision in the Washington Supreme Court is unfortunate, but certainly not unexpected. It is in character with that court's prior rulings, plainly rooted in racism and dedicated to the proposition of white supremacy."

Despite the collision between courts, Boldt himself remained confident his ruling would stand. "Judge Boldt has great respect for the state's jurists, but there can be no doubt what the outcome will be if the state and Federal courts clash," noted Dr. Richard Whitney, one of Boldt's technical advisers. "This is the same argument for states' rights in every civil rights issue from Mississippi to Boston and they've gotten nowhere."

In response to the judicial clash, the NWIFC demanded that the federal government take over the salmon fishery. Boldt assumed control on September 1, 1977. Billy relates the story:

> As of today, Boldt said, "I'm taking your right away, state of Washington. You do not manage the fish anymore. The United States government is managing the salmon. I'm going to give you a number to call, a hotline. Right now, the National Marine Fisheries is out in the water with the Coast Guard. They're throwing all the boats off the water, right now, as we speak. And you do not manage this resource anymore." ...
>
> Slade Gorton went back to Dan [Evans]. And Dan said, "What happened?" He said, "Well, they just took our right away from us." And Dan said, "You better make sure you get that right back."

"They had to change laws—all the RCWs," Billy continues. "They had to do all kinds of things before the judge gave them their right back. But he took everybody off the water. Nobody is fishing anymore, illegally or nothing. They were cheating each other out here."

But, to the dismay of the tribes, Boldt took his responsibility a step further. Responding to a request by President Carter's new task force, Boldt reduced the tribes' allotted share by 5 percent. Indians were stunned and angry. "I've never seen an Indian come out on top," Billy snapped. "They've got it just as bad as the non-treaty fishermen who are so-called going bankrupt."

To Leo Krulitz, solicitor of the Interior Department, and President Carter, Billy argued that the proposed reduction undermined the 1974 order, "depriving tribes further of their treaty and economic rights, and sacrificing the welfare and escapement needs of the salmon resources of Puget Sound." Billy agreed to comply with the reduction, but warned that the cut diminished the federal government's reputation with the tribes.

In fact, it seemed no one was happy with the reduced allocation. Non-Indian gillnetters accused the government of luring them with "sucker bait." A 5 percent reduction of the Indians' share would never put an end to their economic hardships, they argued.

Nonetheless, the Coast Guard, National Marine Fisheries Service, and federal marshals moved to Washington waters. "We ended up taking over the fishery by court order and injunction and then we brought in U.S. marshals from around the country," Waldo says.

"They were raping the fish, just raping," Billy says. "There was no law and order or nothing."

Almost twenty-five hundred fishermen were served with notices to obey fishing orders or risk being held in contempt. According to attorney Mason Morisset, by the end of the 1977 fishing season, some "183,000 salmon had been taken illegally by the state licensees." Further, the state adopted regulations that limited Indian fishermen "for conservation," writes Morisset but at the same time, allowed non-Indians to fish nearby areas: "Non-Indian fishermen took 95.3% of the 1978 illegal catch."

According to a report by the NWIFC, a pattern had developed to control allocation and put more salmon in the hands of non-Indians: "The State would announce a predicted run size for an expected run of fish and establish the number representing one-half of the harvestable fish which would be the entitlement of the non-Indian fishermen under the formula of *U.S. v. Washington*. But again and again, after the season had commenced and non-Indian fishermen had taken the number of fish assigned to them under that formula, the State would announce that its earlier predictions had been too optimistic—that there were not enough fish left for the Indians to achieve their share."

WHEN THE United States Commission on Civil Rights met in Seattle in October 1977, tension was palpable. For hours it heard testimony on the fishing rights struggle and Native problems with white society. "There's a new breed of people that wants to run us out of the country," charged Forest Kinley, a Lummi Indian.

"[Whites] talk about the Panama Treaty and these other treaties all over the world," Billy said in exasperation. "They don't know that in their backyard there's a treaty right there that's being violated. . . . Your neighbor right down there is an Indian. He's got a treaty and he's a human being."

Among the first to testify was Slade Gorton. "Why are we here? Why are you here?" Gorton demanded. The Commission never bothered to include a single representative from the non-Indian commercial or sports fishing industry, Gorton pointed out. In its attempt to improve the lives of Native Americans, Gorton says, the state was simply "substituting one form of discrimination for another."

In his own testimony before the Commission, Billy was outspoken and direct. He characterized the evolving proposed fisheries settlement as a document that "isn't worth the powder to blow it to hell. And that's really my feeling about it." "One of the things in that last report of the task force—and all it is is a political document—is that it takes our enforcement," Billy continued. "It takes away our usual and accustomed fishing areas, and it also takes away our management."

MR. ALEXANDER: Do you feel, in a sense, betrayed or cheated by the Federal Government? . . .

BILLY: Well, you know, if you take the politics out of the management of salmon, we wouldn't have this purse seiner out here talking about a generation of him being in the fishery; we'd have salmon right now. These salmon would have been protected and the politics stayed out of them.

Now, with this piece of document right here, you'll have the politics right back in them, and you'll have the Indian right out of business.

Right now, today, I am a manager, an equal manager with the state of Washington, and I have something to say on that Nisqually River as far as the salmon are concerned, the enhancement programs that go on, on that river stream, but before I didn't have nothing to say.

If I accept the task force report right tomorrow, as it stands, or the legislation that probably will be enacted, it will put us out of the management business, it will put us back into no fish. The other two species that only remain on the Nisqually River will probably no longer be there in a matter of a few years.

The media picked up on the hostility between the Indian tribes and non-Indians. "We are here," Billy told the Commission of the Indian people.

"Us non-Indians are here, too," countered Howard Gray, director of the Interstate Congress of Equal Rights and Responsibilities.

The NWIFC believed that the violence on the water was a scheme to send the Boldt Decision back to court. In August 1978, senators Jackson and Magnuson sent a letter to Secretary of the Interior Cecil Andrus: "As you know, the implementation of the so-called 'Boldt Decision' has caused four years of conflict and controversy in Washington State . . . it has become impossible to provide adequate protection of the resource with present enforcement capabilities. . . . In

1976, illegal non-Indian fishing accounted for an estimated 34 percent of the total non-Indian catch in all of Puget Sound . . . adequate escapement levels necessary for the perpetuation of the resource are in jeopardy . . . while we work together for a long term solution, we must urge your very serious consideration of less than full implementation of the Boldt decision for this year."

THE WORK OF THE Carter task force ended with a proposed settlement in the late 1970s. "We came out with this proposal and we had hit the mark pretty well in a lot of respects," Jim Waldo recalls. "There was this deafening silence while everybody sat there trying to figure out what they wanted to do or not do.

"At that point, I got together with Billy and some of the tribal leaders. They had some issues with a couple things we recommended. So, we talked about them and I explained why I thought they would work out to their benefit. I remember Joe DeLaCruz and Billy and Dutch Kinley saying, 'What do you think we ought to do?' I said, 'I'll leave it to you to decide whether this is good enough. But if I were you, I would recommend just saying you're studying it for awhile. You're going to be getting calls from federal people telling you, you have to decide, but you can take some time with this.' They did."

"We realize that not everyone will clutch this proposal to his breast with enthusiasm," said John Merkel of the contentious spirit, "but it will provide a fishery that is better than the chaotic situation we have now." Merkel's assessment was a gross understatement.

To Billy, the settlement plan fell apart at the most basic level. It "fails to satisfy one of its main goals which is to fulfill Indian-fishing rights," he declared. The Puget Sound Gillnetters Association expressed shock and disbelief: "We feel the general concepts of the proposal are tantamount to a government declaration of segregations of race and areas as a national policy," said Phil Sutherland, association president.

The plan reduced the tribal allocation, limited the size of the non-

Indian commercial and troll fleets, and paid bonuses to non-Indian fishermen who quit the business. It adopted a new management system with regulators that included the Departments of Fisheries and Game and a tribal commission. It replaced ancestral fishing grounds with smaller tribal commercial management zones.

In addition, the settlement called on most tribes to give up fishing for steelhead commercially. Sports fishermen flocked to Magnuson: "We don't like a lot of this, but they're pretty close to what we want, the steelhead. If we could just get all the tribes off steelhead, commercial fishing, we could support this package."

Magnuson made the change. "At that point, everybody started climbing on planes to go back and see people in the agencies and the congressional folks, including the tribes," Waldo says. "If you'll change these three or four things I can support this. So, it was pretty clear our effort was over." In good humor, Waldo recalls task force members adding a last page to their final notebooks with the lyrics to the Johnny Paycheck song, "You can take this job and shove it."

BILLY BOARDED PLANES to Washington, D.C., often after the Boldt Decision, representing tribes, meeting with crucial players in the fisheries dispute, and working closely with longtime friends Suzan Harjo and Sue Hvalsoe, both Carter appointees. Harjo recalls a concerted effort within the Justice Department to persuade Indians to agree to a lesser allocation: "Of course, federal people can make it sound very attractive if you go in their direction," Harjo says. "It was very heavy handed. Billy wanted to keep track of who was eating with whom. We would drive around town in Sue's little Volks-wagen. . . . You'd see tribal leader X with the Justice Department or someone from the Hill. It was just fascinating to see the groupings of people. It tells you something, especially when, at the next day's meeting, someone would be telling you to agree to something less than 50 percent. Collectively, we had a lot of information."

The three quickly recognized that they weren't the only group keeping tabs on adversaries. "There were probably people who were circling us!" Harjo laughs. "Billy was able to arm up the people who didn't want less than 50 percent. The treaty says 'in common with.' It was big business and big bucks. Billy was able to be circumspect in meetings and on the lookout for something."

IN EARLY 1979, Judge Boldt again sent shockwaves through the Northwest as he relinquished his authority over the fishing rights case. "He did WHAT?! the Puget Sound Gillnetters Association exclaimed. Boldt stepped down noting the present status of the litigation, his health, and the timing—the fact that Washington was between salmon seasons. Boldt had faced a strong backlash for his handling of the case. Later, questions arose about his mental health."We are firmly convinced that his decision was not a matter of personality, nor of private conviction, and that any judge given the same evidence and arguments would have reached the same conclusion," the Northwest Indian Fisheries Commission said.

THE HERITAGE OF Indian tribes and Washington's multi-million-dollar fishing industry hung in the balance in February 1979. Slade Gorton's voice was brisk and clear, as he addressed the United States Supreme Court in the most important case of his political career. The collision in the courts had escalated. Now, a related court case over fishing rights appeared before the justices. The highest court in the land had agreed to review the 1974 Boldt Decision. Gorton took the floor with confidence. He argued that the treaties did not secure Indians an allotted percentage of fish, but equal access to the fishery. The key words "in common with" ensured neither Indians nor non-Indians would be discriminated against.

Gorton's adversary was Mason Morisset, who addressed the court with candor, bluntly stating that he disagreed with the attorney general on just about everything, even basic facts. Paraphrasing Judge Belloni, who presided over an all-important, related fishing rights case in Oregon, Morisset quipped: "This case might make sense if we ignored all history, law, facts of the case and the behavior of states of Washington and Oregon."

According to Morisset, Indian treaties guaranteed Indian nations a right to a decent living: "I think the important thing for us to get across is that we must construe the treaty as a whole. . . . It was designed to guarantee that the Indians would continue to make a good livelihood fishing." Morisset argued that instead the state of Washington had preempted the Indian fishery since 1890, when salmon fishing was first outlawed during certain parts of the year. He described a regulatory scheme that took salmon from Indian tribes year after year. The tribal attorney argued that treaties were "unbreakable contracts" and secured half the harvestable salmon and steelhead catch to tribes.

The U.S. Supreme Court upheld the Boldt Decision on July 2, 1979, with a stern warning that federal officials would step in, should the state choose to ignore the order. In doing so, it noted the dramatic findings of the court of appeals that had previously upheld the Boldt Decision: "The state's extraordinary machinations in resisting the decree have forced the district court to take over a large share of the management of the state's fishery in order to enforce its decrees. Except for some desegregation cases [citations omitted] the district court has faced the most concerted official and private efforts to frustrate a decree of a federal court witnessed in this century. The challenged orders in this appeal must be reviewed by the court in the context of events forced by litigants who offered the court no reasonable choice."

Non-Indians were disheartened. Fishermen scrapped plans to fish Puget Sound that summer and headed north to the wilds of Alaska. "I don't think it's gonna work," said one fisherman in dismay. "The guys won't just sit by."

Neither would the salmon. For all the energy spent debating the justice of Boldt's decision, "the salmon is the loser," the *Washington*

Post declared, as the number of fish spiraled downward. Some thirty different jurisdictions in the United States and Canada shared control over the salmon. The intricate industry suffered from an excess of commercial licenses and still-limited knowledge of the importance of the environment and habitat. Biologists and Indians alike sounded a warning: certain wild salmon species were endangered.

Chapter 12

Bridge Builder

Billy has the flawless timing of an orchestra conductor. He understands when to push, when to quit, and when to laugh, letting the tension out of a room like a balloon that slowly deflates. Tom Keefe, a longtime friend, compares his striking ability to read people to the talents of a gypsy fortune teller. "In some ways, I think Billy Frank is a lot like Barack Obama," assesses Keefe. "They are both similar to a Rorschach test. They tend to be what you want them to be, but not deliberately. I don't think either sets himself up to do that. With Billy, I think there's a unique simplicity about him, and how he views life. I don't think he even graduated from high school, but he's brilliant. His brain works on levels that mine doesn't even approach. He sees events and situations against a larger background, rather than in the crisis of the moment."

As 1980 neared, Billy's star rose. He settled into American politics as a back-slapping, handshaking, joke-telling tribal leader with a disarming way to win support for the Pacific salmon. Once, at a Red Lion in Portland, Billy spoke to the power companies and utilities about the dangers of cheap electricity and dams. "You see these god damn light bulbs?" he asked, pointing up at the ceiling. The crowd nodded in response. "I don't see no god damn fish swimming out of those god damn light bulbs." The audience howled. "He had great timing

Billy moves from the riverbank to the State Legislature where he testifies in 1989 in support of Curt Smitch, the Booth Gardner appointee to head the state Wildlife Department. The Seattle Times *called Smitch's confirmation hearing "one of the stormiest in the state's history."*

when things were getting real hairy in a room, or just going up and giving somebody a hug. He's a great hugger. And even in the tense moments, [he'll say], 'I think we ought to listen to this a little bit longer,'" Bill Wilkerson says.

Billy could charm just about anyone, even one of the most influential men in the U.S. Senate. Keefe saw it firsthand as legislative director for Warren Magnuson. Keefe had persuaded his boss to retain a sharp attorney named Sue Crystal, a law school graduate with red hair and a vivacious personality to match. Crystal had just finished an internship with the Senate Appropriations Committee. Assigned to a delicate tribal funding case with the committee, she walked into Keefe's office. "Do you know who Billy Frank is?" she asked.

Keefe laughed, "Do I know who Nelson Mandela is? Yeah, I know who Billy Frank is. I went to St. Martin's College just up the hill from Frank's Landing. I could practically smell the tear gas from my dorm room!"

Crystal was pushing Keefe for a legislative earmark that would allow an Indian school at Frank's Landing to run independently, limiting interference from the Nisqually and Puyallup Indian tribes. "Billy was kind of a hot potato at the time," Keefe says. "The whole fishing rights battle was a major headache for our congressional delegation. Politically, it wasn't a very popular thing to get involved in. I worked Magnuson a little bit on it, about the school, and about Billy Frank and his dad. As a result, I kind of opened the door for Magnuson to get to know Billy as a human being, rather than as the renegade symbol of this seemingly endless struggle. They became really good friends."

When the Senate recessed, Keefe typically flew home to the Pacific Northwest. Typically, Billy waited on the airport drive in a big red Chrysler to provide one of "Professor Frank's Windshield Seminars," a crash course on the environmental hazards facing the salmon.

Once, on the banks of the Hoh River, Billy called the 50 percent allocation to the tribes meaningless without any fish. "What we should have done," he told Keefe, "was all pile into my canoe and taken a ride up the Nisqually River, or the Hoh or the Puyallup, to where Mr. Weyerhaeuser and Mr. Simpson and Mr. Georgia-Pacific was destroying the salmon's nursery, while we were fighting over the harvest downstream. Time is running out for the salmon."

Keefe urged Billy to meet with Magnuson and sell him on the urgent need to improve salmon habitat. After one session, Maggie sat puffing his cigar and turned his bulky frame toward Keefe, "Your friend Billy really makes a lot of sense."

Those sessions with Billy altered Keefe's view of the fish and its relationship with the tribes. As the "white guy in blue suits," Keefe attended a myriad of weddings, funerals, and feasts with Billy all over Indian Country. "I was really struck by the odd mix of deep poverty overlaid with great pride, and the central role the salmon played in their survival as a community."

THE FRAGILE STATE OF Pacific salmon grew more delicate still. Presenting themselves solely as fish advocates, biologists and resource managers had sounded a warning in the *Seattle Times*: "All citizens of this state are bound to lose with the present course of salmon and steelhead management." There were other factors killing off salmon to be sure, experts acknowledged. However, the tangled web of fishery managers threatened irreparable harm to the runs. "It appears that control of fishing by state and federal courts, state and federal agencies, international organizations and Indian tribes has been inadequate," authorities warned. Experts called for a decisive and clear management structure: "Such a plan is essential and the need is urgent. If it is not initiated soon, the salmon and steelhead runs of the state of Washington may well cease to exist."

Proposed solutions took various forms. Tribes attacked one congressional proposal to decommercialize steelhead as a scheme to abrogate treaties. Billy sharply chastised Congressman Don Bonker for the bill, and used the media to debunk myths and kill the legislation. Taking steelhead off the commercial market would be a violation of treaty rights, Billy shot back, even if the fish could still be used for ceremony and subsistence. Supporters of the proposal argued that Indian nets were destroying steelhead runs, while sportsmen paid for the resource. Billy refuted the claims. Taxpayers, even the non-fishing kind, funded steelhead programs through federal grants used to research the species. Because of the Boldt Decision, tribes invested resources to track and manage the runs. That effort would cease, Billy warned, if Indians could no longer sell the fish.

Magnuson, meanwhile, proposed the Salmon and Steelhead Enhancement Act, calling for a widely accepted management plan for Northwest fisheries. Maggie's bill also offered a "buy back" of commercial licenses furnished by the state.

Billy supported Magnuson's bill, with some adjustments, and took heat for his endorsement. Tribal members distrusted Magnuson because of his earlier stance on Indian fishing. As Hank Adams explains, "In 1964, both Henry Jackson and Warren Magnuson introduced resolutions into Congress to extinguish these treaties and/or to buy out, to either place all Indian fishing under state control and regulation and alternatively to buy out all treaty rights and extinguish them relating to fish."

The Salmon and Steelhead Enhancement Act passed three days before Christmas in 1980, just weeks after Magnuson's defeat by Slade Gorton. "I really look back on that legislation as the Magnuson/Frank blueprint for the future in restoring our salmon runs for everyone, but it mostly depended on Magnuson's re-election," Keefe recalls. "We did get some license buy-backs, but the Reagan era brought big cuts in domestic discretionary spending, so the restoration of spawning grounds and destroyed rivers and streams didn't happen. Spending money on habitat restoration in the Pacific Northwest was never going to be a Reagan priority, and with Magnuson's defeat, we just ran out of time."

Billy and Magnuson's friendship produced tangible results. In 1980, the site of Wa He Lut Indian School at Frank's Landing transferred into federal trust status. The lot adjacent to the Landing was now a permanent location for the school. In 1987, Frank's Landing was deemed eligible for federal funding to aid in education at Wa He Lut. Their friendship was also key in the passage of the Northwest Power Act of 1980, says Adams. The law targeted dams on the Columbia River and required a regional energy conservation plan mindful of salmon.

Generally speaking, Magnuson became more favorable to Indian interests because of Billy, says Adams. "By the end, when Senator Magnuson came to know Billy, he found that he liked Billy and began to see Indians in a different way. You had Warren Magnuson fighting as strongly for Indians as he ever fought against them at the end of his Senate career."

THE 1980 SENATE RACE between Magnuson and Gorton was Billy's first major foray into mainstream electoral politics. He campaigned relentlessly on behalf of his new friend, Warren Magnuson, and doggedly against his longtime adversary, Slade Gorton. For all his power and prestige, Magnuson found himself in the fight of his political life.

Maggie's well-worn senate seat had long held a political giant— one-half a super-duo with Scoop Jackson. The two were coined the "Gold Dust Twins." The moniker reflected sizable contracts and federally funded projects the two senators secured for Washington State. Maggie's role as chairman of the Appropriations Committee greatly influenced how the federal government divided a half-trillion-dollar budget. "He is scrupulously fair with federal funds; one half for Washington state, one half for the rest of the country," quipped Walter Mondale.

Magnuson touted his experience as appropriations chair in the campaign. "But federal fiscal restraint has become attractive even to voters in Washington," observed *Time Magazine*. "As a result, Magnuson's pork-barrel record is no longer the asset that it was in past campaigns."

In a clever spin, the Gorton camp declared it was time to give Maggie a gold watch and elect "Washington's next great senator." Because Gorton was known for his vehement opposition to the Boldt Decision, the campaign focused on the lingering bitterness over the fish wars. "Sportsmen for Gorton," they printed on bumper stickers.

Pundits mused that the presidential race was too close to call. But Ronald Reagan handily defeated Jimmy Carter in a landslide that sent Magnuson—and a dozen or so Democratic Party senators— packing. "Vote Republican for a Change," the party appealed. Voters listened.

At a fundraiser in early 1981 to pay off campaign debt, Magnuson's wife, Jermaine, noted beautiful flowers scattered about that would soon go to waste. She leaned toward Adams, "Can't you load up as many as you can and take them to Billy's families at Frank's Landing?"

As the years went by, the friendship between the retired senator and the tribal leader grew. Billy helped commission a totem pole, carved by master craftsmen from the Lummi Nation, to present to Magnuson on his eighty-sixth birthday. The yellow cedar work of art still looks out toward Puget Sound from Maggie's home on the south slope of Queen Anne Hill. It reveals the story of the senator's rise as a friend of the environment, the tribes, and the fish.

"Billy always took the time to drop in on Senator Magnuson, bring him some smoked salmon and just sit and share stories about the state," Keefe remembered. "They were quite a pair."

When complications related to diabetes took Magnuson's life in May 1989, his wife personally invited Billy to the memorial service, a grand affair at St. Mark's Cathedral in Seattle. One thousand people bid the longtime politician farewell.

MORE THAN A YEAR after the Boldt Decision was upheld by the U.S. Supreme Court, tribes celebrated a second crucial court victory. Phase II of *U.S. v. Washington*, the environmental question, was decided in the fall of 1980. An excess of legal issues during the original trial had prompted Judge Boldt to parcel certain questions of merit for later consideration by the court. Phase II focused in part on the government's responsibility to maintain adequate fish habitat and in part on hatchery fish. Judge William Orrick ruled in favor of the tribes on both counts. If the government backed out of its responsibility to provide suitable salmon habitat, Orrick opined, Indian fishermen "would eventually be reduced to the right to dip one's net into the water . . . and bring it out empty." Hatchery fish should be allocated, Judge Orrick further held, because they existed to replenish dwindling numbers of wild fish.

Big business flinched at Orrick's decision. Anticipating a lengthy appeal process that would put business permits on ice, sixteen companies formed the Northwest Water Resources Committee. The committee filed an amicus brief in the state's appeal of the opinion.

Tribes viewed the friend-of-the-court brief as anything but friendly to their treaty rights. "If the big guys want to negotiate with the tribes, they shouldn't be doing it with one eye on the courthouse," Keefe told Billy. They decided to fight back with something the business world clearly understood: money. Keefe and Billy pitched the idea of a national tribal boycott to Bob Rose, reporter for the *Spokesman Review*. Pleased with his article, they made a flier to circulate at a national conference of tribal leaders. That's when they bumped into Art McDonald, director of communications for Puget Power, in an elevator at the *Spokesman Review*. The bespectacled, affable spokesperson looked surprised to see them.

"Billy, what are you doing here?" McDonald asked.

Keefe handed him the flier.

"We're calling for a national boycott of your company and their friends," Billy told him, as the elevator doors closed.

THE NATIONAL CONGRESS OF AMERICAN INDIANS met at the Sheraton-Spokane Hotel in May 1981, attracting some of the most influential leaders of the day.

It had been ten years since Joe DeLaCruz, longtime chairman of the coastal Quinault Indian Nation, famously demonstrated against the logging of tribal land by blocking access to the Chow Chow Bridge, a main route to tribal timberlands. He supported the boycott and called Billy to the podium. "I encouraged the NWIFC and Billy to come to NCAI to make a presentation and a motion to boycott these corporations. Billy made the motion; I seconded. It passed unanimously," DeLaCruz said.

"We're going to boycott!" Billy bellowed from the podium.

The Colvilles had already agreed to pull fourteen million dollars out of Seafirst Bank, and branded the company's involvement a disservice to every tribe. "We don't want them [Seafirst] using our money to fight other Indians. We're all brothers," vowed Mel Tonasket.

"Then something wonderful happened," Billy said at the time. "All the kids over at Washington State said that they were willing to boycott the bank, too. This sort of thing tends to spread and it did, to other campuses."

Billy describes what happened next. At the NCAI meeting in Spokane, someone suggested the NWIFC chairman fly to Anchorage and meet with Cook Inlet Corporation, a Native-owned company and landholder that started in 1970. During Billy's presentation in Alaska, someone in the back stood and said, "I move we pull $80 million from Seafirst Bank." It was seconded and passed unanimously.

The plane had yet to touch down in the Northwest when the phone rang. Mike Berry, president of Seafirst Bank, was desperate. "Before I jump out of the seventeenth floor of the Seafirst Bank in Seattle, I've got to sit down and talk with you," he told Billy when they connected. They agreed to meet at the bank headquarters on 4th Avenue in downtown Seattle. Billy sat on one side of the table "with all the Indians." The "good old boys' club" sat on the other in white shirts and ties.

"I want you guys to roll up all of your shirtsleeves," Billy said. "I want your sleeves up because I don't want any hidden cards. You have to start moving forward with recognition of the tribes and the treaty in the Northwest, and lay out an agenda we can follow. Recognize this treaty is here to stay, and get away from trying to abrogate it. Be an advocate for us." The talk opened the discussion to co-management. The bankers agreed to testify against bills proposed by Slade Gorton and Don Bonker to abrogate treaties.

Berry would later compare filing the amicus brief to kicking over a hornets' nest. "Mike Berry was a really decent man," says Keefe, "who realized they were heading down the wrong road. Jack Larsen from Weyerhauser took the lead in changing course. He turned out to be a thoughtful and reasonable guy, with no previous anti-treaty baggage.

Things started to improve once Billy got a seat at the table, and Jim Waldo found his niche as the go-to guy for keeping folks talking instead of litigating. My feeling was, better late than never."

THE END OF 1981 brought hope. Two days before Americans would sit down for Thanksgiving dinner, corporate heavyweights and two dozen tribal leaders sat down for lunch at the Washington Athletic Club in Seattle. Nerves were frayed, recalls Waldo, especially among the tribes. "What's the harm in a meeting?" Billy had asked. "What's wrong with talking with these folks?"

"At that time in tribal country, negotiating with the folks on the outside, meant that they had something valuable that someone else was about to take away from them," Waldo says. "There were political risks for tribal leaders, even in sitting down and negotiating. You wouldn't think of that if you came from a different culture. But if you think about theirs, and how poorly any treaty agreement that they'd ever made had worked out, it actually made a lot of sense. They were willing to meet; but they were very nervous. We could not call it a negotiation."

Astute facilitators recognize how seating arrangements impact group dynamics. At the Washington Athletic Club, Waldo and Billy sat tribal leaders next to business heads. "Well, what happened, of course, is that they started talking," Waldo recalls. "All of these people hadn't made it as far as they had as tribal leaders or business leaders by being inept. So they start out, 'Tell me about your tribe or your business? What's your family situation?' Then they started talking about their kids and playing ball and whatever else. It was quite animated. Of course, the tribal people, Billy being one of them, were quite eloquent. You could see they were having quite an impact on the business folks. They were talking about how important salmon have been and are to them, and why. The business leaders were responding to that and saying we have no need to harm your interest, but we just want to be able to go on about our work."

Slowly, executives and Native leaders peeled off from the room to break afternoon engagements. "It was an excellent meeting," concluded Joe DeLaCruz. "In a nutshell, we spent four hours getting to know one another. Now, I think, there's good reason for dialogue."

According to Waldo, Billy played a crucial role at the WAC: "Billy has no need to hear himself talk. When he decides to say something, it's for a purpose. Sometimes, he will make, in effect, a speech about the importance of salmon, or the tribes, or the history. Often, what he's doing is articulating for other people that aren't from that community, what's on the mind of the tribal leaders in the room. Billy also has a keen sense of when to try and figure out a way to just say, in essence, we've done as much as we can do here today. That is a gift. It's an art, not a science."

"We can keep winning in court," Billy had suggested that day, "but it won't protect the life of that salmon. If we continue in the direction we're going, there won't be any fish there." The corporations eventually agreed to back out of the Orrick appeal.

BILL WILKERSON, an enthusiastic, longtime government executive, sits in his home office in Olympia where two pictures hang on the wall. One is a portrait of Joe DeLaCruz; the other is an image of Billy. "He trusted me at a time when I had done nothing to earn his trust," Wilkerson says. "He supported me during some real tough times, when it probably wasn't in his interest to support me. Billy took a chance on trusting the state, and trusting me, when the history showed that we had done nothing to earn it. And it worked for him and for me." When Wilkerson earned his 1982 promotion to the controversial and often thankless role as director of the Department of Fisheries—like Evans and Boldt, Wilkerson was burned in effigy—tension remained palpable between the state and tribes. Many public employees grew up with the fish wars and associated Native Americans entirely with that conflict. "Probably the leadership understood that none of this was easy and that they had to deal with the tribes," Wilkerson says. "But you had a bureaucracy that not only didn't understand it, but didn't like it."

Although most people focus on the fifty-fifty allocation of harvest prescribed under the Boldt Decision, Wilkerson sees the shift toward the environment as the decision's true legacy. If the fish couldn't survive the streams, Indian fishermen would never see their share. "They harvested in the streams," Wilkerson explains. "Everybody understood that if you caught all the fish that you could catch to meet escapement levels, you would basically cork tribal fisheries. Or they would be severely limited. When the Boldt Decision came out, the tribes were catching about three percent of the total harvest and the court said they have to get 50 percent. That meant, you had to return more and more fish to the streams, where they were fishing."

But oversight of the fish runs remained a glaring problem. "The bottom line was that the tribal biologists weren't really managing the fishery," Wilkerson observes, "nor was the department. The court was. That again made no sense whatsoever."

In the winter of 1983, Governor John Spellman sat down with Wilkerson for his annual checkup. It was a Spellman ritual with agency department heads.

"Bill, how's everything going? How's it been?" Spellman asked.

"I've been to court seventy-eight times," Wilkerson told Spellman of the onslaught of court cases involving the Department of Fisheries. "We won three of them. And they weren't very important cases, those three. So, I personally think it's kind of ridiculous, this process that we've been sucked into, or nailed ourselves into."

Spellman, a lawyer himself, didn't care for the performance much either, Wilkerson says, "and he sure didn't like the political chaos around it."

The conversation ended when Spellman gave his full support to Wilkerson. "If it doesn't make sense to you, frankly, it doesn't make much sense to me either," the chief executive said.

"I think we need a real serious plan; the relationships are terrible," Wilkerson said. "If you want me to, I'll develop a plan for you to bring some folks together to at least have a discussion about where we ought to be focusing our attention." Spellman agreed.

The communication was sorely needed. Strife on the water still held the attention of national media at times. *Life* magazine devoted a four-page spread to the story in 1983, with Willie Frank Sr. prominently pictured deep in thought, every bit the elder. "On the rivers of the Northwest it's white man vs. Indian," the magazine related. "Why does anyone go fishing with a gun?" one Indian woman asked in the story. In a showing of persistent stereotypes, a sportsman declared, "Take all these Indians out and scalp 'em."

A BREAKTHROUGH occurred on a glorious March day at Port Ludlow in 1984. Inside tense courtrooms of the past, black-and-white battle lines were clear. At a peaceful resort on the shores of Ludlow Bay, the state and tribes would attempt to find the gray and leave the mediation up to Jim Waldo, whom both sides trusted.

Tribes were suspicious of the state. Billy brought Wilkerson to pre-meetings with Native leaders. "I basically told them that I had shown them, over the course of the time that I was both deputy and director, that I wanted to make some sense out of this thing. They knew that I was somewhat serious about trying to change things," Wilkerson says.

Wilkerson admitted, with brutal honesty, that the state had made mistakes. "I think we've made a lot of serious resource errors in preparation for the litigation. Because we're preparing for court, we're not focused on the resource. I think you are as concerned as I am about the conservation."

At least three people on Ludlow Bay were sanguine. "The most optimistic people in the room were Billy Frank, Jim Waldo, and Bill Wilkerson, and it probably stopped there," Wilkerson laughs, "but we were willing to give it a try. We first had to identify all the things that we had done over the last few years that had created the awful atmosphere. One of the top issues was a lack of respect."

A cooperative spirit soon took hold. Eventually, onetime adversaries found common ground. Both groups recognized shared interests in conserving the resource and securing a treaty with Canada. Both groups acknowledged they'd be far better off working the issues out themselves. They agreed to leave attorneys out of the conversation.

"If I hadn't been here and if you, as a news reporter, wrote everything that happened, I wouldn't believe it when I read it," said one shocked attendee.

"We don't want nobody coming through that door that's going to be negative," Billy insisted. "We don't have time to sit here and talk about the past. Some days it looks pretty gray. But there is always a little blue sky that opens up. You don't expect giant steps, just little ones."

"Billy was just the glue in a lot of ways," Wilkerson says of the more collegial atmosphere that began at Port Ludlow. "He kept the tribes coming to those discussions. He was chair of the Commission [NWIFC]. If we were dealing with north Puget Sound, Billy was making sure that all of the tribal leaders that were involved in that, and the biologists, were in the room. I made sure that my north Puget Sound staff was in the room. We just kept working on it. We didn't get to leave until we had agreement on the season.

"The bottom line was it was working. We went to the Fisheries Advisory Board three times that summer after being there eighty times, or seventy-eight times, the year before. We developed enough belief at Port Ludlow to try this. Then, we applied it to Puget Sound and we did it."

An encore arrived that May when an agreement was reached on a joint plan to manage chinook salmon fishing in Puget Sound, a milestone hailed as the greatest fisheries management achievement in a decade.

Eventually, the pre-season meetings became known as the North of Falcon Process, since Washington manages salmon stocks from Cape Falcon, Oregon, north to the Canadian border. "Nobody leaves happy," Billy says, "but it's better than going to court." Eventually, the Northwest Renewable Resources Center formed—a team of tribes, industry, and environmental and government interests that serves to mediate and problem solve. Eventually, the tribes and the state became allies in forming a U.S.-Canada coalition.

Washington's congressional delegation noted monumental progress. "We weren't bringing them the number of problems that we were always bringing them in the years before," Wilkerson says. "So, they were [supportive], 'Keep going. Keep going, Billy, keep doing what you're doing.' Governor Spellman was rock solid. He stood behind me all the time. The tribal leaders were standing behind Billy."

But stalled negotiations and collapsing agreements with Canada over a much-needed U.S.-Canada salmon treaty worried everyone. The chinook, in particular, were in real trouble.

Chapter 13

Resilience

Billy is sometimes compared to the Energizer Bunny, the immortal character that came to life in 1989 beating the drum for the long life of Energizer batteries. Billy's own ability to keep "going and going and going" is perhaps more remarkable noting the blows that could have swayed him off track. The elder has been dealt his fair share of grief.

In the early 1980s, Billy and longtime wife Norma separated. The couple had a hard time, says friend George Walter. "I think they had a disappointing marriage in that they didn't have children [biologically]. I think that Billy always made sure that he cared for her, took care of her. She was part of the whole team down at Frank's Landing for a long time." Despite the parting, they maintained an amicable spirit. Billy still cared for Norma as she suffered from diabetes, a chronic disease that afflicts Native Americans more than any other ethnic group. "I did what I had to do and there was no inference, argument, or anything," he says of their split. "We never had an argument."

Billy's relationship blossomed with Sue Crystal, the "larger-than-life" Magnuson aide." Her and I was just side by side," Billy says. "She did what she does, and she let me do what I do. We just complemented each other, and kept on going."

"She was like a force of nature coming into his life and completely turned everything upside down," says Patricia Zell, a longtime close friend of the couple.

Billy and Sue married Indian style in a ceremonial symbol of their commitment. "That was good enough for us," Billy says. Crystal once likened her relationship with Billy to a peaceful boat ride on the river.

Their relationship was somewhat unexpected, Zell says. "They were from such dramatically different backgrounds. Their temperaments were night and day." Crystal was the only child of Jewish parents who exposed their daughter to every educational opportunity. She earned her law degree at the University of Washington and eventually immersed herself in politics. "Having worked with Warren Magnuson and Ralph Johnson, she was more politically savvy than Billy," says Zell. "Billy learned from her." Zell describes Crystal as "a man's woman" with off-the-charts intelligence who never pulled any punches with Billy. She was a voracious reader. Books from every genre were scattered about the house.

"I knew Sue when she worked for Maggie," Bill Wilkerson says, "and then I knew her, of course, when she worked for the state. Bright, go-getter, real, solid—you always knew what Sue thought, very strong, adored Billy. She was agency director for a long time, and very good at it. She knew healthcare backwards and forwards. She was a neat gal and I always liked her. She had people who didn't like her, but it's because she articulated her position and advocated it."

Tom Keefe once asked Crystal about the difference in age between her and Billy: "Billy is twenty years older than you. What do you guys talk about?"

"What do you mean what do we talk about?"

"You're from different generations. You probably don't even listen to the same music."

"But Thomas, we're in love! Music doesn't matter."

"I used to grind her pretty hard on it," confesses Keefe, "but she took it in stride and called me the big brother she never had. Billy and Sue had a very special relationship, full of love and laughter. When Willie came along, it just got better."

BILLY FRANK JR. PERSONAL COLLECTION

"The way she treated me, I couldn't imagine anything else," Willie III says of his mother. "I was always her number one priority. I've never seen anybody like her, the way she cared for people." New son Willie with Sue Crystal and Billy

Like his dad, Billy fathered a child late in life. He was fifty-one, in April 1982, when William Frank III arrived, with an uncanny resemblance to William Frank II. It was one of the great days of his life, Billy says. Paying homage to a family lineage that reaches back to territorial times, the new baby took both names of his grandfather, Willie Frank and Qu-lash-qud.

The Frank family eventually moved to Johnson Point, a short distance from the Landing, the only place Billy has ever really considered home. Juggling high-pressure jobs with high-pressure family demands, Billy and Crystal depended on good friends. Keefe recalls one instance when he dropped Crystal off at the airport. She closed the car door and leaned in to Willie, a toddler of one. "OK, Willie. Now, Uncle Tom is going to take good care of you."

Willie took one look out the car window at his mother, toting her luggage down the long departure corridor, and one look back at Keefe sitting behind the steering wheel. "He screamed at the top of his lungs until I got to my house in Seattle," Keefe vividly recalls. "I told Willie afterward, 'I never, ever experienced a kid who did not inhale! I thought you must have been breathing through your ears, because you screamed for forty minutes straight.' I mean, my head was ringing when it was over."

In a display of the communal lifestyle that Billy has lived, Norma often watched Willie, and the two shared a bond. "Oh yeah, she just loved that guy, you know," Billy says. "She loved kids beyond belief," agrees Georgiana Kautz, Norma's younger sister. "Not only did she adopt, she took care of Willie."

In 1983, when Willie was a toddler, a gall bladder ailment sent his namesake and grandfather to the hospital. The elder, the last full-blooded Nisqually Indian alive, was 104 years old. Doctors were at first reluctant to operate. "He was in pain. After we had all talked about it, they finally decided to go ahead and operate," said granddaughter, Alison Gottfriedson. "After the surgery, the doctors came back and talked to us. They were astounded at his good health, and said he went through the operation very well." Even so, the long life began to take its toll. "While some of his family were at the hospital, I suggested that they look at Gramps' hands," said Hank Adams. "They were young hands. They were not 104-year-old hands. They were hands that labored for Indian people all of his living days."

On June 17, 1983, Willie Frank Sr. died. By most accounts, he'd lived 104 years. Word of his passing spread as his body lay inside the Wa He Lut Indian School with candles burning on each end.

"Dad gave us 104 years of his life. That's happy times. Happy times and great times," Billy observed, thankful for the many years spent together. Billy had shared coffee with his father every day of his adult life. "We accept that death is part of life. You gotta be sad and you gotta be happy. You gotta cry and you gotta be glad. That's the way we're going to be here today."

If the measure of a man can be gauged by the number of people who pay him final respects, Willie Frank Sr. left an indelible mark on Indian Country. His passing brought 450 people to Nisqually. Indians from many nations—Makah, Quileute, Lummi, Skykomish, Squaxin, Elwha, Chehalis, and more—joined a host of dignitaries that included Dixy Lee Ray, governor of Washington, and high-level bureaucrats from the Department of Fisheries and the Bureau of Indian Affairs.

"He didn't rob us when he left," Adams reflected. "He left us with strength and energy. It is not the end of an era, because Gramps's life was so involved with bringing new resources to his people . . . to bringing an appreciation of us to people who aren't Indian . . . to enhancing our understanding of people who can't know what it is to be Indian."

Billy stood alongside the casket, holding his fourteen-month-old son Willie in his arms. Two of the most important people in his life shared little more than one year together on the planet. "That's the one thing I really wish," says Willie III, "that I could have had a chance to know my grandpa. Even the people I talk to at Nisqually, who really weren't supporters of the Landing, they've all said, 'Your grandpa was one of a kind. There's never going to be anybody like him. He was special.'

"He never cussed. He never talked down to people. He never talked bad about people. It's so hard, in this day and age, to even think that anybody could be like that, especially dealing with tribal politics. I mean, god dang. I see people—they'll run somebody

Willie Frank Sr. and Billy are not the only Franks to make history. Collectively, family members survived assimilation, fought for treaty rights, and founded an Indian school to preserve their heritage. Seated: Angeline and Willie Frank; standing: Billy, Maiselle, and Andrew.

down—and then, the next hour, they're sitting next to them, talking to them. What is that? A lot of fake people, it seems like. He definitely wasn't. Him and my dad both, they're definitely not that kind of person."

After the procession had made its way from the Nisqually Tribal Center to the actual burial ground, a Lummi elder bade farewell, calling on nations to honor the memory of Willie Frank Sr. and fight for their land once again: "I am no stranger to this man we are laying to rest here. He never had golden peace down here with the federal government and the state. It's high time we get together and start suing the state and federal government. Look at the land they've stolen from us. They never ask. They just take it. Somebody has to pay for it.

"This is the land of our treaty rights, our fishing rights and hunting rights. They're after it. But the state can't begin to scrape up enough money for our fishing rights."

"I knew Dad would pick his own time to die," Billy reflected at the graveside.

Shortly afterward, in a letter to the *Tacoma News Tribune*, the family acknowledged the outpouring of tributes:

> To the editor, The family of Willie Frank Sr., thanks the hundreds of people who helped us honor Grampa Frank in the time following his death. Your generous gifts of drumming and songs, flowers, food, memorial donations . . . his teachings of Indian treaty rights and human rights, and dreams for Indian community life, will not be lost or forgotten. We thank each of you. The Family at Frank's Landing.

WILLIE FRANK III and his older siblings grew up in different worlds. The chaos and violence of the fish wars had diminished during Willie's childhood. The struggle for treaty and fishing rights still consumed courtrooms, but the debate largely played out in face-to-face meetings between adversaries who were now communicating. Billy stopped going to jail. Violence on the riverbank quieted.

This new spirit of cooperation handed Billy a new opportunity as a father. He had time to give his child. "It was a different day, and a new day," says Billy. "We took Willie skiing. We'd go to baseball games. We'd go see [Ken] Griffey. We were always there. We'd load the kids up and take them to the ballpark. Of course, you can't do that anymore. It will cost you 100 to 200 dollars to go there now!"

Early on, Willie shuttled back and forth between Flagstaff, Arizona, where his mother worked for the federal Navajo-Hopi Relocation Commission, and Washington State. "I remember starting preschool down there. We would stay down there for a month and then come back. It was split up. My dad and I would drive down there to go see my mom. She'd work part-time down there, and then she'd work up here also. Then, once I got into kindergarten, I came back up here. That's when she got a job for the state."

"As a mom, the way she treated me, I couldn't imagine anybody else," Willie says. "I was always her number-one priority. She worked for the governor. She was like, the governor's healthcare policy person, and she always made time for my dad and myself, regardless of whatever it was. She was always there for us.

"The one thing my mom always told me was, 'You've got to finish high school. You've got to go out and get your education. It's going to be very important.' There weren't a lot of people in our family that went to high school, finished high school. Out of the younger generation of kids, the twelve or thirteen of us, there's probably only three or four that graduated from high school."

Crystal was a stricter parent than her husband, and the bulk of the discipline fell to her. "Once Dad raised his voice, that was it. I knew whatever I was doing was wrong. My mom was the one that gave me the discipline."

"That's right," agrees George Walter. "I can remember Billy taking Willie down to Lake Fair and just saying, 'Oh here.' Give him a twenty-dollar bill, or whatever, and off he went. No question about spending it wisely. 'Come back if you need more.' Just very generous and very open with him. But I think that that actually is illustrative not of just Billy's parenting of Willie, but actually his approach to things, our approach to things. If something doesn't go right, instead of getting upset about it, figuring out how to take advantage of what's happened and keep going."

BILLY AND SUE's household was, at times, characterized as a perpetual sleepover, an inviting place that welcomed family and friends, especially displaced friends. "I had friends; most of them didn't have a good home life, and she took them in and cared for them," Willie says. "One friend, his mom worked like two or three jobs. He never had a dad. He spent a lot of time with us. My mom really took care of him almost as one of her own. . . . Another friend, his mom pretty much sent him packing right after high school. It was like, literally, the day after high school, she said, 'You're out of here. Good luck. I raised you for this long, and now you're on your own. My mom said, 'You know, Joe, we're not going to let you. You can come live with us.'"

One day, when Willie was in junior high school and playing YMCA basketball, his mother delivered earth-shattering news: "I want to coach."

"'What?!'" The news stunned Willie. Mom wasn't much of an athlete. "She couldn't dribble a ball; she couldn't even catch a ball," Willie says. But he soon realized what the offer was all about; his mom wanted to spend time with him. His teammates agreed, and the wife/mother/attorney took on a fourth role: coach. "We'd pretty much just scrimmage," Willie recalls. "There were eight, nine, ten of us. We'd just have enough to practice. It was pretty funny. It wasn't about her coaching. It was just about being around us."

BY 1986, NORMA's diabetes had worsened. High levels of glucose in the blood can lead to severe medical problems. Despite the grim report from the doctor, Norma kept her spirits up: "Like I told the doctor, she'll be at the Sonics, the Mariners or up watching our kids—she's not going to give up until she has to. And she didn't," says Georgiana Kautz. "Even when she was sick as hell, she'd make sure she spent time with me," says Norma and Billy's son, Tanu.

"When old man Bill died, they came and got me down at the end of the road. When I got down there, it was Norma laying in the road; she'd had a heart attack. And I kept yelling for her to wake up. And then we took her to the hospital. Then, it was deterioration. The kidneys were bad. They would give her blood transfusions. Her kidneys would give out if you operated on her heart, so it was just a matter of time." Three years later, as Norma neared the end, Kautz began bargaining to keep her sister alive: "If you live, I'm not going to smoke anymore. I'm not going to do this . . ."

Norma Frank passed away on March 22, 1986. Roughly three weeks later, Billy lost his mother, Angeline Frank, at the age of ninety-six. He'd lost three people close to him in as many years. "We had a good life, with Dad and Mom, and all of us together," Billy says.

Chapter 14

The Negotiator

The 1980s found the United States and Canada in an icy cold war over salmon. Rivals seethed at the thought of compromise. Billy played the role of consensus builder with the longest of odds. A treaty between the two countries "is only as good as people want it to be," Billy said. "It is a one-time-only opportunity to rebuild the fish resource." Friend George Walter scribbled down Billy's approach:

1. Look for answers that don't cost a lot of money. You'll never have much.
2. Understand the art of negotiation. Respect your adversaries enough to look for answers they can *actually* support.
3. Bring people together. (Alternatives usually involve buckets of money, even more time and someone in a black robe giving orders.)
4. Avoid hitting people over the head with a stick, regardless of any temporary gratification. The outcome is almost never positive.

"We could have gone down a track that was totally involving antagonism, fighting and everybody running up their attorneys bills," Walter says. "Billy advocated approaching things in the working together, drawing consensus arena. And that's really the only thing that ultimately works." The approach served Billy well through a series of historic settlements that marked the mid-1980s.

THE EVERGREEN STATE is extolled worldwide for its thick blankets of trees, its pristine and roaring rivers, and the jewel Billy characterizes as the golden egg, the Pacific salmon.

"Can you name another icon?" asks Bill Wilkerson, former head of the Department of Fisheries. "I can't name one. Washington is identified with it, and it's still a big industry." Consequences of no salmon, or fewer salmon, run deep. "There are parts of Puget Sound that would be hugely affected economically," Wilkerson says. "Bellingham is a good example, where there's a huge fleet. Seattle. People don't realize how important that marine fleet is to the Seattle economy. Ballard. It used to be Ballard exclusively, and down there at Fishermen's Terminal, it's still one of the biggest terminals in the world."

Washington chinook and coho were generating big dollars, but too much of the money lined the pockets of Alaskans and Canadians who intercepted the fish during their long migration north. "Many of the Chinook salmon produced on Grays Harbor find their fate in the nets of Alaskans and Canadians," noted the *Aberdeen Daily World*. "So many, in fact, that there has not been a season specifically for Chinook on Grays Harbor in five years. The Alaskans jealously guard their share, while the Canadians won't budge until the Alaskans make some concessions, and the Washingtonians say their countrymen to the north better face facts. The energy that various user groups have wasted squabbling amongst themselves strikes us as a latter-day tragedy of the commons, with little for the common good."

ENERGIZED BY breakthrough sessions at Port Ludlow in 1984, Billy and Wilkerson remained hopeful as the United States and Canada stood on the brink of an historic pact to thaw a cold war twenty years on. An accord could control interception. "It was our stocks that migrated up the coast into Alaska and then back down through Canada and Alaska, particularly our chinook and coho," Wilkerson explains. "We hated it. Our fish were being intercepted in both fisheries."

But the spirit of cooperation had yet to travel north. "We have been waiting twenty years for a U.S.-Canada Treaty," Billy grumbled. "Somebody has got to make sense out of protecting this resource!"

With a $400 million fishery along the West Coast at stake, drafted agreements between the two countries collapsed. Talk of a salmon war spread. The runs would never recover, biologists warned. After all, in eighteen years, Native spawning grounds lost 80 percent of their returning chinook. "What brought it home to me," says Jim Waldo, an attorney and facilitator in the post-Boldt era, "were the statistics from one day in 1976, when 750,000 salmon were caught by Americans and Canadians in the Fraser River. It's obvious that no fishery could long withstand that kind of pressure."

A truce, however, was a complex proposition at best, layered with emotions and politics. Salmon that originate in Washington rivers are indeed swept up on the high seas by Alaskans, Canadians, the Japanese, and the Russians. But interception works multiple ways. Washington fishermen can also intercept another host country's salmon, and do.

Unbeknownst to the fish, as they travel beneath the surface of the water, they pass through a tangled political web of jurisdictions. Charles Wilkinson, a longtime professor of Indian law, was so struck by the jurisdictional hopscotch that he took up the issue with the Committee on Indian Affairs of the United States Senate.

Today, salmon recovery in the Pacific Northwest is a patchwork quilt of many dozens of Federal and State statutes, tribal and international treaties, and county and city land use plans and regulations. Once in writing an article about the Columbia River, I found that a Chinook salmon born in the Lochsa River in Idaho would have to pass in its life's journey 8 dams on the Columbia, 16 passages in all out and back. And that the Chinook, in its return journey as an adult harvestable fish, would pass through no fewer than 17 separate Federal, tribal, State and international jurisdictions. Thankfully, Sammy, as I affectionately came to call my imaginary salmon, did not need a separate passport for each jurisdiction."

"And we had no treaty," sums up Bill Wilkerson. From the state of Washington, the pact was in the hands of Wilkerson, Billy, Tim Wapato, head of the Columbia River Intertribal Fish Commission, and Levi George, a Yakama, among others. "I can remember talking to Billy and Tim one night and saying, 'We're going to have to get more political about this thing.' We had a treaty agreement that fell apart, I think, in '83," Wilkerson recalls. "None of us were talking to each other, so we didn't know why. We didn't have each other's perspective. We were relying on the tribes to push the conservation arguments; we were pushing the allocation arguments. But there was no coordinated effort whatsoever. Wapato agreed to provide the staff to form this coalition, and he was dead serious about it. Fish weren't getting back to the Columbia. Internally, we were avoiding the litigation, we were campaigning like crazy about why what we were doing was right."

"Judges and lawyers haven't gotten us a damn fish!" an energetic Billy told the tribes. Wilkerson remembers Billy's speeches. "He had a few doozies. I would always get him, 'Well, I thought you did number 305 particularly well and effectively today.' I mean, it was all exaggeration, and he would laugh about it."

But Billy kept the tribes at the table, Wilkerson says. "He was the tribal leader. The Northwest Indian Fisheries Commission was kind of the focal group, and the Columbia River Intertribal Fish Commission that Tim Wapato ran. They were the two quote 'management entities' for the tribes.

"He always knew the right time to give one of his speeches," Wilkerson recalls. "He was so respected in the Canadian delegation because they had a tribal delegation. He was Billy Frank to those people, one of the top tribal leaders in North America. . . . It happened pretty fast once we had the president of the United States and the Canadian prime minister saying, 'Get it done.'"

A marathon negotiating session at a hotel in Vancouver, British Columbia, capped a long and frustrating process. In March 1985, President Ronald Reagan and Prime Minister Brian Mulroney, signed the highly anticipated Pacific Salmon Treaty, ending, at least temporarily, the fishing feud between the United States and Canada.

"The president really did want something tangible to take with him to Canada," said Slade Gorton, at that time a U.S. senator, of the treaty's expedited route through Congress.

"This is the best deal possible for all sides given the state of the industry and the resource," declared Garnet Jones, Canada's top negotiator. "This gives us the ability to truly manage stocks on a coast-wide basis."

The deal was made with three guiding principles: minimize interceptions, minimize disruptions of existing fisheries, and manage the fishery to conserve stock. The newly formed Pacific Salmon Commission that would navigate issues consisted of eight members, four from each country. Among its provisions, the treaty reduced the fish harvest in Canadian and Alaskan waters by roughly 25 percent. "Everybody gives a little," said then-U.S. Senator Dan Evans. Not everybody was satisfied. "To make this treaty happen, Alaska bled," said Earl Krygler, a delegate from the Alaska Trollers Association.

Politics can intervene, even for an optimist like Billy. The elder has a long history with the Nisqually Tribe. Over the years, he held various positions including vice chairman, council member, and fisheries manager. Then, in 1985, there was a falling out. "[The tribe] cut my funding," Billy recalls. "But I've got a bigger picture in my mind." The NWIFC reorganized in 1985, allowing Billy to be elected as chairman at large.

BILLY'S POSITIVE attitude helped secure an agreement with the timber industry in the mid-1980s. For all the importance of forest products to the Washington economy and American life—an industry association assessed that "on average each American uses three pounds of wood products per day"—the timber industry wreaked havoc on salmon habitat. Felled trees muddied rivers and stole shade salmon need to thrive. Thinking they were assisting salmon on the path of their migration, timber crews were required to remove logs from streams and rivers. But the effort backfired. The removal disturbed gravel beds and spawning places for the fish.

The tribes pushed for more protection of streams through buffer zones, selected areas that would remain off limits to logging and farming. Billy struck up a friendship with Stu Bledsoe, the man at the helm of the Washington Forest Protection Association (WFPA). Stu liked Billy. Billy still played tough. "They were drawn into the room by Billy's organizing the state's largest tribes and the Alaskan Native corporations to threaten withdrawal of money from the banks in Washington State if they continued to oppose Indian rights and management goals in relating to timber, water, wildlife," says Hank Adams. Communication was key. But the boundaries were clear.

Bledsoe, a former legislator and familiar figure in agriculture circles, continued to be impressed by the Nisqually Indian. "He was very confident that he could trust Billy, and he wasn't sure about me," Wilkerson laughs. "Billy and Stu had a really rock solid relationship. I was the least solid, because I knew him the least. So, Billy I would call him truly the glue on that one."

Billy also worked toward a compromise with Joe DeLaCruz. As chairman of the Quinault Indian Nation, DeLaCruz valued both timber and fish. With a vested interest in timber harvest, however, he opposed exceptionally restrictive practices in the industry. "He and Billy sat down," Wilkerson recalls. "They were negotiating with each other about what was OK and what wasn't OK. Those two guys closed the deal from the tribal standpoint, Billy and Joe. Billy accepted the fact that we would be the regulator, but wanted to be at the table."

In July 1986, again at Port Ludlow, representatives of the timber industry, tribes, environmentalists, and governmental agencies found middle ground. Six months and sixty meetings later, the Timber,

Fish and Wildlife Agreement was announced on February 17, 1987. The new pact over the use of Washington's tree-covered landscape struck a balance among competing interests and spurred an historic shift in how Washington managed its natural resources.

In assessing Billy's contribution to the negotiations, Wilkerson says, "He's made himself a credible spokesperson for the resource and I can't tell you what value that has. He's the guy that's been there the whole time. He's been through all of it. I saw him lighten the load in the room a lot of times. And everybody knew they were dealing with a leader, but they also knew that they were dealing with a great character. I personally think great characters are really . . . hard to find, great characters that really influence things are even rarer I think. And he is one of those.

"I think he wanted to protect those fish," Wilkerson continues. "He wanted respect for the tribes. He genuinely likes people. He's one of the greatest politicians I've ever known, truly, because he knows that, face-to-face, he's a retail politician. He's great at it. I don't know that he knew that about himself, but I know he knows it today."

In hindsight, Billy says he helped introduce a culture of long-range thinkers: "Us Indians are gatherers. We're harvesters. That's our life. We want the farmer and the timber industry to be like us, and they have been. The farmer is a neighbor of ours who thinks out a hundred years. And the timber industry, the growth of trees are one hundred, two hundred years. We want that mindset, that you sustain the life of the salmon, sustain the life of the shellfish, of the water. Sustain all of those trees up there and all of the farmers. If the farmers disappear, the guy that's building the houses will be there. And he'll take that land."

ALL WAS NOT WELL in the Nisqually watershed, however. Forest land that borders the Nisqually River had evolved into a minefield with a volatile history. Environmentalists had battled the Weyerhaeuser Company over a proposed log-loading port near the wildlife refuge. (Despite Weyerhaeuser's court victory, the logging market diminished before the plan could be realized.) Tribes were urging buffers at the river's edge—no farming, no logging—while farmers and loggers strived to protect their livelihood. The tribes proposed a strict plan for land use, but timber interests concluded, "The river is healthy, so leave it alone." It looked like everybody was ready for an absolute shootout," says Stu Bledsoe. "Everybody had their armor on." The state formed the Nisqually River Task Force and tasked the group with finding common ground to protect the largest stream that drops into Puget Sound.

In an old barn, Billy and 19 others handpicked by the state, sat at the front of a U-shaped table. The room held a mix of interests: tribes, businesses, arms, Fort Lewis, as well as the power and timber industries.

Jim Wilcox, who was anxious about his 1909 family farm, remembers one "particularly stormy session," when tempers rose. "I'll never forget the night. Billy Frank got up. He said, 'We've got to stop this right now. I want everybody to know that we want Weyerhaeuser Timber Company to continue to operate and own the land along the river. We want Wilcox Farms to keep farming. We don't want to do anything that's going to put them out of business.'"

"I told people condemning the people's land is not a good thing and the Nisqually Tribe doesn't want to be part of that," Billy adds.

Billy's declaration eased tension. Following his lead, the task force moved forward with a protection plan that required no new laws or regulations. Wetlands were recovered to nurture fry and a compromise was reached on buffers. "Basically, the landowners said, 'Come to us and tell us what's wrong and we'll show you an existing regulation that covers it,'" says Milt Martin with the state Department of Ecology. As a result, Wilcox recycles manure that is generated near the river to keep the water free of the waste. The tribes and Wilcox cleared a beaver dam together to make way for the salmon. As of 2012, roughly 75 percent of the delicate shoreline that runs from Tacoma Public Utilities' LaGrande Dam to the mouth of the Nisqually River is protected, more than seven times the protected acreage in 1977.

In August 1989, the healing continued. Federally recognized Indians tribes and the state of Washington secured a Centennial Accord, to find mutual solutions and recognize Native sovereignty.

FOR ALL BILLY's willingness to negotiate, his tough stand on treaty rights remained. The tribes did not and will not abandon the salmon, says Wilkerson, ever: "The biggest war that they fought since statehood is the Boldt Decision. They're never going to walk away from all that emanated from it, including co-management."

Clear Creek Hatchery

Mount Rainier rises like a snowy giant from the Cascade Range, spreading its rugged surfaces over the foothills and one of the most diverse ecosystems in North America. As climbers claw their way toward its summit, an invisible web stretches beneath, connecting every piece within its grip. From the mountain to the sea, this intricate world is linked, a concept we must understand, Billy says, if we ever hope to save the salmon. "We live along the river in these mountains, along these hundreds and hundreds of watersheds, our Indian people," he says. "Everything that's floating out there has got a meaning to it. Everything in this watershed is important."

Rainier stands as the great water source of the Nisqually watershed where a delicate dance is always underway between mountain, land, river and life. "My eyes sparkle as Dad's did, whenever I connect with that place in my heart where the Nisqually flows, timeless and sure," Billy has said of this homeland.

Powerful cycles directed by nature never stop. Rain and snow fall from the sky, absorbed into land and feeding the rivers. Miles of fragile shoreline offer a living space for fish. Salmon, in turn, fill waterways with nutrients and feed wildlife. Salmon are an indicator species. With every mile they swim, salmon reveal the health of the watershed. Dirty water, degraded habitat, and warm water can make

Nisqually Land Trust

it impossible for the runs to survive. Even subtle changes can make the difference over time in a watershed. Fallen branches or scattered debris can alter the path of water and provide resting space for fish. Trees that line the river's edge shade the water. Remove them and the temperature will climb. At seventy-seven degrees, salmon will die.

The fish have adapted to slow, natural change throughout history. But keeping pace with the dramatic and sometimes erratic advances of humans is something else. Sprawling urban areas and giant dams have had a staggering impact on drainage and devastated multiple species. In the late 1960s, the spring run of the Nisqually River's chinook was extirpated.

"It's the habitat," Billy says. "The habitat is disappearing and has disappeared. If you looked out on that bay, it looks beautiful. But underneath is a forest—field grass, everything, it's all gone. It's gone by just society and overpopulation."

Here, in an ultimate act of teamwork, Billy and a host of organizations are trying to turn back the clock across 720 square miles of watershed. They secured agreements with land users and at the same time proposed a hatchery, a place where additional fish could be propagated and reared to satisfy demand. "The Nisqually was the only large stream in Puget Sound that didn't have a hatchery," explains George Walter, an anthropologist and longtime employee at the Nisqually Tribe. "Rates for fishing for chinook and coho were pegged to harvest hatchery fish. Our natural fish swimming with them were harvested at a high rate. At least in those days, the only way to get Chinook back in decent numbers to our fishery was to have a hatchery."

YOU COULDN'T FIND a better spot for the hatchery Billy and Walter proposed. Clear Creek, the small tributary to the Nisqually River, is flush with springs and strong flows. Old maple and cedar trees surround the stream, shading and cooling the water. Salmon could thrive at its temperature, an ideal fifty degrees in winter and fifty-two degrees in summer. Its half-mile course is a short trek for fish migrating to the Nisqually.

But obstacles stood in the way. The country was mired in the worst economic slump since the Great Depression, and the small tributary cut across a swath of Fort Lewis, the 87,000-acre military base near Tacoma. It was all once Nisqually land, of course. But in 1917, because of World War I, the bulk of the reservation was condemned so that a military base could be built. The Nisqually people were forced from their homes, and Clear Creek has flowed across military land ever since. "Fort Lewis immediately said no," Walter recalls. "We couldn't possibly have a hatchery here; it would interfere with training."

"I had to fight my way back up into getting that hatchery," Billy says of wading through red tape. Doors shut. "The Pentagon in Washington, D.C., wouldn't talk to me anymore. Nobody would talk to me."

Billy and Walter tapped a burly congressman from Bremerton. Since 1976, sixth district voters have been sending Norm Dicks to Congress. His booming voice and gregarious manner have made him

Never accused of being soft spoken, Congressman Norm Dicks is a powerful force and advocate of Billy's in Washington, D.C.

an institution. Dicks held a seat on the Appropriations Subcommittee on Interior and Environment.

Billy made the case for a hatchery to Dicks and Dan Evans, then a U.S. senator. Both men contacted the Pentagon, and the $650,000 feasibility study for a potential hatchery site slid through Congress.

Although the Clear Creek location won the endorsement of the U.S. Fish and Wildlife Service as expected, Billy and Walter met more resistance from the military. They asked for reasons in writing and responded to each concern. Still, the military refused to budge. To move the army, Billy took some of his own advice. When Joe Kalama, Billy's cousin, was a young up-and-comer, Billy used to tell him to order oatmeal three times a week, dress so he's not shaming the tribe, and leave every negotiation with a chip in your pocket, a card you could play later.

In negotiations over the proposed hatchery, Billy leveraged two properties with questionable ownership within the boundaries of the military base. When the Nisqually Reservation was condemned, the land was divided into thirty allotments and held in trust by the U.S. government for individual Indians. But two properties could not be included in those proceedings. One was Nisqually Lake; the other was a cemetery. "Willie Frank Sr. deeded the one-acre cemetery to the United States in trust for the Nisqually tribe," explains Walter. "In other words, the title to this one acre was held by the U.S. and thus could not be condemned in state court, without the explicit agreement of the U.S. and with the U.S. being a party to the proceedings. And, the U.S. was not a party to the condemnation.

"Nisqually Lake was considered a navigable water body when the reservation was allotted," Walter continues. "Therefore, all of the allottees' deeds included a description that ended the property at the edge of the lake. The lake and its bed were not allotted, and therefore remained tribal/community property, again held in trust by the U.S."

The ownership was unclear, says Walter, but the U.S. Army was still using the area for training. "They were shooting over the reservation from Rainier," Billy adds. "You could hear the rounds go over. Every now and then, a round would be short and land on the reservation. And one landed right up where the casino is right now. I'm telling these guys, 'We're going to stop all this. This is political.'"

Billy met again with Dicks and played his hand. "I own two titles to that property over there. I'm going to ask the federal judge to stop all the impact at the firing range and everything."

Considering that the sitting federal judge at the time was Jack Tanner, the militant African American who had represented the "renegades" during the fish wars, a settlement undoubtedly appealed to Fort Lewis. "This one acre and Nisqually Lake are both right in the middle of where the ownership of the United States and of the Army was ambiguous," explains Walter. "The very idea that the tribe might make an issue of the two pieces of property forced a quiet settlement."

"You own those two pieces of land?" Dicks asked.

"Yeah, got the title for them."

The tribe and the U.S. Army struck a deal: "We wanted to put the hatchery in," Billy remembers, "and we wanted the federal government to build that hatchery." The army wanted the two pieces of property.

The proposal arrived at the chairman's desk at the Military Construction Subcommittee in Congress. Ron Dellums, a liberal anti-war African American congressman from Berkeley had taken his seat in Congress six years earlier than Dicks.

"Are you telling me that you want me to take land from the United States Army at Fort Lewis and give it to the Nisqually Indians?"

Dicks nodded.

"Right on, brother!"

"It was helpful to find something that they could say that [the U.S. Army] got. And they reduced a risk for some adverse judgment," Walter says. "The two pieces of property that they did not have clear title to would have been a shoe horn potentially."

The federal government paid more than $11 million for a state-of-the-art facility at Clear Creek. Tacoma Public Utilities pays for hatchery operations, as part of a settlement for damaging the Indian fishery on the Nisqually River.

On a ninety-nine-year lease, the unlikely pairing has coexisted. "In the middle of the night, rangers will infiltrate the hatchery and hop the fence and basically capture the building," Walter says. "There's nobody there."

The hatchery opened with great fanfare in 1991 and instantly drove harvest numbers up. Out of four million fish released annually, the Indian harvest jumped from roughly two thousand to as many as twenty thousand. Billy's three-part plan to clean up the watershed—bring the fish back, clean up the river, build a hatchery—was coming to fruition.

Thanks to the Clear Creek hatchery, the Nisqually culture is alive. Like their ancestors, Indians can still fish the river. In fact, the hatchery is billed as the most successful chinook hatchery in Puget Sound, says David Troutt, director of Natural Resources for the Nisqually Tribe. Without it, he says, the tribe would never meet its harvest goals.

Yet it is only the first step, Troutt cautions. Modern science is leading hatchery managers closer to nature as biologists confront a powerful truth: the most advanced technology and the largest harvests of hatchery fish cannot possibly compensate for the absence of habitat and be sustainable through generations. Salmon, hatchery or wild, depend on a healthy environment to survive. Cool water, clean gravel, and strong flow are vital. In a white paper distributed by treaty tribes in 2011, Billy and the tribes opine that by restricting harvest, the federal government has glossed over the source of the real problem, habitat loss and degradation:

> An example is the Nisqually River, with its headwaters in a national park and its mouth in a national wildlife refuge. It is one watershed in Puget Sound where we have made significant habitat gains in recent years. More than 85 percent of lower river estuary habitat has been reclaimed through cooperative federal, tribal, and state work to remove dikes; nearly 75 percent of mainstream river habitat is in permanent stewardship.
>
> Despite this massive cooperative effort, research shows that young ESA-listed salmon and steelhead from the Nisqually River die before they can reach Seattle, just 30 miles away. The main cause is believed to be a lack of nearshore habitat caused by ongoing development practices.

In the years that followed the opening of the hatchery, Congress paid for an independent group of scientists to study the state's entire hatchery system. Experts urged a major facelift. Among its more than a thousand recommendations, scientists underscored the need to view hatcheries as an addition to habitat, not a replacement. "The old model was, we figure out how many fish we want to catch, and we'll build hatcheries that will produce the fish that will go out and be caught," said Barbara Cairns, executive director of Long Live the Kings, which oversaw the project. "We need to stop thinking about hatcheries as factories that produce fish, and start thinking about them as tributaries of the watershed in which they reside."

In *Salmon Without Rivers*, author and biologist Jim Lichatowich takes it a step further, acknowledging that humans have not only failed to recognize the importance of the whole picture but have tried to manufacture elements that can only be created by the forces of nature:

> Fundamentally, the salmon's decline has been the consequence of a vision based on flawed assumptions and unchallenged myths—a vision that has guided the relationship between salmon and humans for the past 150 years. We assumed we could control the biological productivity of salmon and "improve" upon natural processes that we didn't even try to understand. . . . The natural limits of ecosystems seemed irrelevant because people believed they could circumvent them through technology. . . . Since the turn of the twentieth century, the natural productivity of salmon in Oregon, Washington, California, and Idaho has declined by 80 percent as riverine habitat has been destroyed. To confront this loss, we need a different vision, a different story to guide the relationship between salmon and humans.

Hatcheries have brought much-needed stability to runs, but can in no way replace wild fish. Years of producing salmon in artificial conditions have created a lesser fish, one that is hand-fed and not as adept at clearing natural barriers. When fish return to Clear Creek, for example, humans, rather than nature, choose which female fish will procreate. Humans strip the eggs and mix them with sperm in a bucket, before incubating them, securing them in troughs, and releasing them to the wilds of the ocean. The result, says Troutt, is a simpler fish and a less diverse run.

To keep pace with this new way of thinking, Clear Creek will now carefully combine some of its hatchery fish with wild salmon to create a more natural species in the runs it artificially propagates. These salmon will depend even more on a healthy watershed to survive, from the summit of Mount Rainer to the depths of waterways.

Chapter 16

Submerged

The highest flood ever recorded on the Nisqually River lashed out in heavy rains during the winter of 1996. Rivers swelled across the Pacific Northwest in one of the century's great weather disasters. Floodwaters stole lives and damages mounted.

The Nisqually had already breached its banks when the floodgates at Alder Dam opened. A mighty release of water pushed a wall of debris cascading down the river. The powerful force gained momentum, downing alder and cedar trees, destroying homes and damaging septic tanks. "The whole of Franks Landing looked like a bomb had hit it," recalls Tom Keefe. "In front of Maiselle's house, the entire riverbank had been ripped away, carving a fifteen foot deep ravine up near her house."

Debris and logs rose from the water like claws when Billy, in a wool hat and parka, boarded a jet boat to survey the aftermath and check on his sister Maiselle. The floodwaters surrounded homes, in some cases rising to windows and the wheel wells of parked cars. Billy maneuvered the jet boat up to Maiselle's home and shouted above the hum of the motor, "Woo-hoo! We're coming in!"

Frank's Landing was home to generations of family. One by one, Billy checked on stranded family members. Despite staggering losses of homes and personal property, the family weathered the flood.

In 1996, record floodwaters bury Wa He Lut Indian School. "The whole of Franks Landing looked like a bomb had hit it," recalls Tom Keefe. With the help of Slade Gorton, U.S. senator and onetime foe, a new school rises from the damage, inspired by a Native longhouse.

"You live along the river, you live with floods," Billy says in hindsight. "This is what our land is. It isn't up on the hill, or over there, or anywhere. It's right here. Of course, now hundred-year floods are coming sooner and sooner."

The big flood of 1996 also made a mess of things at Wa He Lut Indian School. When the school doors opened twenty years before, Maiselle fulfilled a dream. In 1974, she brought a teacher to the Landing. The educator and four students were the seeds of Wa He Lut. Vowing to instill Native pride and confidence in its students, Wa He Lut took its name after the wiry warrior who got even with the betrayer of

Chief Leschi. It was Willie Sr.'s idea. "Nothing defeated Wa He Lut the man, and so nothing will defeat our school," he reasoned. Teachers at the Indian school strove to give students a better education than many Native children were receiving in the public schools, especially during the struggle for treaty fishing rights.

Then came the flood. "The school was completely wiped out," Billy remembers. "The smoke shop was wiped out. Everything was wiped out. We were devastated."

Beneath the surface, floodwaters weakened the foundation of portable classrooms beyond repair. A sea of muddy water poured into the new school gym, a $1.5 million project that had just opened its doors that September.

The flood destroyed the riprap that held the bank in place. Wa He Lut received $402,000 from the Federal Emergency Management Agency, but it wasn't enough to build a new school.

After his tenure in Magnuson's office, Tom Keefe had become superintendent at Wa He Lut. Casting aside hard feelings, he contacted a member of Slade Gorton's staff. The influential veteran of the U.S. Senate held a powerful seat on the Appropriations Committee. As Keefe candidly admitted to the staff person, Gorton certainly didn't owe him any favors. There was no love lost between the senator and the tribes. Gorton's role in the contested Boldt case was engrained in tribal memory. Indians said he was still causing trouble. In 1995, Gorton slashed federal assistance for Native Americans almost 30 percent. Even so, Keefe and Billy managed to work a deal with the senator.

"It was an easy call to make," Gorton said. "Whatever my disagreements with the tribes, there is no question that the federal government should provide the best possible education." Gorton secured roughly half the cost of the new school, $2 million. The Bureau of Indian Affairs financed a grant for $2 million of the total construction cost. Building the school was a complicated proposition. "It's sitting on sand," Keefe explains. "It's basically sitting where the river used to flow. We had to build it up to a hundred-year flood stage. Even with

Andrew McCloud Jr. and Billy inspect new riprap at Frank's Landing after the flood of 1996.

LAURA MOTT

Inspired by her own experiences at Chemawa Indian School, Maiselle, Billy's sister, founds Wa He Lut to preserve Indian culture.

what's there now and the beautiful school, it's still sitting in a zone where that whole place could be washed off any time. With Mother Nature, It's impossible to engineer against these kinds of things."

"We got back in business again," Billy says, "with the help of the United States Congress, Senator Gorton, all our delegation, Congressman Norm Dicks. I mean, we just got in and we built that school in two years."

The school was transformed from a scattered group of modest trailers to an 18,000-square-foot gathering center inspired by an Indian longhouse. "After the flood, we all agreed to rekindle the spirit of the Indian long house, which allows for no bitterness about the past,"

Keefe says. "Now, the challenge for Franks Landing is to put that long house spirit into the new building."

The roughly 125 students who attend Wa He Lut are exposed to Indian languages and culture. "We're proud of that school," Billy says. "We have dictionaries of our language. These little kids are talking Indian now." The school is primarily funded through the Bureau of Indian Education and receives supplementary funding through an agreement with the North Thurston School District and the smoke shop at Frank's Landing.

Over the years, Wa He Lut has struggled with low academic assessment scores, but school spirit remains strong. Billy is an active school board member and maintains a strong presence. Inside hangs his famous canoe. "Looks pretty good up there; there's a lot of memories riding in that canoe," Billy said as the symbol of the fish wars was hoisted to the school ceiling.

A COUPLE OF WEEKS before the dedication of the new Wa He Lut Indian School, Sugar Frank pulled his brother Tanu aside. "The Muckleshoots are looking for you," Sugar told him.

Kerry Marquez, a Muckleshoot, was scouring historical documents for Muckleshoot children who had been adopted outside the tribe and lost in the system. She discovered a letter from Norma Frank requesting enrollment for her child, Tanu Frank. On a whim, Marquez called the Nisqually Tribe. It turned out that Marquez is Tanu's biological cousin. She had been looking for him for years. Tanu connected with his cousin and aunt and eventually met his biological mother, Georgina Daniels. Billy says he and Norma had no idea Tanu's biological family had been searching for him. Eventually, to enroll in the Muckleshoot Tribe, Tanu took his birth name, John Elliott. Today, he considers himself fortunate to have reconnected with his biological mother and for the life he had with "Ma"— Norma—and for his continuing relationship with Billy. "We were lucky to have him as a father," says Tanu. He's all about his family and his extended family."

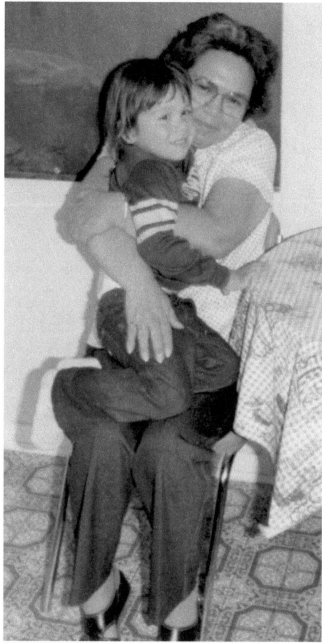

GEORGIANA KAUTZ PERSONAL COLLECTION

Norma and son Tanu Frank.

Chapter 17

The Tough Guy

Along with his happy-go-lucky persona is tough Billy, a man who is unafraid to stand up for treaty rights or salmon, regardless of his opponent's stature.

When Republican Ken Eikenberry tossed his hat in the ring for governor in 1992, Billy didn't mince words: "People supporting Ken Eikenberry for governor must be doing so for one of two reasons. They either want to destroy the natural resources of this state, or they don't really know Ken Eikenberry." Billy accused Eikenberry of opposing cooperative management with the tribes and predicted that if elected he would drag them to court.

While their mutual admiration is readily evident, there are even spats between good friends Norm Dicks and Billy. Dicks calls them family disputes. He'll push Billy, he says admittedly, when he wants more out of the tribes. "One of the things I wanted the tribes to work on with the state and feds was marking of salmon," Dicks says. The tribes were initially reluctant. "They have a certain number of hatcheries of their own. I wanted them to mark their fish, which means you clip off the adipose fin. We got the money to get the Pacific Salmon Recovery Initiative, which Al Gore and I had put together. Now, all these fish are marked. The reason that's so important is that you want to distinguish between hatchery fish and wild fish."

HANK ADAMS PERSONAL COLLECTION

He may have targeted Ken Eikenberry in the 1990s, but Billy's relationship with former Governor Dan Evans couldn't have been better. Once on the opposite side in the fish wars, Evans traveled to Maryland in 1992 to present Billy with the Albert Schweitzer Prize for Humanitarianism.

Another example came in the mid-1990s, when Billy took the podium in the old Executive Office Building next door to the White House. "We are not interested in preserving salmon as museum pieces," Billy told the crowd. "We are fishermen—we always have been, and we always will be. We need fish to harvest." The June day in 1997 marked the beginning of a new relationship between the United States and Indian tribes with issues involving the Endangered Species Act.

But behind the scenes, Billy had had a run-in with Bruce Babbitt, the former governor of Arizona sworn into office as Interior secretary in 1993. Under the ESA, any taking or killing of listed species is illegal. Many species of salmon are listed, including species on Indian reservations.

"A basic part of Indian law is that you read those words as the Indians would have understood them," attorney Charles Wilkinson believes. "You read a federal statute in favor of the tribes. The Endangered Species Act never mentions tribes, and it never mentions abrogating treaty rights to take salmon." According to Wilkinson, both sides could make the case that the ESA should or should not apply to treaty tribes. Wilkinson continues:

> We sent this long letter to Babbitt asking for formal negotiations. We ended up having top-level people go. After an agreement was reached, Babbitt asked, "Is there anything else?"
>
> Billy stood up, "Yes, I have one last thing. Do you have the energy to do this? Will you give this a priority? If we're in these goddamn negotiating sessions, and we reach an impasse, can we call you at home to have you break the impasse? Can we tell your officials to get off their goddamn asses and agree with those Indians and work it out? Don't have a blockade here! Do you have the energy?" Babbitt said yes.

Under terms of the ESA Secretarial Order signed in June 1997, federal authorities must defer to tribal plans for ninety-five million acres of Indian land when enforcing the ESA. Moreover, the order put systems in place to assist tribes in protecting habitat with the benefit of science and technology. Indian lands, "are not federal public lands," the agreement states, "and are not subject to federal public land laws."

"For too long we have failed to recognize the needs of Indian tribes to be consulted and part of the process from the beginning, and the traditional knowledge they can share about species, habitat and conservation," Babbitt said.

Ironically, the breakthrough agreement was the first secured with Natives in the Indian Treaty Room in the White House Executive Office Building. According to Babbitt's staff, a peace treaty with the Balkan states was secured in 1947, but "no treaty with Indians ever was."

"Signing the equivalent of a treaty here today gives new meaning to the name," Babbitt said. "It is my hope, from this day on, that we will banish forever the traditional treaty process that has been one-sided, overbearing and not infrequently unfair."

Billy stood in a light-colored jacket, accented with a bolo tie, and signed the historic agreement for the tribes.

Meanwhile, the state of Washington requested an exemption from the Endangered Species Act known as a Habitat Conservation Plan. The HCP was historic and pertained to more than one million acres of Washington timber land. Under the HCP, some logging was allowed. The tribes had requested changes and though some were made, others were not. "If that level of timber harvesting was too high and is hard on the runs, there's not much you can do about it," says Wilkinson. Babbitt pushed for Billy to attend the accompanying press conference. When the day arrived, the elder was absent. "Where's Billy?" Babbitt asked. "Billy is not coming. He's not supporting this," the secretary was told. Babbitt was not happy.

THREE YEARS LATER, fresh from a U.S. Supreme Court victory that validated the rights of treaty tribes to clams, oysters, and other shellfish, tough Billy emerged yet again. The elder came out swinging for Senator Slade Gorton. With casinos humming, Natives from the Pacific Ocean to the Atlantic amassed a war chest to unseat their longtime foe.

Their tool was the First American Education Project (FAEP), founded by Billy, Quinault chair Joe De La Cruz, and Ron Allen, then chairman of the Jamestown S'Klallam Tribe. "The fight is fair and square. The consignia is clear: 'Dump Slade 2000,'" blasted *Indian Country Today*. With Native issues pending in court, the tribes were

convinced that ousting Gorton would keep the country from sliding backward. Major tribes and the National Congress of American Indians banded together in an effort to raise $1.5 million and defeat the senator. When a thousand people gathered at the University of Washington, they were filled with rhetoric to send Gorton packing.

To Gorton, public tongue-lashings from Billy and the tribes were nothing new. Still, he refused to back off the mindset that Natives are quasi-sovereigns, not sovereigns. It was a matter of law, Gorton said, not race. The tribes called him General Custer and labeled him an Indian fighter. On the Navajo Reservation, they compared Gorton to Kit Carson, who "rounded up the Navajos in 1863, burned their food supply, cut down their orchards and marched the starving tribe to a holding area in the desert of southern New Mexico."

The tribes accused Gorton of suffering from a bruised ego after his 1979 defeat in the U.S. Supreme Court and carrying a vendetta against them ever since. "Then, when he did win a case against Indians, such as his victory mandating tribes to tax their non-Indian customers, the tribes ignored the Supreme Court decision, contending tribal sovereignty against state taxation. Apparently, Gorton took his Indian defeats personally," declared an editorial in *Indian Country Today*.

In 1995, Gorton had whacked Native federal assistance by nearly 30 percent. In 1997, he appended two riders onto a sweeping $13 billion government spending package that waived Natives' sovereign immunity from civil lawsuits and forced those earning higher wages to give up federal assistance. "My provision would restore citizens' constitutional right to due process . . . it would not alter the tribes treaty-protected right to self-governance," the senator said.

"The primary sponsor of the legislation is a U.S. senator who has made every effort conceivable to destroy the tribes throughout his career," Billy said at that time. The elder and leaders from three hundred tribes met in Washington to oppose Gorton's provisions. Gorton pulled the provisions after an agreement was reached to take up tribal sovereign immunity during the next session.

Sizing up the political landscape in 1998, Billy surmised, "Whether he knows it or not, Senator Gorton has done the tribes a favor. He brought us together and underscored the need for Congress to get to know us better."

When 2000 arrived, the tribes were out for blood. Some surprising supporters came to Gorton's defense. Tom Keefe said the tribes unjustly attacked and slighted Gorton, forgetting the senator's crucial role in rescuing Wa He Lut Indian School. "Thanks to Slade, they have an award-winning design by one of the Pacific Northwest's premier architects, Bassetti Associates, state of the art classrooms with computers, and a soaring commons area where Billy Frank's old canoe hangs on permanent display."

But the tribes' massive effort, coupled with a strong campaign by a forty-one-year-old multimillionaire, ended Gorton's long senatorial run. Maria Cantwell parlayed $10 million of her Real Networks fortune into victory. When the heated contest tipped in her favor, Ron Allen called it a new day:

> The defeat of Slade Gorton, and the politics he represented (that of division, blame and castigation of the powerless) is a double victory for Indian Country. First, through the FAEP, Indian people educated the public about Gorton's true record and exposed the type of politics he practiced, while aggressively promoting Indian issues and positions in the media.

Second, and perhaps more importantly, Gorton's loss sends a message across the U.S. that politicians who so aggressively fight to destroy Indian sovereignty and mistreat Indian people will do so at their own political peril.

It was a new day for the U.S. Senate to be sure. Cantwell's victory guaranteed the chamber's first fifty-fifty party split in more than a century.

THE TOUGH GUY isn't always popular. For all Billy's fame, there are jealousies and resentments in Indian Country. Some feel his contribution is overstated. Plenty of Indian fishermen have stories to tell about the fish wars. Once, when stopping for lunch at the Nisqually Elders Center, an older gentleman sat in the corner looking out the window. "I understand you've known Billy for a long, long time. May I talk with you?" a writer asked.

"You don't want to talk to me about Billy Frank," the elder grumbled, refusing to say more.

Jim Johnson, a state supreme court justice, says he considers Billy kind of a con man. "He was fun to have around and a character," Johnson says in retrospect, "but his dad was the real fisherman. I never saw Billy Frank fish." Next to Gorton, Johnson is a well-known target in Indian Country. The self-assured justice took on the tribes with zeal in representation of the state. "I got shot at more in the AG Office than I ever did in the Army," Johnson says.

"Just as worthy of celebration is the defeat of Jim Johnson in his bid for position 3 on the Washington State Supreme Court," Billy declared, after Johnson's narrow defeat in 2002. "It would have been a travesty for this man to gain a seat on the state's highest court. . . . The fact is that he is an 'Indian fighter'—a longtime opponent of Indian rights, as evidenced by his quarter century history of litigating against the tribes in Washington, as well as in other states across the country."

Once Johnson and Billy found themselves on the same side in a court case, and the two were cruising in a state plane over the Nisqually River, so that Billy could reveal the precarious path of the salmon to the judge. As the plane hovered above Frank's Landing, Billy joked, "You can drop me off right here! I could land at my house."

"Don't!" Johnson hollered. "Billy, they'll all think I've pushed you!" A couple of tough guys shared a laugh.

"You were always there for me"

The clock was ticking, but no one knew. The nagging cough stubbornly resided in Sue Crystal's lungs where it had lingered for months. Enough was enough. It was January 2001 and Billy suggested a trip to Hawaii, where the American Indian Resources Institute was holding a Tribal Leaders Forum "We'll get in the sunshine and get you rid of that cough." Good friend Patricia Zell joined them. The small group traveled toward the sandy North Shore in a rental car. Sue, in the front passenger seat, pulled out a special wooden box.

"I brought this along. I want to share with you," Sue explained. "It's what the boys gave me for Christmas." "The boys," Willie's close circle of friends while he was growing up, had become family to Billy and Sue. The couple extended a lifeline to the young men during overnights and heart-to-heart talks. In appreciation, they gave Sue a beautiful wooden box with a note inside from each of them. "They were getting daily life lessons in how to be," says Zell. "You study hard. That didn't come from Billy; it came from Sue."

In a community weighed down by drug abuse and high school dropout rates, Sue offered support and direction: "You're going to make something of your life. You don't have a choice here," she told them. "Don't think of this drinking and drugs. You're not going to do it."

MARY RANDLETT

Billy, Sue Crystal, and Willie Frank III. "Our family was together, real close, and we just loved one another and depended on each other," says the Nisqually elder.

"All my friends were her kids," Sue's son, Willie, recalls. "She made sure that every one of my friends had a home when they came to the house. She took them in and she cared for them. One friend—his mom worked two or three jobs. She had three or four kids. She had cousins living with them, aunts and uncles. He never had a dad. He was kind of—whatever is left over. He spent a lot of time with us. My mom really took care of him almost as one of her own.

"My other friend—his mom pretty much sent him packing right after high school. The day after high school she said, 'You're out of here. Good luck. I raised you for this long. Now, you're on your own.' My mom said, 'You can come live with us.' He's always been like my brother. We've known each other since fourth grade. Him and I have always been really close, and we still are today."

As the rental car hummed along, Sue pulled each note from the box and read it aloud. "Each letter made our hearts cry—in a happy way— over the beautiful way in which each boy so sincerely expressed his love for Sue," says Zell.

"You were always there for me, if I was down or needed advice," the boys wrote. "I wouldn't be who I am today, if not for you."

Four weeks later, when Washington rains replaced the Hawaiian sun, doctors diagnosed Sue with stage four kidney cancer, a baffling and deceptive disease known for its lack of warning and resistance to chemotherapy. Renal cell carcinoma forms in the lining of small tubes within the kidney. By the time doctors discovered it in Sue, the cancer had invaded other parts of the body. "Your mother and your dad should be living a long life," Billy says, thinking of his own parents. "I told Crystal all the time, 'You've got to outlive me.' And we took care of each other. I mean, Jesus, she never smoked or anything. We took good care of each other all the time, and all of a sudden, this happened. She'd been going to the doctor, but they didn't tell her that she had cancer."

From what doctors have pieced together about the disease, Sue didn't fit the mold. While its root cause is unknown, smokers, the obese and those struggling with high blood pressure are at risk. None of these descriptions applied to Sue.

"Finally, when they found out that she had cancer, we just tried to beat it," Billy remembers. "You keep saying, 'I need some warm weather and it will knock this cold out.' That's the way you think. But we could never make that happen. That cancer was eating her. We tried chemo and all that."

Willie's friends came and sat with Sue every day, holding her hands, offering to go grocery shopping or clean the house.

As they did each year on America's birthday, Billy and Sue threw a bash on the beach outside their Johnson Point home. Friends say she was grateful to watch fireworks light up the sky from the deck outside her window.

The disease progressed. Friends and family came to pay tribute. "On her death bed, she had sage and sweet grass and also the Star of David," Hank Adams said. "She had those things with her to the end. Now, both Indian and Jewish things go with her on this journey." Billy sat at the end of her bed rubbing her feet.

"She got weaker and weaker and weaker, and then died," Billy recalls. "God dang. And here's Willie, a young man. The cancer come and took her away. That was a big, big blow to Willie and I. We were all so close together. Not only that, but all of our family was together, real close. We just loved one another and depended on each other."

"I always tell people, you never realize how valuable your time is with somebody until they're gone," Willie says. "The one thing I regret is that people didn't tell me how sick she really was. If I would have known that, I would have been by her side every day. I would have sat there every day. I think about it now, if I could have just one more hour, even an hour, that would be fine. The way she treated me, I couldn't imagine anything else. I was always her number one priority. People ask me, 'Could you explain your mom?' I say, 'I really can't, I've never seen anybody like her before, the way she cared for people.'"

Sue Crystal died at only forty-eight years of age, remembered for her energy, her advisory role to two governors, and her contributions to Indian affairs and health policy. Gary Locke, former governor, called the loss overwhelming.

"As a person, she was one of the strongest, boldest personalities that I've ever come across," Zell says, "yet she was also very soft, loving and compassionate. . . . Crystal opened new worlds to Billy, and that made him stronger in his local world here."

"When Susan died, I never found out she died until after the fact," says Billy's son, Tanu. "I understand. Dad was too broken up." "For a long time, I just couldn't talk about her," Billy says. "I'd get emotional. And I'd just stand up, and I've got to say something in different forums, and god dang, I just couldn't say anything. Finally, I got to where I can talk."

Tanu was able to offer Billy some comfort: he was going to be a grandfather. Tanu's daughter was named Crystal, in honor of Susan.

Sadly, in April 2002, Crystal Elliott died from Sudden Infant Death Syndrome or SIDS, the baffling unexplained death of a child under age one.

Willie III, meanwhile, had enrolled at South Puget Sound Community College. "I probably shouldn't have gone back to school right away. My grades weren't in it. I ended up going through, and I got good enough grades to pass for that quarter. I got my AA and I didn't want to go anywhere out of state or anything, I wanted to be close to my dad, so Evergreen will be a good choice." Willie graduated in Native American studies and considers the education "the best thing he could have done with his life." Willie is now vice chairman of the Nisqually Tribe and has developed a following of his own.

Sue Crystal would be proud, Billy says.

Chapter 19

The Catalyst

You can follow the reach of Billy Frank Jr. from the floor of the Pacific Ocean to the snowy peaks of Alaska. He is a familiar face in both chambers of Congress and the only tribal member who can pull strings to secure an appointment with the head of the National Oceanic and Atmospheric Administration, says longtime friend Patricia Zell. The fact is most people like him. Billy has personally known every U.S. president since Jimmy Carter. "I've sat you next to Alice Rivlin [Budget Director], Billy, because I know you and the salmon need the money," Bill Clinton said, during the 1995 Pacific Rim Economic Conference in Portland.

"Presidents, we just outlive them, but we always stay the course," Billy muses. "We're working for the natural world out here."

Mike Grayum has a trove of Billy stories at his disposal that span four decades:

> In D.C., in the elevator, in the Capitol Building, wherever you are, all of a sudden somebody cries out, "Billy!" and puts the hug on him.
> "Who was that, Billy?"
> "I don't really know."
> We're walking down the street in downtown Tacoma, across from the museum and the courthouse. I think we'd been in a restaurant.

To Billy Frank
With Best Wishes,

Bill Clinton

HANK ADAMS PERSONAL COLLECTION

Known for his charm and gravitas, Billy counts several American presidents among his friends.

Three young ladies come walking from the other way. They got 20 or 30 feet from us and they said, "Oh my god! That's Billy Frank!" And they're jumping up and down, screaming, running up and throwing their arms around him. Billy, of course, is returning the hugs. We get done with that and walk on.

"Billy, who was that?"

"I don't know."

Billy keeps close friends in high places, like Dan Inouye, an influential U.S. senator from Hawaii. Inouye is convinced Billy helped turn around the stereotype of Native Americans in Washington, D.C. "If he'd been born 150 years ago, he'd be a chief," the senator says.

Early on in a twenty-year friendship, Inouye climbed cautiously into a boat on the Nisqually River with the elder for an excursion across Pacific Northwest Indian Country. Plenty of differences stood between them. Billy is open, Inyoue reserved. The senator is not someone who warms easily upon introduction, clarifies Patricia Zell, a friend of both men. But he responded immediately to Billy, after observing him at a private dinner party with Warren Magnuson.

Because Inouye sacrificed a limb on a battlefield during the Second World War, he worried that day in the boat. His one arm could have thrown him off balance. But the new chairman of the U.S. Senate Committee on Indian Affairs gave Billy undivided attention, as they visited tribal reservations of the Makah, Nisqually, and Yakama. "You need to accept gifts. I don't care what the ethics rules say," Billy told Inouye. The Nisqually then related his anger over the fish wars, the incessant fighting for every scrap, and the jail time.

INOUYE MADE more than a dozen trips to Washington State in the midst of one of the century's largest land agreements with an Indian tribe. In the sweeping Puyallup Land Claims Settlement Act brokered in the late eighties, tribal members gave up claims to prime real estate in Tacoma in exchange for a $162 million dollar settlement.

U.S. Senator Dan Inouye tours Pacific Northwest Indian Country with close allies Billy Frank Jr. and Patricia Zell.

Around meetings, Inouye, Zell, Billy, and his wife, Sue Crystal, met for breakfast or lunch at a restaurant near what was then the Tacoma Sheraton. On one occasion, the senator handed the waitress his credit card. "When the waitress approached the table, she eyed both men closely," Zell recalls. "Then, she stepped back looking mystified." The credit card clearly belonged to a U.S. senator.

The waitress looked directly at Billy. "Which senator are you?"

Zell says Inouye appeared somewhat taken aback by the assumption, but the faux pas never bruised his ego. The story still gets laughs.

INOUYE AND BILLY also collaborated on a struggle for treaty rights in Wisconsin not unlike the conflict in the Pacific Northwest. The Chippewa Indians have a long history spearing spawning walleyed pike on the lakes of Wisconsin, boarding their canoes with lanterns fastened to their helmets. Like Northwest Indians for whom gillnetting is part of their heritage and culture, the Chippewas revere spearing. By way of three nineteenth-century treaties, the Chippewas ceded land to the U.S. government, but retained their rights to harvest timber, to hunt, and to fish off Indian reservations.

Walleye is not revered by tribes alone. It is a sportsman's trophy. Named for its prominent and wide-set eyes, the often twenty-pound walleye is sought after at night, as it forages dark waters.

Protests erupted for years after a 1983 federal court opinion upheld treaty rights of the Chippewas at 178 lakes in northern Wisconsin and enraged non-Indian fishermen. Individual demonstrators and organizations like Stop Treaty Abuse, scattered across the shores, taunting Natives, hurling racial slurs and making death threats. In escalated cases, bombs and sniper fire were used. Sports fishers charged the Indians with capitalizing on treaties to rob lakes of fish in a tourism-dependent territory. But state Department of Natural Resources records revealed otherwise. While sports fishers took in more than 650,000 walleye in 1989, Chippewa Indians speared just 16,000.

After an especially ugly turn of events at a boat landing in 1989, the State of Wisconsin attempted to shut down Native spearfishing by court order. The judge, Barbara Crabb, refused, comparing the turmoil to the struggles of African Americans in the 1960s.

The Chippewas sought out Inouye, then chairman of the Indian Affairs Committee. He, in turn, contacted the committee's chief counsel, Zell, who suggested that the events playing out in Wisconsin were strikingly similar to experiences in Washington State.

With peace on the waters of Washington State, parties from both sides of the conflict cautioned the people of Wisconsin against pursuing a dangerous course of action. A joint report of federal, state, and tribal assessments of the fishery resource was produced with a public education campaign to debunk myths that the tribes were destroying fish in Wisconsin.

On his own dime, Billy joined Northwest fisheries managers, including one-time combatants, and traveled to the Midwest. At conferences, he urged Indians and non-Indians to get together. The tribes are not a threat to the fish, he told audiences.

"Wisconsin doesn't have an 'Indian Problem'! Washington doesn't have an 'Indian Problem,' but the blame is put on us." Billy urged the tribes to speak with a single voice. "If we are not together, nobody will ever hear us and the resource will decline."

The 1983 federal court opinion in Wisconsin established a commission, much like the Northwest Indian Fisheries Commission that formed after *U.S. v. Washington*. Sue Erickson, with the Great Lakes Indian Fish and Wildlife Commission, says input from Billy made a difference. "He was a voice of experience and what the Northwest went through and how it all played out. It wasn't a problem unique to Wisconsin. He was an excellent speaker and ardent about treaty rights," says Sue Erickson. In 1991, the Chippewas sued one of the protesting organizations, Stop Treaty Abuse, and won the case. The judge ordered "a preliminary injunction prohibiting all forms of interference with tribal spear fishing." Protestors lost credibility with the public. The lawsuit and the public education campaign brought more peace to the lakes of Wisconsin.

"We went there to educate, along with our Great Lakes tribes, to educate the governor at that time, to keep from having any kind of killings going on or anything like that. And so we did that, all of us together," Billy says.

BILLY REMAINS a trusted advisor on Indian affairs in national politics, and a catalyst around the world. In 2010, U.S. Senator Inouye nominated the Nisqually Indian for the Nobel Peace Prize: "Through the ages of our species, the intervention of one race of people over another has resulted in the holocausts that time has recklessly forgotten. It is healing left undone.

"Yet, that is what this simple Native fisherman from the Pacific Northwest had done year after year, decade after decade, in village, town, city and various nations—in such a manner that he stirs the blood of all who hear him and he leaves a lesson of love wherever he goes."

Billy also earned high marks for influencing votes at the United Nations in support of a moratorium on driftnets. The thirty-mile traps ensnare marine life, like dolphins and even whales, in massive sweeps of the ocean floor. Dubbed the walls of death, more than thirty thousand miles of driftnet were deployed each day by foreign fleets before the moratorium was secured.

Japan initially fought the ban, noting it would put ten thousand fishermen out of work and make the harvesting of flying squid, a Japanese delicacy, difficult.

A pact was reached at the United Nations in December 1989, for a moratorium everywhere on the high seas after the spring of 1992. Japan agreed to pull half its driftnets by mid-year and the remaining by year's end. The agreement also reduced driftnet fishing in the South Pacific.

Hank Adams and Jolene Unsoeld, the environmentalist and congresswoman who worked at Billy's side, say the elder swayed votes by selling the concept of a sustainable fishery: "There's nothing phony about him. I don't know of anyone [of his stature] who has been at such a detailed level of pushing policy. He certainly mourns for the things we humans aren't doing, but there's no bitterness."

In September 2006, the camera found the Nisqually elder at work in America's northern-most city, Barrow, Alaska. "*These* are our First Nations," he professed, stretching his arms above the icy waters of Prince William Sound. The elder hosted a segment of the 2008 series, *This Is Indian Country,* that demands that corporate America pay the forgotten victims of the *Exxon Valdez* oil spill. Alaskan Natives living in coastal communities were among the hardest hit by the accident. "*These* are our first nations," Billy told viewers. "*These* are our first stories. *This* is where our lives begin."

There is no place on earth like this part of Alaska. Its untarnished surroundings, its stunning landscape, and its marine life lead you far

MICHAEL HARRIS

Billy Frank Jr. won an Emmy for his excursions with Michael Harris filming the documentary This Is Indian Country. *Barrow, Alaska, September 2006.*

away from the gridlock and city skylines that define modern America. The hum of traffic is replaced by the stillness of nature. "This is the soul of indigenous America," Billy said during filming, "places you've probably never seen. Sounds you've probably never heard. People you knew nothing about. . . . This is their home. This is their mountains. This is all of their land here. All of that water is theirs."

Alaskan Natives lost their livelihoods and the means to practice their culture when the supertanker *Exxon Valdez* ran aground on Bligh Reef in March 1989. The 987-foot ship spewed nearly eleven million gallons of crude oil and toxic disaster into Prince William Sound. At the time, the United States had never witnessed a more massive oil spill. Lethal crud spread nearly five hundred miles, coating some thirteen hundred miles of shoreline, devastating marine and wildlife. Seabirds, whales, bald eagles and sea otters died. Fisheries, tourism, and Alaskan Natives paid a price.

Years have passed, and they're still paying. A small army of workers may have combed beaches in a billion-dollar cleanup effort after the accident, but oil remains. Ducks and otters are killed, scavenging the sand for prey and releasing oil. During the shoot, Billy walked the beaches and turned over rocks to discover fresh oil, bathing the once unspoiled terrain. Populations of animals and marine life are slow to rebound.

In 2006, the U.S. Department of Justice and the State of Alaska asked for an additional $92 million to clean up "relative fresh oil" still damaging habitat, but Exxon has disputed the charge. The case is considered "unresolved." In addition to earning Billy an Emmy Award for best host, *This Is Indian Country* drew attention to the lingering impact of the spill, its impact on Alaska Natives, and the 2006 claim.

"I went through all of the villages up there and taped them and getting information and telling the story about them, not me, about them," Billy says. "Don't hire anybody from New York to come out to tell your story. Hire your Indians, the Eskimos or the Natives. Hire them because they have a story to tell."

The documentary moved a little-known story from the coastal communities of Alaska to the small screen. "We come across the bay and here we are, up to our knees in oil," Billy said to an Alaskan Native during the taping. "This oil is supposed to have been cleaned up, and you know your people is living with it 24 hours a day. . . . I'll be back," Billy told him.

AT THE WILDHORSE RESORT AND CASINO in Pendleton, Oregon, tension was palpable. "You could cut it with a knife," recalls Royce Pollard, then mayor of Vancouver, Washington. They were busily planning for the Lewis and Clark Bicentennial in 2004. The uncomfortable environment found meeting goers with their arms crossed.

Billy sat at the U-shaped table with Pollard, historian David Nicandri, trustee Kelso Gillenwater, and Antone Minthorn, chairman of the Confederated Tribes of the Umatilla Nation. Also present were Roberta "Bobbie" Conner, a Cayuse Indian, and historian Allen Pinkham, of the Nez Perce.

The country would soon celebrate the bicentennial of the famed Lewis and Clark expedition. Pollard invited tribes to the upcoming events in Vancouver. Because of the rocky relationship between the Nez Perce and the city of Vancouver, a meeting was called to order.

"Why the hell would we want to go to Vancouver, where Chief Red Heart was held prisoner?" Conner demanded, referring to the eight-month imprisonment of Red Heart that began in 1877, when he and his band were captured in Idaho and transported to Fort Vancouver. The seizure made the *Vancouver Independent*: "Thirty-three Nez Perce Indian prisoners, men, women and children, arrived at the Post Tuesday evening, under the guard of 19 soldiers. The Indian men are all stalwart, swarthy looking fellows, and, no doubt know the exact turn of the wrist in lifting a scalp. . . . The prisoners will be confined in the Guard House until such time as it may be thought best to send them to a reservation."

Pollard says he made the mistake of calling the commemoration a celebration, and "things went downhill from there." In passing, Pollard noted that he was not only the mayor of Vancouver but a retired commander of the Vancouver Barracks.

"You're the guy who held my great-grandfather prisoner," Minthorn declared. A few minutes later, he added, "It's just Native American humor, Mr. Mayor." But the point was made.

Billy interjected, "The mayor has come a long way to extend a hand of friendship. We should not slap the hand extended to us."

"Once Bill Frank broke the ice, things took on an organic quality," Nicandri recalls. In due course, they agreed to meet again. Billy never attended another session, but he had salvaged the relationship. Conner, once decidedly negative, became the enthusiastic vice chairman of the entire celebration. There's now an annual get-together of the two cultures at Fort Vancouver.

"We want to get the history set straight about this country and the Indian people," Billy said to explain the tribes' involvement in commemorating the pivotal expedition across the American West.

Chapter 20

Operation Chainsmoker

Frank's Landing is located in Nisqually, Washington, at an interchange of Interstate 5, near Norma's Burgers, a popular lunch joint, and Schilter Family Farm, where 180 acres of Christmas trees, pumpkins, and pasture lands spread out, paralleling the freeway.

A smoke shop at the Landing operates from a nondescript beige building, bearing the simple sign: "The Landing, A Skookum Creek Outlet." On any given day, you'll find cars pulling up slowly to the drive-through window, where drivers place orders for soft drinks, candy, or cigarettes.

Sometimes, you'll hear shrieks of laughter from nearby Wa He Lut Indian School, the Native cultural center founded by Billy's older sister, Maiselle, in response to children's experiences in public school.

This community is steeped in history, dating back to Muck Creek Village on the Nisqually Indian Reservation where Billy's father grew up. A century earlier, Indians gathered and traded goods at the village, then a major tribal center on the south side of the creek. When the Nisqually Reservation was condemned during World War I, displaced Indians at Muck Creek Village scattered. Among them was Billy's father, who lost his allotment. He eventually bought 6.3 acres of land near the mouth of the Nisqually River. A new community emerged with a sawmill, a blacksmith's shop, a fish landing, and a trading post.

Over the years, multiple generations of the Frank family have lived on the property. The parcel of land became known as Frank's Landing after Billy's father. The smoke shop supports the family and supplies a reliable revenue stream for the school and Indian causes. "We [the families] don't get no federal money of any kind," Billy explains. "That was our income, that smoke shop. And so that was all taken away."

The sale of cigarettes on Indian land has long been disputed. In *Washington v. The Confederated Tribes of the Colville Indian Reservation* (1980), the U.S. Supreme Court held that even on Indian land, states could impose taxes on cigarettes sold to non-Indians. At the time the high court issued its ruling in the Colville court case, cigarette profits were bringing in a much-needed forty thousand dollars to Frank's Landing every year. Billy characterized that verdict as another tactic by the federal government to bring down the Indian people. "This is the way the United States government works," he told a reporter. "They're trying to push us back into the ground. We've come out of shacks into trailer houses. We might have to go into the shacks again."

"There will be very deep hurt as a result of this," agreed Ronald Andrade of the National Congress of the American Indians in 1980.

To avoid further legal disputes, the state of Washington and Indian tribes considered establishing compacts—mutually agreeable terms under which cigarettes could be sold on Indian land. Alison Gottfriedson, Billy's niece, took part in a two-year study. "Alison was one of the two Indian members of a state study commission on tax losses and Indian cigarette sales," explains Hank Adams. "That was under Senate Majority Leader, Sid Snyder, and Brian Thomas. They came up with the original proposals for the compact. . . . One [option] was to just repeal all laws restricting Indian sales of Indian, untaxed cigarette sales." Generally, tax-free cigarettes may be sold on

Indian land only to enrolled members of the same tribe. Who is buying, who is selling, and where the cigarettes are manufactured can all dictate whether a tax is imposed. Even in Indian Country, Indian retailers must impose a tax if cigarettes are sold to non-indians. Because of the friction this has caused between the state and Indian tribes, Washington law gives the governor authority to enter into agreements with certain federally recognized Indian tribes that allow the collection of tribal taxes instead of state and local sale and use taxes. All packs of cigarettes must bear a stamp of some kind that acknowledges a state tax, a tribal tax, or a tax exemption.

The state insists on a tax, in part, to level the playing field between Indian and non-Indian cigarette sellers. Moreover, the tax brings in considerable revenue. Washington smokers pay among the highest taxes in the country. (In 2011, consumers paid more than three dollars in taxes for a single pack of twenty cigarettes.) In 2009, the cigarette tax generated almost $400 million in revenue for the state of Washington.

FEDERAL AGENTS carried out Operation Chainsmoker in 2007. Brandishing search warrants and weapons, they raided shops and private homes in Washington and Oregon.

"They started a task force in Eastern Washington," Billy explains. "They were going to bust Montana and Idaho—cigarettes coming across the border. They put all these federal people on that task force. Then, they picked up our name over there somewhere—the Landing transporting cigarettes. We always bought our cigarettes from Idaho, from the Nez Perce, and the different Indian tribes. We always traded with them. They'd been watching us all of this time, and they come down and raided us that day."

Federal agents converged on Frank's Landing and accused shop owners Hank and Alison Gottfriedson of selling contraband cigarettes to non-Indians. "ATF takes these investigations very seriously," said Kelvin Crenshaw, a special agent. "We are letting the criminal element know we are here, we are watching and we will not tolerate it."

Billy, hours away at the Lummi Reservation in Bellingham, got the call: "The Landing is being raided by the federal firearms and tobacco people!"

Agents with the Bureau of Alcohol, Tobacco, Firearms and Explosives seized more than fifty thousand cartons of cigarettes from the smoke shop that day. "They confiscated everything, cleaned the whole place out," Billy recalls. "I told everybody that the Landing is being raided. At that same time, they were raiding the Swinomish Tribe."

"They seized between one and two million dollars worth of cigarettes," Adams estimates. "They confiscated about one half million dollars in cash from the smoke shop and from the safe at home. . . . They went to Billy's niece, Alison Gottfriedson's house, at gunpoint, and took the granddaughters in their pajamas out on the front lawn. Alison and Hank Gottfriedson were [both] under gunpoint and under arrest out on the lawn. And then [they] took Hank Gottfriedson into the house, just to help locate things so that they wouldn't destroy the house altogether, hunting for things."

"They scared the heck out of my grandkids," Alison recalls. "They took both the computers and they trashed the whole house."

BILLY SAYS the federal raid violated a treaty right to trade freely on Indian land. "We always contend that we don't pay tax. We are exempt from any tax, state tax. What the feds did is they come down on the Landing using state law. They made the raid on the Landing based on charges of not paying tax, laundering money. We're renegades, and the Landing puts 108 people to work every day, that's the school and the smoke shop."

"We didn't have no compact with the state of Washington? We'd been negotiating for two years on a compact with the state of Washington!" the elder says in exasperation.

Adams says at the time of the raid, the Frank's Landing Indian Community had indeed entered into discussions with the Washington State Department of Revenue to resolve outstanding issues surrounding cigarette sales. "We were meeting episodically, either at

Frank's Landing and the Wa He Lut School, or at the Department of Revenue, from 2006 right up until the day of the federal raid."

As a result of the raid, the smoke shop at Frank's Landing shut down for eight months. The family hung cardboard signs in front of the store calling the raid and seizure illegal.

HANK AND ALISON GOTTFRIEDSON were charged with "conspiring to traffic in contraband cigarettes and structuring currency transactions," and pleaded guilty on a negotiated plea. As part of their sentence, they were ordered to pay more than $9 million in back taxes and "agreed to forfeit more than $1.5 million in cash." As U.S. District Judge Benjamin Settle handed down the decision, he recognized Alison's prominent standing in the community.

Adams says the Gottfriedsons had good reason to negotiate a plea. "They threatened to indict her mother, Maiselle, and Billy, a whole bunch of people. . . . Their sentences were issued in February of 2009, and it was no jail time, some community service, and no home monitoring, in other words, no ankle bracelets. So it was no jail, but it was forfeiture of all seized product and moneys."

There's no difference between the fight for fishing rights and the fight for the right to sell goods and services tax-free on Indian land, Billy told a journalist. "They say Alison owed $9 million, but she didn't owe a dime. The federal government violated our sovereign rights. . . . The way things are now, there's nothing to say that our kids won't go to jail, just like Alison did. There's fishing and there's taxation, but it's the same issue."

THE STATE OF WASHINGTON amended a tobacco agreement with the Sqaxin Island Tribe and Frank's Landing that governed the taxation of cigarettes. The Frank's Landing smoke shop reopened after the raid under the amended compact. The Landing holds a unique designation under federal law as a "self-governing Indian Community" that allowed the agreement to move forward. The community at the

Landing has included members of all Medicine Creek Treaty tribes: the Puyallup, the Nisqually, and the Squaxin.

"The Congress acted in 1987 to establish that the Frank's Landing Indian Community is eligible for the Federal programs and services that are provided to Indians because of their status as Indians," explains Patricia Zell, an attorney who handled the legislation, "and that the Community is eligible to enter into contracts with the United States under the authority of the Indian Self-Determination and Education Assistance Act. In 1994, the Congress further amended the 1987 law, to make clear that the Frank's Landing Indian Community is a self-governing dependent Indian community that is not subject to the jurisdiction of any Federally-recognized tribe, with the provisos that the 1994 amendment does not alter or affect the jurisdiction of the state of Washington nor does the amendment constitute the recognition of the Community as a Federally-recognized tribe and that the Community shall not engage in any class III gaming under the authority of the Indian Gaming Regulatory Act." After the smoke shop reopened, the Nisqually Tribe claimed jurisdiction over Frank's Landing and sued the state for amending its compact with the Squaxin Island Nation. Conflict between the Nisqually Tribe and the Landing is nothing new. Billy has often walked a tightrope with the tribe. "Our issue is not with Frank's Landing," insists Nisqually Chair Cynthia Iyall. "It's not with their smoke shop. It never has been. That smoke shop has been there for twenty-five years, and we've never had an issue with the smoke shop. We support the fact that they've been able to run that smoke shop.

"Our issue is with Washington State and the very fact that our tobacco compact . . . shows [the] Nisqually Indian Reservation including Frank's Landing. Frank's Landing is a part of the Nisqually Indian Tribe. When Governor [Christine] Gregoire decided it was okay to sign an amendment that allowed Squaxin Island to come onto our reservation, collect taxes, collect revenue for their tribe, that is a breach of contract, and that's our squawk."

"Understand our position as a tribe with Squaxin Island coming in and collecting on our reservation," continues Iyall. "If they're going to do that with tobacco tax, does that mean then that Governor Gregoire is going to amend our fuel compact, and our gaming compact allowing a casino down in the valley to cut us off? That's what I'm talking about." The case climbed to the Ninth Circuit Court of Appeals and was resolved in favor of Frank's Landing.

"The way I look at it is that it all has to deal with money," says Willie III who currently serves the Nisqually Tribe as vice chairman. "It's all about cigarettes. It's about power. It's about control. In 2007, we got our smoke shop raided. ATF came down. They said we were selling unmarked cigarettes, untaxed cigarettes, and that we needed to figure out our own compact with the state. Before the raid, we were trying to set up our own compact with the state. We were trying to get our own compact with the governor and the state, to go in and sell cigarettes down there like we'd been doing for thirty years. So, 2007 comes and we get raided. Come to find out, Nisqually [Tribe] was the reason we got raided in '07. They sent numerous letters to the Department of Revenue talking about how we're selling unstamped cigarettes down there."

Any friction between the Frank's Landing Indian Community and the tribe doesn't appear to bog Billy down. "In my mind, I don't hold any grudges," he says.

"That's what gets me about the whole situation is that he doesn't hold a grudge," Willie III says. "He'd still do anything for these guys. If they asked him to do something, he'd do it. If they asked him to be a speaker somewhere, whatever it may be, he'd drop everything and do it. It's just the kind of person he is. I've told him that a number of times, 'That's one thing I admire about you, Dad, because I wouldn't be able to do that.'"

"For three years we've been negotiating with the state, the Department of Revenue, and all them. It's just another battle in the life of the Landing," Billy says, shaking it off.

Chapter 21

Hard Truths

In his latest act at the helm of the Northwest Indian Fisheries Commission, Billy has set out to awaken the West Coast to the perils of pollution and the consequences of climate change. It's a matter of accepting hard truths, he says, like a bitter pill or a good look in the mirror when you don't like what you see. To the average person, the truths are invisible, but crippling salmon runs just the same.

For all the progress in the Pacific Northwest, for all the collaboration and emphasis on salmon recovery, Billy's hard truths are these: fish runs remain in crisis and habitat continues to degrade. The problem is one of balance. The world in which the salmon live is compromised faster than it is restored. What's left is a share of fish for treaty tribes no better than four decades ago, when Natives won their long-fought battle over treaty rights.

The bitter pill leaves Billy using the bully pulpit and racking up frequent flier miles to lobby for natural resources, a balanced food chain, and fair management that protects habitat as well as restricts harvest. There's a price to pay for sitting idle, says Billy. And the picture looks grim: fishing boats tied to the docks, tribes with no means to practice their cultural heritage, and swaths of ocean no longer fit for marine life. "What do we tell our children when the fish are gone?" Billy asks.

THE INVISIBLE KILLER cannot be seen from the shores of Hood Canal or the surface of Bellingham Bay, but it's there. At the depths of Puget Sound, oxygen-starved water drives off or suffocates ocean life. The footprint of humans can be traced on the ocean floor, in dead zones, toxic places where fertilizer runoff and wastewater trigger blooms of algae that strip oxygen from the water. Sometimes, the problem is climate change. According to the World Resources Institute, 758 dead or threatened zones exist on the planet. Some 22 can be found in Washington. At Hood Canal, in 2010, oxygen depleted to its lowest level in recorded history.

"The people need to know the truth, but the government won't tell them the truth!" Billy says. The master of thinking big, Billy poses questions for the ages. "How do we clean up the ocean? How do we make a comprehensive plan along that ocean and all our waterways? How do we start getting to where we want to be in the cleanup? We need the people to be there."

It's a problem for the region, where, despite the best recovery efforts, Nisqually River salmon die before reaching Seattle, some thirty miles away. "The rivers and the Sound are being poisoned," Billy says. "Now, the state is cutting $40 million from its fish and wildlife budget. I used to swim in the Nisqually River, but I won't swim in it today. Poison is going down the Columbia River. That dead sea is right off the coast of Florence, Oregon, clean to Kalaloch Beach, in the state of Washington. All dead zone."

In 2010, a task force of scientists assembled by the White House released a special report bearing bad news: dead zones "have increased 30-fold in U.S. waters since 1960." A dead zone off the coast of Oregon, linked to climate change, is ranked third largest in the world.

Educating the public on problems with water quality has proven a monumental task because, often times, pollutants are invisible to the naked eye. For example, in 2006, 80 percent of Washingtonians considered Puget Sound healthy. "They look at the Sound and see the pretty boats and the sun glistening off the water," Billy concludes. Some even fancy the rainbow colors the sunlight creates when it

PUGET SOUND PARTNERSHIP

*The state's chief executive, Christine Gregoire, is counting
on the Puget Sound Partnership to help restore Puget Sound.*

bounces off oily sheens on the water's surface. They don't notice the
lack of feeder fish. They can't see most of the contaminants or the
diminished forests of eel grass under the water's surface."

THE YEAR 2005 handed Billy a new platform for truth telling. The
News Tribune dubbed it an SOS for Puget Sound, when the elder and
a host of regional experts formed a brain trust to rescue Washington's
most famous inlet. Pledging to restore the health of the sound in
fifteen years, Governor Christine Gregoire formed a new agency. The
Puget Sound Partnership has since identified a series of aggressive
cleanup goals like reducing toxins, restoring shellfish beds, and protecting tree-lined shores for salmon.

"An unhealthy Puget Sound means no salmon returning to our
rivers; it means the few shellfish able to survive on our beaches will
be too poisoned to eat," Billy said. He called for a government
crackdown on water treatment plants and advocated the institution
of a zero-tolerance policy for pollution discharge by the year 2020.
Further, Billy pushed for close examination of permits that allow
development near salmon-bearing waters.

Billy has long preached that salmon are an indicator species. Fish kills typically symbolize stress in the environment. Sure enough, when the Puget Sound Partnership formed, trouble signs abounded. The Washington Department of Ecology, after some twelve years of study, found increased levels of pollution in the sediment around the sound. The chemicals are called polycyclic aromatic hydrocarbons (PAHs), toxic byproducts found in car exhaust, emission from coal and wood-burning stoves, or asphalt that can cause tumors in fish. In humans, PAHs can increase the risk of cancer, impair development, or cause reproductive side effects.

Fish are paying the price for spoiled habitat. In 2011, Puget Sound chinook spent their twelfth year on the Endangered Species List and harvest fell to a fraction of its historic high. Throughout history, fifteen chinook populations had already gone extinct. Puget Sound orcas, the killer whales that draw legions of sightseers to the decks of cruisers, joined the chinook as an endangered species. Without the designation, the Center for Biological Diversity says the whale would go extinct in a hundred years. "The status quo will decimate orca and salmon populations," Billy warns. "That's why our agreement to 'tell the truth' is so important."

"But they don't want to hear about the balance of the killer whales," Billy says. "The killer whales need chinook salmon to survive. There's no more chinook salmon. . . . We've killed them all by habitat. . . . The habitat's gone," Billy says. "And we've got to bring the habitat back."

BILLY BLAMES habitat degradation on mismanagement and incessant foot dragging by those in power. He says the lag time in implementing a solution is eroding treaty rights. While tribes increased their percentages of the salmon harvest after the Boldt Decision of 1974, the actual number of fish caught has since dropped to low levels that predate the historic court case. Billy's most recent years have been spent articulating the real threats behind the dwindling numbers of Pacific salmon. Of the four Hs that impact fish runs—habitat, hydropower, harvest, and hatcheries—Billy considers habitat the cornerstone of salmon recovery.

"Many resources in the Pacific Northwest are in trouble because of growing human populations, urban sprawl, pollution, over-allocation of water, climate change and lack of wisdom and vision by non-tribal governments," Billy has told U.S. senators. "Sadly, the federal government has done a poor job, overall, of implementing ESA [Endangered Species Act] with respect to the listed salmon species in the Northwest. Emphasis placed on harvest and hatcheries in the response has been largely misdirected, while the major cause of resource decline—habitat degradation—has been largely ignored. The tribes have grown hoarse trying to get federal officials to understand these things."

Governmental inaction has placed fish on an obstacle course, Billy says. Corroded, decrepit, and so poorly situated that "only a kangaroo could jump that high," culverts are among the worst offenders of healthy salmon habitat, according to the elder. More than a thousand concrete and aluminum tunnels channel water beneath state highways and block more than two thousand miles of salmon habitat. The fish can't get home. Billy and the tribes took legal action against the state to prompt immediate culvert repairs that would guarantee fish passage. "Common sense would tell you to allow the salmon passage," fired Billy. "We need to start fixing them right now. That's all we're asking—fix the culverts."

In 2007, Ricardo Martinez, a U.S. district court judge, agreed. (The Ninth Circuit Court of Appeals called on Washington State to protect fish habitat in 1980. It later vacated the ruling and required a specific case to show the impact a destructive habitat imposes on fish. Treaty tribes filed the culvert case in 2001.) He ruled that abandoning culverts violated treaty rights of Indians. Billy applauded the decision: "The judge's order today said the fish have got to be there. If there's no fish, there's no fishing. We're trying to get the salmon back, make that salmon whole again."

The victory was short-lived. While tribes won the court round, their negotiations stalled with the state. Corroded culverts continued to decay. Tired and frustrated, Billy soon followed a well-worn path back to court. "I'm seventy-eight right now and still in the courtroom all day," he complained, "still talking about fixing the salmon problem. It never seems to get done, and we're running out of time."

From the state's perspective, the issue is not a lack of desire to repair culverts, but a lack of funding in cash-strapped Washington State. "The problem is the cost is just huge," said a spokesperson for the Department of Transportation. . . . We already don't have enough money to maintain and preserve our existing highway system."

To Billy, it's a question of priorities. "There's so much spawning ground up above the culverts that you've closed off, the state of Washington," Billy says. "We're going backward, backward, backward. Their budgets are falling. Their half of the management of our 50-50 split hasn't worked. The tribes are doing lots of things on the watershed. We've got to get the co-managers to do more of the same."

Additionally, Billy sounded the alarm to restrict development in floodplains, another offender of healthy salmon habitat. The necessary levees and dikes for construction there, in many cases, lead to the removal of brush and trees that keep waterways cool for the fish. They create a straight river, instead of a body of water that follows its natural path. Straight rivers mean high-speed flows that limit salmon habitat.

"We have to get creative as thinkers and put thought into what we are talking about, thought into talking for the fish, talking for the animals, talking for the resource," Billy says. "How do we all talk and protect them at the same time and find a balance out there, with all the people that are moving into our country?"

BILLY IS AGAIN taking his message outside the Nisqually watershed and beyond the borders of the Pacific Northwest. "We've got to reach clean down the Pacific Coast, clean to Mexico," Billy says. "We've got to go clean up into Canada, clean up into Alaska. We've got to be the managers, the tribes. They're the only ones that care about the salmon. Salmon is life. It is survival for all of us."

In 2006, Oregon and California reported historically poor salmon runs. The Pacific Fisheries Management Council shut down the salmon fisheries south of Cape Falcon, Oregon. Billy held habitat managers accountable for diverting water to agriculture that could have been used to replenish low water levels: "Fishermen are being punished because of mistakes in salmon habitat management. If we ignore the importance of protecting salmon habitat, the closures, restrictions and resulting economic shockwave that is beginning down south, will head this way. To save our region from the fate of Oregon and California, we must make sure the mistakes of the Klamath River aren't repeated here. Harvest and hatcheries are powerful management tools. But it's the Big H—habitat—that brings salmon back year after year. If we lose sight of the importance of salmon habitat in Puget Sound, we will soon be looking at fishing closures in our backyard."

In 2008, the chinook run in the Sacramento River, once characterized as the hardiest south of Alaska, nearly collapsed. According to the California Department of Fish and Game, the roughly sixty-seven thousand fall chinook marked the lowest run since the 1970s. While several factors were linked to the cause, the damage was clear. As Billy states:

> There's no fish there anymore, going up the river. They're just poisoned and everything else from society doing whatever they do. The tribes are taking in their findings of gravesites and bones along the watershed. They're finding the salmon was there. They're taking the DNA and they're going to prove what was in this river. That's making the case of the salmon, talking for the salmon. Why are these salmon gone? Why didn't you protect them? It's an obligation of the state and the federal government to be doing that, and they're not doing it. They let the poison come down the river.

The only people that care about the salmon is the Indian tribes, the villages along the rivers. Down in California, I'm trying to talk to our tribes. You have to put a natural resource division together within your tribe. Start protecting the water. I think out fifty or a hundred years. Put that in your mind. You're going to start gathering the information. You guys have never moved. You guys are still here. Start putting your areas together. That message is a hundred years out. It is a lifetime.

ON HIS OWN stomping grounds, Billy has been cultivating relationships in the Nisqually watershed, hoping to reintroduce the united spirit of the 1980s: "Right now, in 2010, we're faced with trying to bring that back, that very important relationship between the timber industry, the farmers and all of us. It's disappeared. Weyerhaeuser has moved away. We see a lot of ownership along the mountain range and we don't know who they are. We are not connected with them. So, we've got to bring that back and try to relive another day."

"We are out of balance," says Billy. "We have got to change our ways. How do we change our ways? Everybody goes to sleep when you say change your ways. How do we do that? How do we tell our children that we have to make a change? It's your generation and the next generation.

"This is our country. It isn't nobody else's, it's ours. . . . We take the responsibility everyday of our country and our own backyard. We take the responsibility of that Pacific Ocean that feeds us. We take the responsibility of that mountain that feeds us. . . . We have to do it and the only ones that can do it is us.

"At the end of your life, you should be able to see the salmon running, see the clams squirting, and see the sustainability of our land, sustainability of medicines, and the huckleberries, all of our medicines. It can never disappear."

SLICK AND HUGE, the nemesis of Billy Frank rises from the Nisqually River and gasps. He tosses his catch in the air like a toy before gnashing it with his teeth. "That's the enemy right there," another fisherman blasts from the Landing, as he points his index finger at a California sea lion.

For generations, children have sat in awe of the performing sea lion. They've marveled as it playfully balances a brightly-colored beach ball on the tip of its nose. As Billy will tell you, there is far more to these intelligent creatures than circus stunts. "They're just eating our salmon," Billy says. Every year, a group of sea lions arrives to devour endangered fish in the Nisqually River. "Winter fish, chum salmon, they ate them all. We had to close our fishery down this year. They're just hammering our fish. We're off balance with seals and sea lions. They're all hungry. They're hungry like everybody else."

You can find Billy's whiskered foes from southern Mexico to southwestern Canada. They arrive in Western Washington like unwanted guests around Thanksgiving. They linger until May, often at the Ballard Locks, frothing at the mouth for the endangered fish. Anecdotally, Billy has witnessed a dramatic jump in the number of California sea lions congregating in local rivers. "The most sea lions that I've ever seen in the Nisqually River, in my lifetime, was six. This year, I counted 68 sea lions—big, giant sea lions, eating salmon right at the I-5 bridge."

As a protected species threatens endangered species, government faces a conundrum. California sea lions fall under the Marine Mammal Protection Act. But they're threatening fish listed as endangered. To halt the feeding frenzy, desperate authorities have found themselves using far-fetched tricks, like rubber bullets, firecrackers, and bad music. They even tied a giant fiberglass "Fake Willy" to anchors and buoys, in an attempt to frighten the sea lions into going back home.

"I got one on the back of the neck with a beanbag and he didn't even drop the fish he was eating," grumbled Darrell Schmidt of the U.S. Department of Agriculture. Nothing has worked. The number of sea lions has grown roughly 6 percent each year since 1983; the number of pups has tripled since 1975. "That's off balance," charges Billy. "The state of Washington has sanctuaries for sea lions over here. I don't know what their thinking is. We are not balancing the food chain. The sea lions are hungry. That is why they're in the Nisqually River. But they might have destroyed that run of salmon because they ate so many. There's so many of them that are eating. It's political. They don't even want to hear anything about sea lions."

Some visiting California sea lions may soon meet their fate, however. With government approval, you can remove protected mammals using lethal means. The Northwest states first submitted their plea to the National Oceanic Atmospheric Administration (NOAA) in 2008, only to be sued by the Humane Society. Ultimately, the Humane Society prevailed in court. "Sea lions have been turned into that mythical beast, the scapegoat," the organization accused. "Rather than helping the fish, killing sea lions simply distracts attention from the government's failure to address the much larger and real problems facing salmon recovery." The real problems, the society says, are degraded habitat, poorly run hatcheries, overfishing, and dams.

In May 2011, NOAA addressed the court's concerns and once again permitted authorities in the Northwest to use lethal means to eliminate sea lions that mass below Bonneville Dam. "This is not an easy decision for our agency to make, but a thorough analysis shows that a small number of California sea lions preying on salmon and steelhead are having a significant effect on the ability of the fish stocks to recover," said William Stelle, Northwest regional administrator for NOAA.

"As Northwest residents spend hundreds of millions of dollars each year to protect salmon, California sea lions camp out at Bonneville Dam and other areas along the Columbia River and gorge themselves on endangered fish," argued Doc Hastings, a longtime congressman from Washington's Tri-Cities. "With all other methods exhausted, it is welcome news that NOAA's National Marine Fisheries Service today released letters authorizing the states of Oregon and

Washington to lethally remove California sea lions that prey on endangered salmon."

Facing a second lawsuit, NOAA withdrew its authorization to the states in July 2011. The states resubmitted and the request is under review in 2012.

"The battle to save the sea lions from unnecessary death—and to help the fish by spotlighting the challenges to their recovery that are being ignored—has been a long one, but it is one to which we are deeply committed," the Humane Society says on its website.

Throughout the ongoing legal battle, some thirty-seven sea lions have been removed. Ten were placed elsewhere, one died during a health exam, and twenty-six were euthanized.

KNOWN AS MUCH FOR his energy and sunny outlook as he is for his dedication to salmon, Billy is the first to point to progress in the Northwest. The health of the Nisqually watershed stands as a model for the country with its natural state and protected shoreline. The 2011 removal of a dike there allows a free-flowing Nisqually River to run its natural course for the first time in a century. Human-made log jams along the Mashel River are helping salmon. So many organizations have risen to the challenge of saving the salmon that coordination is an issue.

As an eye witness to history, Billy celebrated an enormous victory for the tribes to revive dangerously low salmon stocks. In September 2011, the National Park Service began the largest dam removal this country has ever attempted. The tribes had waited a century; the planning consumed two decades. The goal is to bring back the Elwha River, a one-time generous salmon producer, which cuts through the state's Olympic National Park. When the Glines Canyon Dam and the Elwha Dam operations opened for business in the early twentieth century, strong runs of Pacific salmon nosedived.

The dam removals are the first of their kind and not without risk. Over the decades, eighteen million cubic yards of sediment built up behind dam walls. Slowly, excavators will chip away at the massive structures. To Billy, the project is well worth it. The three-year simultaneous removal of both dams will free seventy miles of spawning grounds and habitat. Populations of salmon are expected to climb dramatically from three thousand fish annually to more than four hundred thousand.

"All of those who have gone before us, they're looking down on the Elwha, too," Billy says, "and they are witnessing what is happening. And they are smiling."

Congressman Doc Hastings defends the use of dams and says he promotes other recovery plans for the salmon that are "grounded in science and not politics." "I am very skeptical of the removal of dams, period," Hastings told the *Washington Post.*

Billy is not dissuaded. "We're taking the dams out. We've got the Elwha Dam that we're taking out and the Klamath River down in California. There's four dams down there. It has to happen."

Chapter 22

Dreams and Legacies

Somewhere within Billy Frank's eighty-one-year-old frame is that boy out on the river, the one who, at fourteen years of age, defended his treaty right for no other reason than to save the life he knew. As he gutted a bounty of fish, Billy made a split-second decision to stand up for his heritage, just like his father, Willie Frank.

"You can't fish the river with a net, Willie Frank. It's against the law!"

"But I've got a treaty," Billy's father had told state wardens, "the Treaty of Medicine Creek in 1854 with my people. I'm Willie Frank, Nisqually Allottee No. 89."

A decade later, Billy shouted at the state himself, "I live here!"

Before he was old enough to drive, the Nisqually Indian had raised powerful questions about treaties and the supreme law of the land.

Sixty-seven years passed.

THE BIRTHDAY CELEBRATIONS of the Nisqually elder are lavish affairs, with elaborate cakes and guests who include the who's who of Indian Country—and the rest of Indian Country. Dignitaries from every echelon of power are there. As hundreds pour through the doors of the venue, they leave video testimonials for the guest of honor. The scent of salmon fillets wafts through the air as platters of

No one inspired Billy like his father. For all of Billy's achievements, the Nisqually elder sees himself as merely an extension of Willie Frank Sr.

fish and seafood are carted to server tables. Governors and members of Congress mingle in the crowd, speak over microphones, and toast the elder. Everybody tells Billy stories. Everybody laughs. The events go on for hours.

On his sixtieth birthday, in 1991, 350 people honored the elder, and a Department of Wildlife director brought a message from then Governor Booth Gardner proclaiming Billy Frank Day.

When Billy turned seventy-five, Willie saw his father in a suit for the very first time; it was gray and pin-striped. That year, in a sea of Indian blankets and baskets, one guest surprised Billy with a couch. Heaps of presents had to be trucked away.

On his eightieth birthday, Billy suggested that he was well stocked up on Indian blankets. But as the night wore on, there he stood on stage, proudly swathed in layers of blankets and wearing a broad grin.

NORTHWEST INDIAN FISHERIES COMMISSION

*When he turned eighty, Billy challenged the crowd to
raise a million dollars and help rescue the Pacific salmon.*

Organizers that year borrowed a page from comedian David Letter-
man and coined the top ten reasons why it's good to be Billy Frank.
(To paraphrase a few, you get to wear jeans all the time and swear
without consequence. Women adore you, especially lawyers.) Emotional tributes followed and humorous moments, too. "I was surprised
to learn that this was Billy's 80th birthday," Governor Christine
Gregoire, joked that night. "I was sure I saw his signature on the
Medicine Creek Treaty next to Isaac Stevens."

AMID THE UNCERTAINTIES of life, you could take a gamble that
history will remember Billy Frank. Generations from now, people
will hear stories about the fourteen-year-old boy on the river who
grew up to become the guest of honor at those fancy birthday parties.
How will he be remembered? Billy's life parallels the salmon's. It's a
journey of survival and a tale of personal triumph.

His audacious climb to prominence began in an America that
noticed the color of skin. It survived a sometimes violent riverbank
feud over fish and treaties. The resulting court battle raised important
questions on both sides about Indians and non-Indians who fished

Willie Frank III tells youth who marvel at his father's international presence, "Stay in school. He's one in a million."

the same rivers. In the end, it turned out what mattered were the salmon, still struggling to survive the highways of the sea.

"He's the exception to the rule," assesses Billy's son, Willie, of his father's contribution to history. The elder's youngest child, sitting in the vice chairman's seat at the tribe, often teaches the next generation how to avoid the pitfalls of youth. The number of school dropouts remains high in Indian Country, and drugs are commonplace. Of his father's metamorphosis from unknown Nisqually fisherman to international leader, Willie tells them, "Stay in school. He's one in a million."

Billy never finished high school, but helped broker a treaty agreement between the United States and Canada. The state locked him up behind bars and Johns Hopkins University celebrated his contribution to humanity. He was painted a villain and labeled a renegade, then nominated for the Nobel Peace Prize. He's been knocked down as much as any heavyweight boxer, yet he's never left the ring.

"These really wonderful things have occurred in the post-Boldt era," says friend Tom Keefe. "Billy Frank overcame that tendency that exists in Indian Country to have sort of a tragic view of yourself based on the history. Billy decided that he was going to live in the present and that he was going to try to shape the course of the future. And he did."

HANK ADAMS UNDERSTANDS Billy's contribution to history, perhaps better than anyone else. As of 2012, Adams is still living as a relentless chainsmoker, rarely seen without a Winston. He is a news junkie and an historian, who surrounds himself with up-to-the-minute broadcasts of current events and relics of the past. Court orders, images, and artifacts—many pertaining to Billy—stack floor to ceiling in his Lacey duplex. He dedicates hours to his cause, assisting students, writers, and tribes. Adams has been called "the most important Indian" and a "mad genius"—a characterization he finds humorous. "I don't know which one is here with you now," he once joked to an audience of the schizophrenic label.

"What does Billy mean to you?" Adams is asked one day as he sits puffing on a cigarette. "He's like the son I never had," he jokes, forcing a laugh. "Other than my younger brother, he's been as close to me as any of my brothers, but not as close to me as my older sisters. We draw much from the same sources, like his dad. I came late; Billy was thirty-three when I became constantly involved."

Adams once compiled a list of the five most interesting people he has ever encountered. Because his dramatic life has taken him from presidential politics to the civil rights movement, his list includes notable figures, like John and Robert Kennedy, and Dr. Martin Luther King. Where does Billy fall? After all, Adams is the first to tell you about Billy's historic contributions to the Boldt case, the Timber Fish

NORTHWEST INDIAN FISHERIES COMMISSION

Their friendship dates back more than a half-century. Hank was the one "making sure you understood that there was a problem," jokes Dan Evans, former governor. "And Billy was the guy who very quickly started to say, 'This isn't working. We've got to find a better answer.'"

and Wildlife Agreement, his work at the United Nations, and the relationships he has cultivated to bring the fish home and peace to Puget Sound. "If there's a category for best all around," Adams quips, "then I'd give him the jacket."

HISTORY WILL REMEMBER Billy's wizened face, his beguiling laugh, and his animated speech. It will remember the respect he paid to people, even combatants. "From my own personal perspective, I can't believe it wasn't always in him," says Mike Grayum, executive director of the NWIFC. "You don't just turn a switch over night. He must have had that in him all along. It was just waiting for the right opportunity to blossom. It's not like he's a superhero, either. People are just attracted to him. One of the reasons is the way he treats people. He treats everybody like his long lost brother or his closest friend, no matter who they are."

Known for his political acumen, the late Joel Pritchard published a top ten list of leadership skills for anyone dabbling in politics. The five-term Washington congressman targeted prospective candidates. But the list reads like a handbook of Billy's own leadership style: keep your ego in check, lead your staff, do your homework, don't worry about who gets the credit, understand your opponent's position, work in a bipartisan fashion, recognize change comes in small steps, listen, don't take yourself too seriously, and admit your imperfections.

In Washington politics, Billy's leadership style has left an indelible impression on some of the savviest minds in the game. "On this fishing trip, there were four or five of us up one night," recalls Bill Wilkerson, former Fisheries director for the state. "We were talking about the lack of leadership that we're seeing in the political world right now." Wilkerson asked the four, each an accomplished political leader, "Who are the great leaders?" "Three out of the four of us named Billy," Wilkerson recalls. "We're talking about a Congressman. We're talking about myself. We're talking about a former wildlife director, and a former federal leader. We're talking about one other person who has worked with all of these people. All of us named Billy. So, he has a way of being a leader, of being a friend, of being a very strong advocate. That's an art. He has certainly been one of my role models."

"I guess I would encompass leadership in three words," adds Dan Evans, former governor and U.S. senator, "passion, knowledge, and respect. Passion without knowledge isn't very much; knowledge without passion isn't very much; the respect part is not just to respect those who you report to, or your colleagues. Respect those who report to you or those who are in opposition to what you're doing. You've got to respect your opponents, as much as your friends. That doesn't happen very often. It's the measure of those guys, like Billy

Frank. They don't just despise or hate. They respect opponents. Now, they sure as heck figure out a way to bring them around if they can."

"No matter how intractable a problem appears, I think Billy has helped instill a culture –not only within the tribes, but beyond them. We are going to work together until we get something worthwhile accomplished," says Jim Waldo. "That's both persistence and dedication to getting results. Billy's not interested in getting along to go along. The result has to be real accomplishments, real benefits."

Indian Country can be tough. Although Billy is unquestionably revered by most Native people, some take exception to the attention and adulation he has attracted. At times, he has been criticized by his own tribe. "I wasn't even born back then—but I have a big concern with our own people not standing up for their rights," says Willie. "I mean, we're getting trampled with our fishing. They have us fishing up on the reservation when we should be fishing on the whole river."

Nonetheless, Billy has earned respect on the national stage from Indians, says Dick Trudell, a Native activist and attorney who goes back forty years with the elder. Trudell, who is executive director of American Indian Resources Institute, describes Indian Country as a place where vastly unique individuals and tribes have been forced to speak as a single voice, for sheer survival. Billed as any kind of national leader of the group is no small feat, he says: "On the national scene, I don't know anyone like him. He's a humble person who knows where he's going. He doesn't back off of anything. I think he works for the larger society. He's not just fighting for fish for the Indian people, he's fighting for fish for the Northwest."

If not for his uncommon traits, Billy's uncommon journey might have ended differently. "There are people that do get frustrated with my dad," acknowledges Willie. "He has this mentality to work it out. Don't bitch and moan and fight. That's not going to get us anywhere. They went through all that. They went through the fishing wars. I see people, younger tribal leaders, that don't have that same patience. They say, 'It needs to get done now. We've got to do it now.' It doesn't work like that. It takes time. You've got to be patient for things."

The rocky history could have made a cynic out of Billy or an angry man. "He just doesn't get mad," attests Sugar. "He just walks away from it. He's strong. He can have people yell and scream and call him all kinds of names, and he just smiles and walks away. Sometimes, I can't handle that." Maybe patience and understanding run in the blood. "Grandpa was really calm and collected too," surmises Sugar of the family gene pool. "He really didn't get excited. I never did see Grandpa get mad when I was a young kid."

AFTER THE BOLDT DECISION in 1974, Billy rose to his potential. Ramona Bennett, a Puyallup Indian who led the 1970 Puyallup encampment, believes Billy's contribution to history will never be matched. No future leader of the Northwest Indian Fisheries Commission will have lived the struggle like Billy. "I know the other people that the other tribes were pushing to the front," Bennett says, recalling the candidates who competed for the top post at the NWIFC. "For them, it would have been prestige and a job. For Billy, it's his life. They won't have the life experience that he has. They'll be someone who stepped into the position after the resources have already gained a high level of protection."

AT EIGHTY-ONE YEARS OLD, assessing affairs and taking stock, Billy lives with few regrets. He holds both an abundance of hope and continuing concern for the Indian people. He longs for a balanced world with peace between Indian tribes. "What's happening now is the Indian tribes don't have an enemy out there. They're their own enemy. We're suing each other. We're fighting one another. It's tribe versus tribe. And the courts don't want any part of that. They've said that."

Poverty refuses to release its grip, and drugs continue to plague families. "Meth is one," Billy says. "Them are problems that interfere with community, and it's big time. It interferes with families. We haven't got out of that rut we're in. You've got to work on that. You've got to work on it and get the community together."

Billy remains encouraged that the tribes will turn the tide and that his children will help encourage healthier choices. "We're going to make that happen, and Willie will be part of making that all happen. You clean yourself out. Your mind is set in that bigger picture. Some of them are living in little pictures, and you've got to go beyond that. Some of these Indian kids, they can take recovery, but they can't get away from it. Something is there. They've got to have a drink. They've got to have something, I don't know, some kind of mental or physical thing. And they die. That's too bad. I don't know how to get them over that. I see a lot of our kids committing suicide. Jesus, if we just could talk to them kids before they actually commit suicide. But maybe you can't do that . . . I don't know."

Although Billy has never been one to lecture his kids based on his own experiences, Willie has independently chosen to stay away from drinking. "He never preached to me about alcohol or anything. He said, 'You're going to learn on your own. There's nothing I'm going to be able to tell you. I've experienced it all and been through it all. You're going to learn all this stuff on your own.' And I did. I just got tired of being hung-over and feeling like crap the next day. My life's not worth that, to be drinking like this all the time. One day I woke up and said I don't want to do this anymore."

OF THE MAJOR VICTORIES the tribes have won in Billy's lifetime, perhaps none is more important to the Nisqually elder than the Boldt trial.

"We're not done with the *U.S. vs. Washington* yet. We've got big plans out there. We're now working on the home of the salmon. That's the culvert case. Judge Boldt kind of laid that out—the decision on salmon, the shellfish, and the habitat. Forty years later, we're still going strong on implementing his decision, as well as working all of our watersheds. It's taken a hundred years to do that. It's just not overnight."

The Boldt case has a far-reaching legacy, factoring into numerous cases around the world, like the 1994 treaty rights case of the Chippewa Indians upheld by the U.S. Supreme Court. *U.S. v. Washington* has also impacted indigenous people in Canada, New Zealand, and Australia.

"The tribes are staying the course," Billy says. "Whatever funding they got available, they do not move off the course they're on. That's putting these watersheds together, working with the local governments and the federal governments and the state, and still doing what they're doing. They've got their technical people out there. They are putting data in the water. They are making their case every day. Their case is science."

"To be honest with you, I don't think there would be a fisheries resource today that looks anything like it without the power and the persuasion of the tribes," says Bill Wilkerson, former state Fisheries director.

LIFE HAS COME FULL CIRCLE for Billy. All of his life, he heard stories about the grave miscarriage of justice against Nisqually Chief Leschi, hanged for the murder of A. Benton Moses, a territorial militia man, in 1858. "We always talked about Leschi on this river, all of us kids," Billy remembers. "We knew what the history of Leschi was. He was one of our people that we talked about and looked up to." Leschi maintained his innocence at the gallows, and through the ages the Nisqually people have openly attacked his conviction and execution. The hanging left a cloud over the tribe for more than a century.

In 2004, Billy and ten other witnesses took the stand in a tribal effort to correct the historic record and clear their leader of murder, 146 years after the killing. Two witnesses, both Leschi consanguine and extended-family descendants, broke down in tears. "So many generations of Nisqually people have had to live with this," said Cynthia Iyall, Nisqually chairwoman. "For the older people, it was hard to even talk about. You could see the pain in their faces. You could see the anger."

In a rare event, the state had convened a Historical Court of Inquiry and Justice. The events took place in a time of war, Chief Justice Gerry Alexander concluded: "Chief Leschi should not, as a matter of law, have been tried for the crime of murder." The exoneration was not legally binding, but the verdict lifted the cloud.

"Tell the truth," said Billy. "That's all we've ever said. That was a great day, great time in our lives."

WILL HISTORY DELIVER another Billy Frank? Billy is far more concerned with his message, and passing the torch to the next generation. "If you can make your children understand, they will get the message. They will respond to the message. Survival is fishing on the river down here."

"My son Willie," Billy says, "and my son James—Sug is what I call him—these people are automatic leaders. They're raised like we were. Oh, they get wild. But pretty soon they become who they are. They're responsible. I don't have any worry about that. My son Willie, he's on the Tribal Council. I never trained him to be on the council. I never trained him to be responsible and look after his people, but that's exactly what he's doing.

"Willie is a good boy; he wants to look after everybody. The problems of the reservation . . . they're not easy to address. You've got to address them a long ways out."

Willie, engaged to a Northern Arapaho woman from Wyoming, may someday add to the prolific Frank family tree. "Somewhere in your life you make a decision," Billy says. "Am I just going to keep going? All of a sudden I'll have an eighth blood, or no blood. All of our people are Nisqually people, Puyallup, and Squaxin Island. We try to keep that bloodline together. . . . My sons, Sug and Willie, we're all together. We have sweat lodges. We have ceremonies. We've got Wa He Lut School. We're teaching our language. All of these things are happening. It's exciting for us to think that we're still holding together. We're still a community."

LIKE HIS FATHER, who impressed a judge at age 103 with his gravitas and body of knowledge, Billy is in it for the long haul. Sometimes age catches up to him, family says, but he refuses to slow down. "He's his

BILLY FRANK JR. PERSONAL COLLECTION

Sugar and Willie share a moment with Dad.

own man. You can't tell your elder what to do," Sugar laughs, leaning over a table at a healthy lunch place, a favorite haunt of the family's. "I think his businesses keeps him young and he's just got a lot of energy. A lot of the people that he grew up with ain't got the energy, they've got problems. But I think it's keeping him alive all that work he does."

John Elliott, Tanu, appreciates Billy's "natural ability to be a people person and to speak his mind while honoring other cultures."

"The dream for me one day is to be able to sit back, and hopefully with my dad still here, and not have him worry about anything," says Willie. "He's worked hard his whole life and I'm hoping one day he doesn't have to. He can just sit back and enjoy life."

"I think every day I get up and I'm happy I'm still here and still being able to talk to you and talk to everybody," Billy says. "I'll never retire. That's just not in my blood. I know people have to retire. They get tired. But I don't get tired. This is part of my life and it just energizes me."

IF THE LEGEND OF Billy Frank lives, a violent storm will unleash, rolling across the Pacific Northwest in the year 2032. Another Billy Frank will arrive, a half-century after the last. But all good legends are full of twists. "I already told him. I'm not going to wait until 50 to have kids," Willie jokes. "I do want to carve my own path. I thought about it years before. Maybe it's not dealing with tribal politics. Maybe it will be something else, I don't know. There's nothing I'm going to be able to do that's ever going to be able to top what my dad has done, and what he's meant for the people."

"Nobody can replace my life," Billy acknowledges. "But I couldn't replace my dad's life. I couldn't replace my grandpa's and beyond. It's just a different time. We think out one hundred, two hundred years. It takes a thousand years for a cedar tree to grow. That's how our thinking is. I don't have any plans in leaving this place."

"He made Indians understandable to non-Indians in an unprecedented way," says Susan Hvalsoe Komori, an attorney for the Nisqually Tribe. "When they see Billy, they can imagine the reason the Constitution pays respect to the Indian treaties, and why it is honorable to continue to respect them. There is no one else I can think of who can do that with such natural grace and humility."

"The resolution of this case is a tribute by all parties to the vision of Bill Frank, Sr., a Nisqually elder who at the age of 104, testified in the Centralia jurisdictional hearing. Mr. Frank recalled the river's former majesty and importance to the Nisqually Tribe, and eloquently expressed his desire for restoration of that irreplaceable resource. Unfortunately, he died soon after that case concluded. His spirit and vision, however, live on in his son, Bill Frank, Jr., who has devoted his life to achieving cooperative solutions to Northwest fisheries disputes. Bill Frank, Jr. has spoken forcefully and effectively for the Nisqually Tribe since the beginning of this case. Since 1977, he has served as Chairman of the Northwest Indian Fisheries Commission. His extraordinary achievements were recognized in 1992 when he was awarded the Albert Schweitzer Prize for Humanitarianism."

Judge Stephen L. Grossman
Federal Energy Regulatory Commission

PAINTING COMMISSIONED BY TOM KEEFE, BILLY FRANK JR. PERSONAL COLLECTION

Three generations of Franks come together in 1982. "I really wish I could have had a chance to know my grandpa," says Willie Frank III of the last full-blooded Nisqually Indian.

BILLY FRANK could prop up his heels. He could sit back and delve into an archive of famous stories and revel in countless awards. He *is* eighty-one years old. But Billy is still in the ring, poised to protect a treaty right debated to this day. The feet are planted, the fists are clenched. Billy is still that fisherman out on the riverbank, raising hell over Indian treaty rights and salmon.

You can hear him cussing at sea lions. You can watch him marvel at the eagles. You can see him passing on lessons where the salmon run. "What I tell the kids is, 'You're a dreamer. You might not know your language. You might not know who you are. You're a Nisqually Tribal Member. You've got to know your own history. You've got to know what we're talking about from way back, to where we are today. We work together to protect this watershed. That's our life, from the mountain to the sea."

"I don't believe in magic," Billy once said. "I believe in the sun and the stars, the water, the tides, the floods, the owls, the hawks flying, the river running, the wind talking. They're measurements. They tell us how healthy things are. How healthy we are. Because we and they are the same. That's what I believe in.

"Those who learn to listen to the world that sustains them can hear the message brought forth by the salmon."

Acknowledgments

I count my blessings because I have direct access to some of the most comprehensive collections of Washington history in the world, and librarians and archivists who are among the finest in their field. Rare books, maps, and special collections of eras long gone are held at the State Archives and the State Library. These treasures include an oral history with Willie Frank, Billy Frank Jr.'s father, a man born a decade before statehood; an investigation ordered by the governor into a violent skirmish on Billy's riverfront property at Frank's Landing; books that document the early life of the Nisqually, Billy's ancestors; and superb reporting of the treaty fishing rights that sent Billy on to the Northwest Indian Fisheries Commission and a place of respect around the world. I am especially grateful for our staff at the Washington State Library who assisted in research and proofread the manuscript. I thank Anne Yarbrough, Brian Frisina, Kathryn Devine, and Marilyn Lindholm.

Billy's story may be a tale of personal triumph, but reliving a sometimes difficult past is never easy. I thank him for his candor and his commitment. With honesty and humor, Billy's children provide a unique perspective on their father and his legacy. Hank Adams, an historian with vast knowledge of Indian Country and Billy's sprawling family tree, appears throughout this book. Adams sits on a trove of documents and images of his own that were invaluable in the writing of *Where the Salmon Run*. I thank him for his time, his patience, and—most of all—his wry sense of humor. Patricia Zell managed, with all else, to provide insight into this subject from the start. Her thoughtful guidance, inspiration, and suggestions are much appreciated. Lois Allen worked miracles at the Northwest Indian Fisheries Commission as Billy's right hand that carried this book to completion. Tom Keefe provided rich detail in many chapters, especially in the era that followed *U.S. v. Washington*, when Keefe worked as legislative director for U.S. Senator Warren Magnuson. George Walter, a longtime employee of the Nisqually Tribe, contributed immensely with his knowledge of Nisqually history and natural resources. I am grateful for Llyn De Danaan. Her vast knowledge of local history is captured in the forthcoming work, *Katie Gale's Tombstone: Landscape, Power, and Justice on Nineteenth Century Oyster Bay*.

I thank attorneys Jim Waldo, Mason Morisset, and Stuart Pierson; Tony Meyer and Mike Grayum at the Northwest Indian Fisheries Commission; Cynthia Iyall, David Troutt, Joe Kalama, and Georgiana Kautz with the Nisqually Tribe; former Governor Dan Evans and former Fisheries Director Bill Wilkerson for providing the state's perspective and insight.

I thank an exceptional team at the Office of Secretary of State that includes Dave Hastings, a first-rate archivist, Carleen Jackson, Laura Mott, Brian Zylstra, and David Ammons. This program exists because of the vision of Sam Reed, secretary of state, and Steve Excell, assistant secretary of state. The work of Lori Larson, chief researcher at the Legacy Project, appears on every page. The sagacious advice of my teammate John Hughes is present throughout.

In this economic downturn, I am especially grateful to our volunteers Stephanie Benna and Roger Easton. Both diligently read the manuscript and offered crucial feedback.

Where the Salmon Run is a collaborative venture greatly improved by the contributions of the University of Washington Press. The overall guidance of director Pat Soden and acquisitions editor Marianne Keddington-Lang as well as the fine copyediting of Julidta Tarver and the design and layout directed by Veronica Seyd greatly enhanced this work.

Billy Frank Jr. Family Tree

The tree of the prolific Frank family spreads its branches from the beaches at Mud Bay to the foothills of Mount Rainier. Billy's parents left hundreds of descendants behind. Billy and his siblings raised a combined total of thirty-seven children.

Like most Indians, Frank family members have married both within and outside their tribes, and the blood of many Northwest treaty tribes flows through the tree.

Bridges, Alvin (1922–1982). Brother-in-law. Fishing companion. Mentor. Activist. Married Billy's sister Maiselle and raised three activist daughters at Frank's Landing.

Bridges, Theresa "Maiselle" McCloud (b. 1924). Half-sister and second mother to Billy. Activist. Daughter of Andrew McCloud Sr. and Angeline Tobin Frank. Founded Wa He Lut Indian School.

Bridges, Valerie (1950–1970). Niece. Daughter of Alvin and Maiselle Bridges. Activist.

Information compiled from the Social Security Death Index, U.S. Census, Bureau of Indian Affairs, newspaper accounts, and interviews with family.

Crystal, Sue (1953–2001). Wife. Mother of Willie Frank III. Attorney. Staff member for U.S. Senator Warren Magnuson. Legislative budget analyst. Aide to two Washington governors.

Cush, Ida Tobin (1901–1987). Aunt. Sister of Angeline Tobin Frank. Daughter of James Tobin and Louisa Kettle Tobin. Former wife of Willie Frank Sr.

Frank, Angeline Tobin (1889–1986). Mother. Daughter of James Tobin and Louisa Kettle Tobin. Married Steve Frederick, Andrew McCloud Sr., Willie Frank Sr. Gave birth to eight children.

Frank, Billy Jr. (b. 1931). Son of Willie Frank Sr. and Angeline Tobin Frank. Fisherman. Activist. Vice Chairman and Fisheries Manager, Nisqually Tribe. Commissioner and Chairman, Northwest Indian Fisheries Commission.

Frank, Ernest (ca. 1906–?). Half-brother. Son of Willie Frank Sr. and Louise Wells. Father of Raleigh Frank.

Frank, James "Sugar" (b. 1961). Son of Billy Frank Jr. and Norma McCloud Frank. Activist.

Frank, Mary Miles (1933–2009). Niece. Daughter of Rose Frederick and David Miles. Biological mother of Billy's children Maureen and James Frank. Married Raleigh Frank, Billy's nephew.

Frank, Maureen (1959–1977). Daughter of Billy Frank Jr. and Norma McCloud Frank. Mother of Ca-Ba-Qhud Dunstan. Activist.

Frank, Norma McCloud (1928–1986). Wife. Married Billy Frank Jr. in 1952. Mother of Maureen, James Tobin (Sugar), and Tanu.

Frank, Raleigh (1929–2004). Nephew. Son of Ernest Frank and Rachel Brignone. Married Mary Miles Frank, Billy's niece.

Frank, Tanu (b. 1976). Son. Adopted by Billy and Norma after the death of Maureen.

Frank, Willie Sr., "Gramps" (ca.1879–1983). Father. Son of Kluck-et-sah and Sarah Martin. The last full-blooded Nisqually Indian. Fisherman. Activist. Historian. Tribal chairman and treasurer.

Frank, Willie III (b. 1982). Son of Billy Frank Jr. and Sue Crystal. Vice Chairman, Nisqually Tribe. Graduate of Native American Studies, Evergreen State College.

Frederick, Ben (ca. 1915–1921). Half-brother. Son of Steve Frederick and Angeline Tobin Frank.

Frederick, Minnie (1914–1926). Half-sister. Daughter of Steve Frederick and Angeline Tobin Frank.

Frederick, Rose "Fritz" (1912–1952). Half-sister. Daughter of Steve Frederick and Angeline Tobin Frank.

Frederick, Steve (1882–1920). Angeline Tobin Frank's first husband. Father of Billy's sister, Rose Frederick.

Gottfriedson, Alison Bridges (1951–2009). Niece. Daughter of Alvin and Maiselle Bridges. Activist. Served on the Puyallup Tribal Council. Chairwoman, Wa He Lut Indian School Board.

Gottfriedson, Hank (b. 1947). Married Alison Bridges Gottfriedson.

John, Herman Jr. "Curly Kid" (1936–2005). Nephew. Fishing companion. Activist. Son of Herman John Sr. and Rose Frederick John. Married Marilyn McCloud, sister of Billy's wife Norma.

John, Herman Sr. "Buck" (1914–1945). Brother-in-law. Cousin. Son of Joseph John and Lizzie Frank John. Married to Rose Frederick. Paratrooper who died in combat during World War II.

John, Joseph (ca. 1877–?). Uncle. Married Lizzie Frank. Father of Herman "Buck" John Sr.

John, Lizzie Frank (ca. 1885–1926). Aunt. Sister of Willie Frank Sr. Married Joseph John.

Kautz, Georgiana "Porgy" (b. 1941). Sister-in-law. Married to Neugen Kautz. Natural Resources Manager, Nisqually Tribe.

Kautz, Neugen "Nugie" (b. 1938). Brother-in-law. Fishing companion. Activist.

Kettle, Sally (ca. 1844–?). Maternal great-grandmother.

Kettle, Sitkum "Old Man Kettle" (ca. 1831–1903). Maternal great-grandfather. Leader of a band that formed the Squaxin Island Tribe. According to the Bureau of Indian Affairs, a member of the Satsop Tribe.

Kluck-et-sah "Frank's Indian" (ca. 1847–1896). Paternal grandfather. Nisqually Indian allottee.

Martin, Sarah Paternal grandmother. Died in childbirth during Willie Frank Sr.'s early years.

McCloud, Andrew Jr. "Sonny" (1921–2009). Half-brother. Son of Andrew McCloud Sr. and Angeline Tobin Frank. Fisherman. Lineman. Activist. Veteran of World War II. Married Edith Kanine McCloud and raised twelve children.

McCloud, Andrew Sr. (1884–1927). Angeline Tobin Frank's second husband. Fisherman. Father of Billy's three older siblings: Andrew, Maiselle, and Don.

McCloud, Don (1926–1985). Half-brother. Son of Andrew McCloud Sr. and Angeline Tobin Frank. Fisherman. Activist. Married Janet Renecker McCloud and raised eight children.

McCloud, Edith Kanine (1924–2010). Sister-in-law. Married Andrew "Sonny" McCloud and raised twelve children.

McCloud, Janet Renecker (1934–2003). Sister-in-law. Member of the Tulalip Tribes. Activist. Founding member of the Survival of American Indian Association. Married Don McCloud and raised eight children.

McCloud, Jack Sr. (1929–1994). Brother-in-law. Fisherman. Activist.

McCloud, Victor Vern (1920–1921). Half-brother. Son of Angeline Tobin Frank and Andrew McCloud Sr.

Mills, Clarence Sidney (b. 1948). Married Billy's niece, Suzette Bridges. Activist. U.S. soldier who served in Vietnam.

Mills, Suzette Bridges (b. 1947). Niece. Activist. Council member, Puyallup Tribe. Wa He Lut School Board.

Shippentowner-Games, Nancy McCloud (b. 1953). Niece. Daughter of Don and Janet McCloud. Activist.

*Tobin, Harry Great-grandfather. Father of James Tobin. Irish. Logger and miner.

Tobin, James H. (1856–1927). Maternal grandfather. Oyster baron. Minister, Indian Shaker Church.

Tobin, Louisa Kettle (ca. 1861–1931). Maternal grandmother. Midwife and healer.

---

*According to James Tobin's death record, Harry Tobin is listed as James's father.

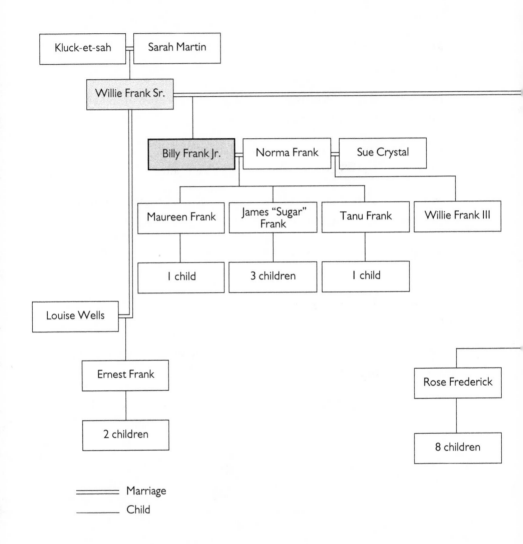

Note: This chart has been simplified to illustrate Billy Frank Jr.'s lineage. For example, the subject's uncles/aunts, cousins, nephews/nieces, and grandchildren are not included to allow for space. The former spouses of Billy's parents have been included if children resulted from the marriage.

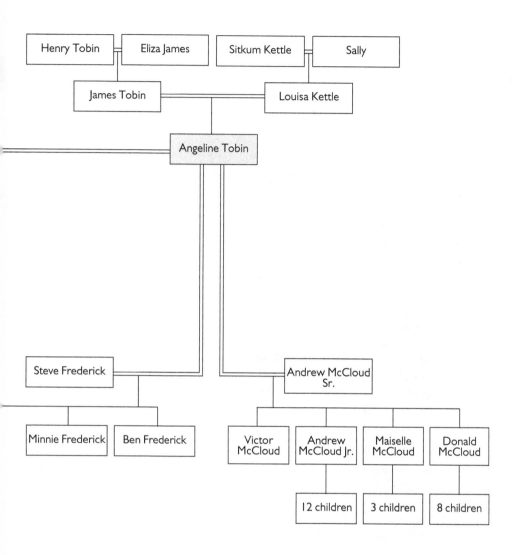

Source Notes

Unless otherwise noted, all interviews were conducted by the author.

PROLOGUE

Overview of the salmon: U.S. Fish & Wildlife Service, www.fws.gov/pacific; National Oceanic and Atmospheric Administration, www.nmfs.noaa.gov; Northwest Indian Fisheries Commission, Report to the United States Presidential Task Force on Treaty Rights in the Northwest (1977); Billy Frank Jr., interviews, 9, 10 Mar 2010. "The person who had to walk the farthest": Bill Wilkerson, interview, 18 Aug 2011. "I've heard of Uncle Billy": Presentation of *As Long As the Rivers Run*, Olympia, 1 Dec 2010.

INTRODUCTION

Billy Frank Jr., interviews, 9, 10 Mar 2010. "I will write it down in the treaty," Stevens comments during treaty negotiations: *Indian Sentinel* 2, no. 1, p. 329; Society for the Preservation of the Faith among Indian Children, Bureau of Catholic Indian Missions (U.S.), Jan 1920. Indians as "super citizens": Francis Paul Prucha, *American Indian Treaties: The History of a Political Anomaly* (Berkeley : University of California Press 1994). American Indian issues in the state of Washington: hearing before the United States Commission on Civil Rights, vol. 3, Hearings Held in Seattle, Washington, 19-20 Oct 1977; Alexandra Harmon, *Indians in the Making* (Berkeley and Los Angeles: University of California Press 1998); Tom Keefe, interview, 13 July 2011; Frank interview (2010); George Walter, interview, 1 Dec 2010; Zelma McCloud, interview, 26 Jan 2011. Christine Gregoire, at Billy's 80th birthday party, 12 Mar 2011. See alsoWilkinson interview (2010); Willie Frank III and James Tobin (Sugar) Frank, interviews, 20 Jun 2011.

Chapter 1. Spirit of the Father

Testimony of Willie Frank Sr., Federal Energy Regulatory Commission, Frank's Landing, 4 Aug 1982. Description of Willie on the witness stand: Susan Hvalsoe Komori, interview, Jan 2010; Walter interview (2010). "Me and the river are the oldest things": *Seattle Times*, "Willie: A Tribe's Last Link with Its Roots, 9 Jun 1979. For background on the Nisqually Tribe and the importance of salmon, see Barbara Lane, *Political and Economic Aspects of Indian-White Culture Contact in Western Washington in the Mid-19th Century*, vol. 1, Report for U.S. Justice Department (May 1973). For background on the first-salmon ceremonies, see Pamela T. Amoss, "The Fish God Gave Us: The First Salmon Ceremony," *Arctic Anthropology* 24, no. 1 (1987): 56-66; American Friends Service Committee, *Uncommon Controversy: Fishing rights of the Muckleshoot, Puyallup, and Nisqually Indians* (Seattle: University of Washington Press 1975). On the life of Isaac Stevens, see Kent D. Richards, *Isaac I. Stevens: Young Man in a Hurry* (1979; report, Pullman: Washington State University Press, 1993). On Donation Land Act and treaty signings, see Cecilia Svinth Carpenter, "Treaty Time at Nisqually," Washington State Historical Society, www.stories.washingtonhistory.org/treatytrail; Fay G. Cohen, *Treaties on Trial: The Continuing Controversy over Northwest Indian Fishing Rights* (Seattle: University of Washington Press, 1986); William J. Betts, "When Whites, Indians Signed First Treaty," *News Tribune*, 19 Aug 1962. For assessments of Stevens's character: Charles Wilkinson, interview, 16 Apr 2010; Hank Adams, interview, 1 Apr 2010; Georgiana Kautz, interview, 2 Dec 2010. ". . . a man who would stoop": Clayton Fox, "Isaac: Treaty Maker Extraordinary," *Daily Olympian*, 26 Apr 1973. On ten treaties signed in total including agreements with Joseph Palmer, see Fronda Woods, "Who's in Charge of Fishing?" *Oregon Historical Quarterly* 106, no.3 (2005). On the beginnings of the canning industry, see Northwest Indian Fisheries Commission Report (1977). ". . . every dollar invested": Russel Lawrence Barsh, *The Washington Fishing Rights Controversy.* (Seattle: University of Washington Graduate School of Business Administration, 1979). On the homicide of Quiemuth, see *Tacoma Sunday Ledger,* "Diary of James Longmire, Pioneer," 1892; *Morning Olympian,* "James Longmire Is Dead," 1897; Washington State Historical Society, "Leschi Justice in Our Time," www.stories.washingtonhistory.org/leschi. "This, ah salmon": Judith Espinola, "Voices of Washington State: The Recollections of Native American Willy [sic] Frank," Oral History, Collection of Washington State slides and tapes, Washington State Library. (1979). Early life of Willie Frank Sr.: Nancy Butterfield, "Mourners Bid Final Goodbye to Willie Frank, *Olympian,* 22 Jun 1983; *Seattle Times,* "Willie: A Tribe's Last Link with Its Roots," 9 Jun, 1979; Flossie Loutzenhiser, "Oldest Nisqually Recalls Tribe's Old Days," *Tacoma News Tribune and Sunday Ledger,* 24 Feb 1966. "Every year they come up to spawn" and "Let me tell you about": Willie Frank Sr., interview with Carol Burns, 1969. On Willie Frank Sr.'s experience with the white man, see Adams interview (2010); Norman Clark, *The Dry Years: Prohibition and Social Change in Washington* (Seattle: University of Washington Press, 1988). For background on Indian boarding schools, see "Kill the Indian and Save the Man," Digital History, www.digitalhistory.uh.edu/database/article_display.cfm?HHID=557; *Seattle Times*, "Tribes Confront Painful Legacy of Indian Boarding Schools," 3 Feb 2008; National Public Radio, "American Indian Boarding Schools Haunt Many," www.npr.org. "At Fort Peck": Adams interview (2010); Frank interview(2010). "He had other Indians with him": Willie Frank Sr. interview with Burns (1969). Description of Willie in the school band: Frank interview (2011). "When they put": Alison Bridges Gottfriedson, interview with Lois Allen and Melissa Parr, March 2009. Description of *slahal:* Willie Frank Sr. interview with Burns (1969). On the condemnation of the Nisqually Indian Reservation, see Letter from the Acting Secretary of the Interior to the President of the United States Senate, Senate Reports Allotted Nisqually Indian Lands, 66th Cong., 3d Sess., 6 Dec 1920-4 Mar 1921. For background on Fort Lewis, see Globalsecurity.org, Military, Fort Lewis; Senate Reports, 66th Cong., 2d Sess., 1 Dec 1919-5 Jun 1920; Yelm History Project, "Tacoma, the City of Destiny." "I'm Willie Frank and I've got a treaty": Mike Lowry, In Memory of Willie Frank, *Congressional Record*, 4 Aug 1983. On the legend of Bill Frank, see Tom Keefe Jr., "Willie Frank (1879-1983)," *Seattle Weekly*, 22-28 Jun 1983.

CHAPTER 2. "I LIVE HERE"

"Star Spangled Banner" signed into law, see, Smithsonian, www.si.edu/Encyl-copedia/SI/nmah/starflag.htm. Childhood setting: Frank interview (2010); Herman Dillon, interview, 9 Sept 2010; Testimony of Billy Frank Jr. (1973), *U.S. v. Washington.* "My dad always told me": Charles Wilkinson, *Messages from Frank's Landing* (Seattle: University of Washington Press, 2000). "When you set a gillnet": Testimony of Billy Frank Jr. (1973), *U.S. v. Washington.* "My parents lived": Frank interview (2010). "He'd take us down": Frank interview (2010). Description of Angeline Frank: Frank interview (2010); Sugar Frank, interview (2011); Angeline Frank, Oral History with Winona Weber, 28 Sept 1980, University of Washington Special Collections. "They were very close": Maiselle Bridges, interview with Hank Adams (2010). Description of Billy's childhood upbringing: Adams interview (2010); Mary Miles Frank, Oral History with Kathy Bruneau, 20 Aug 1980, Center for Pacific Northwest Studies, Western Washington University, Bellingham. Description of Maiselle's upbringing at Mud Bay: Maiselle Bridges, interview with Llyn De Danaan, 1 Aug 2000. Description of Maiselle's departure for Chemawa Indian School: Keefe interview (2011). Enrollment record, Theresa Bridges, Application for Enrollment to Non Reservation Schools, Reproduced at the National Archives and Records Administration-Pacific Alaska Region (Seattle) 7 Jun 1939. Don McCloud at Chemawa: Nancy Shippentower-Games, interview, 2011. Maiselle's experience at Chemawa: Carol Burns, interview, 21 July 2010. Death of Herman Buck John: Adams interview (2010); *Valley News*, "Five County Soldiers Are Killed in Action," 11 Jan 1945. Fire at the Frank home: Ray Mccloud, interview, 4 July 2011. 1945 arrest on the riverbank: Frank interview (2010), Wilkinson (2000).

CHAPTER 3. SURVIVAL

Description of the 1950s: Frank interview (2011); Walter interview (2010). "She took care of": Sugar Frank interview (2011). Description of Norma's upbringing and "You're out there": Kautz interview (2010). "Their approach": Epps Garrett, *To an Unknown God: Religious Freedom on Trial.* (New York: St. Martin's Press, 2001); John Echohawk, interview, 2011; Vine Deloria, *American Indian Policy in the Twentieth Century* (Norman: University of Oklahoma Press, 1992). "They were terminating tribes": Department of Commerce, Marine Protected Areas Federal Advisory Committee, 15 Feb 2005, p. 229; Sugar Frank interview (2011); Adams interview, 1, 22 Apr, 2011; Kautz interview (2011); Ramona Bennett, interview, 12 Mar 2010; Suzan Harjo, interview, 4 July 2011.

CHAPTER 4. SURVEILLANCE

Description of the Washington fisheries: Department of Fisheries, "A Program for Conservation of Fish and Wildlife Resources through Indian and Federal Relations," Washington State Library, 2 June 1961. "What this adds up to": *Daily Olympian*, "Fish Dangers Seen By Biggs," 14 Jan 1962. For a summary of fishing rights and the law, see Alvin Ziontz, *A Lawyer in Indian Country* (Seattle: University of Washington Press, 2009). Tribal perspective on diminishing runs: Frank interviews (2010, 2011). "A few individual": *Skagit Valley Herald*, "Battle Lines Drawn in Fish Test," 14 Dec 1960. "Nice to hear": Alvin M. Josephy Jr., *Now That the Buffalo's Gone* (Norman: University of Oklahoma Press, 1984), p. 192. Opinion reaction and protest: *Daily Olympian*, "No Salmon, No Santa," 23 Dec 1963. "Anyone who thinks": *Daily Olympian*, "Fish Dangers Seen By Biggs," 14 Jan 1962. "Some are now": *Seattle Times*, "Indian Netting May Destroy Sport Fishery," 14 Jan 1962. Description of underground society: Frank interview (2010); Sugar Frank interview (2011); Alison Bridges Gottfriedson interview with Parr and Allen (2009). Description of Game Department: Keefe interview (2011). "Mom and Dad, they were our": *Puyallup Tribal News*, "Maiselle Bridges: Matriarch of Treaty Rights," May 1996.

CHAPTER 5. RENEGADES

Adams interview (2010). "We are certain the Indians": Bradley Shreve, "From Time Immemorial," *Pacific Historical Review* 78, no.3, Aug 2009. "We're not depleting": *Daily Olympian*, "Indian Band Defies Game Department," 22 Jan 1964. "They must think the salmon": *Seattle Times*, "Truce Ended, Nets Going Back into River, Nisquallys Declare," 21 Jan 1964. "We had the power": Josephy (1984), p. 194. ". . . skinny Indian kid": David E. Wilkins, *The Hank Adams Reader* (Golden: Fulcrum, 2011). Analysis of Billy Frank Jr. and Hank Adams: Dan Evans, interview, 22 Nov 2010. "In the early 1960s": Marlon Brando, *Songs My Mother Taught Me.* (New York: Random House, 1994), p. 377. Brando; "If the Indian fishermen feel": Herb C. Williams and Walter Neubrech, *An American Nightmare* (Seattle: Outdoor Empire Pub., 1973). "probably is going to drive": Yelm History Project, 1964-Yellowstone

May Be Next If Indians Follow Settlers' Way, Letters to the Editor; www.yelmhistoryproject.com. ". . . rare as the dodo bird": Remarks by Governor Albert D. Rosellini to a Gathering of Washington State Indians, 3 Mar 1964, Washington State Sporstmen's Council Papers, University of Washington Special Collections, Indian Affairs Folder, Box 3. "Marlon Brando is coming": Ziontz (2009), p. 50. For a comprehensive review of the treaty fishing rights cases, see Northwest Indian Fisheries Commission Report (1977). "We'd rather fish than": Shreve (2009). Indian fishing rights: Hearings before the Committee on Interior and Insular Affairs, U.S Congress, 5, 6 August 1964. "Your rivers are being destroyed": Bob Hart to fellow sportsmen, Washington State Sportsmen's Council Papers, University of Washington Special Collections, Indian Affairs Folder, Box 3.

CHAPTER 6. CANOES AND CLASHES

Personal experiences of subject on the Nisqually River: Frank interview (2010). Description of canoe and carver: Don Hannula, "Renegade Indian: Bill Frank's Long Journey," *Seattle Times*, 10 May 1985. "This is just" and "We're going to shoot 'em": *Daily Olympian*, "Net Warfare Warms Up," 9 Sept 1965. ". . . a man without country": Don Hannula, "The Indian Problem The American Americans: The Great White Man Promised a Great Day—Will It Come?," *Seattle Times*, 30 Jun 1968. "The Indian is more free": Treaties Made, Treaties Broken, Documentary, Educational Media Collection, University of Washington (1970). "Those bastards rammed us": Wilkinson (2000), p.33. Description of October 7 boat ramming: Affidavit of William Frank Jr., Washington State Library, 7 Oct 1965. Details of canoe confiscation and return: Frank Haw, interview, 7 Apr 2010; Frank interview (2010). The "Battle of Frank's Landing,": Evans interview (2010); Janet McCloud, "The Last Indian War-Part 2," NIYC Papers, University of New Mexico Center for Southwest Research, Box 19, Folder 18, 1997, p. 1. "Blood was flowing freely": see, Letter from Armon C. Koeneman, Game Protector, to Walter Neubrech, Chief of Enforcement, Department of Game, Department of Game files, Washington State Archives, 18 Oct 1965. "The people aren't": *Daily Olympian*, "Game Agents, Indians Have a River Bank Bash," 14 Oct 1965. "There was a huge" Bridges Gottfriedson interview by Parr and Allen (2009). ". . . criticized the state": Don Hannula, Statement to Norman E. Mattson, Inspector, The State-Indian Skirmish of October 13, 1965, 21 Oct 1965, Washington State Archives. "The thing that upset me" Statement to Norman E. Mattson from Jim H. Siburg, The State-Indian Clash on the Nisqually River on October 13, 1965, 10 Nov 1965; Susan Hvalsoe Komori, interview, Jan 2010. "If something isn't done": *Auburn Citizen*, "Federal Men Ask Citizen's Help in Civil Rights Probe," 20 Oct 1965. "You've got to follow": Evans interview (2010); *Seattle Times*, "Indians Found Innocent of Fish-In Incident," 19 Jan 1969. Attacks against Frank's Landing 1963 to 1970: Wilkins (2011), p.52. "We've gotten so fond of them": *Life*, Feb 1983, p. 81.

CHAPTER 7. AS LONG AS THE RIVERS RUN

"I don't think up to now": *Seattle Times*, "Fishing Not Indians' Big Problem - Evans," 28 Jan 1966. Description of rally: *Survival News*, "Night Rally," 14 May 1966. "I think our ancestors": *Seattle Post-Intelligencer*, "The Indians Make It Hot for Gov. Evans in Effigy," 30 Jan 1966. On state politics: Evans interview (2010); Frank interview (2010). "Tribal leaders of the many": Sovereign Immunity Hearing before the Committee on Indian Affairs, U.S. Senate, 105th Cong. 2d Sess., 7 Apr 1998, Seattle. "biting brand of" and "American had gone all over": David L. Bicknell and Richard L. Brengle, *Image and Event* (Des Moines: Meredith, 1971), p. 322. "I deplore these": Associated Press, "Comedian's Fishing 'Deplored,'" *Seattle Times*, 8 Feb 1966. "This is going to be" and "I fail to get very excited": *Tacoma News Tribune*, "No Attempt Made to Jail Dick Gregory," 7 Feb 1966. "This is for Evans": *Daily Olympian*, "A Fish for Governor Evans," 18 Feb. 1966. "We are not fighting": *Jet* Magazine, 3 Mar 1966, p. 61. ". . . officials performed a": *Seattle Times*, "Public Loses Patience in Fish-in Feud," 16 Feb 1966. Martin Luther King in Atlanta: Adams interview (2010); Frank interview (2010). Poor People's Campaign announcement: Board of Trustees, New York, NY, May 1968, urj.org//about/union/governance/reso//?syspage=article&item_id=2237. Meeting at Frank's Landing on Poor People's Campaign: *Seattle Times*, "Indians Urged to Join Poor March," 16 May 1968. "*Puyallup I*": *Puyallup Tribe v. Department of Game*, 391 U.S. 392 (1968). "We expected the doors": *Seattle Times*, "Washington Indians among Poor Who Stormed Supreme Court," 31 May 1968. 1968 encampment at Frank's Landing: Don Hannula, "Nisqually Fishing Confrontation Now 46 Days Old," *Seattle Times*, 20 Oct, 1968; Harjo interview (2011). "Right up to the Boldt Decision": Gottfriedson interview with Parr and Allen (2009)."A lot of people" and "and now another": Burns, *As Long as the Rivers Run*. "This thing is clear out of perspective": *Seattle Times*, "6 More Arrested in Indian-Fishing Clash," 18 Oct 1968; Haircuts given: *Seattle Times*, "Nisqually Fishing Confrontation Now 46 Days Old," 20 Oct. 1968. Letter from Hank Adams, Survival of the American Indian Association, to Governor Dan Evans, and force exceeding sixty officers: see Dan Evans Papers, Washington State Archives, 17 Oct 1968. Fact-finding committee, interview with Billy at Frank's Landing: see Dan J. Evans papers, 2S-2-448, Washington State Archives. Phone call regarding purchase of Frank's Landing: United States Government Memorandum to Superintendent, "Telephone call from Mr. Neubrech," Billy Frank Jr. Files, Bureau of Indian Affairs, 13 Dec 1968.

CHAPTER 8. TAKEOVERS

Harjo interview (2011). Phone call from Willie Frank Sr: Dean Chavers, *Racism in Indian Country* (New York: Peter Lang, 2009), p. 65. Takeover at Fort Lawton: Burns, *As Long As the Rivers Run*; Frank interview (2010); Sugar Frank interview (2011); Adams interviews (2010, 2011). 1868 Sioux Treaty: Adams interview (2011). ". . . military person touched anyone was to help them off the post": *New York Times*, "Indians Seized in Attempt to Take Over Coast Fort," 9 Mar 1970. "Is it true": *Seattle*

Times, "Indian Attack on Fort Fascinates World Press," 9 Mar 1970. "The whole country": Jack W. Jaunal, *Images of America: Fort Lawton* (Charleston: Arcadia, 2008). Death of Valerie Bridges: Adams interview (2010); Kautz interview (2011). ". . . determine by string measure" and "In her lifetimes": *Daily Olympian,* "'She Was the Strongest': Miss Bridges Fought for Her Beliefs, 21 May 1970. "The trial meant so much to her": *Seattle Times,* "Indians Pay Tribute to Drowning Victim," 20 May 1970. Puyallup encampment 1970: Burns interview (2010); Adams interview (2010); Frank interview (2010). Testimony of Billy Frank Jr., *U.S. v. Washington,* 384 F.Supp.312 (1974), *U.S. v. Washington,* Court Transcripts, Testimony of Walter Neubrech, exhibit testimony g-16. "It's a sad thing" and "If anyone lays": *Seattle Times,* "Shots Fired, 60 Arrested in Indian-Fishing Showdown," 9 Sept 1970. "They were all up on the highway": *Seattle Times,* "Fish-Camp Raid Etched in State History," 7 Sept 2010. "Your face burned": Gottfriedson interview with Parr and Allen (2009). Hank Adams shooting: Adams interview (2011); *Seattle Times,* "Rumors Cloud Facts in Report of Shooting," 11 Apr 1971; *Seattle Times,* "Indian Activist Sues Officials for $20 Million in Shooting Incident," 7 Aug 1971. "I can't identify him" *Tacoma News Tribune,* "Adams Suit One of 4 Dismissed by Judge," 24 Jun 1972. *Daily Olympian,* "Hank Adams Shot While Tending Net," 19 Jan 1971. The 20-Point Proposal: Adams interview (2011); Frank interview (2011). Trail of Broken Treaties: Adams interview (2011); Frank interview (2010); Bennett. interview (2010). BIA a "dumping ground": *Washington Post,* 31 Oct 1972. "For nearly a month": Vine Deloria, "Old Indian Refrain: Treachery on the Potomac," *New York Times,* 8 Feb 1973. "I want to get his feelings" and "I really believe": *Seattle Times,* "Thurston County Man Speaks for Indian Reformers," 26 Nov 1972. Department of Game takeover (1973): *Seattle Times,* "Indian Netters Fish On, Wonder," 4 Feb 1973. Scene inside Department of Game: Frank interview (2010); Adams, Hank, Eulogy of Alison Bridges, 2010. "When Judge Goodwin": *Daily Olympian,* "Face to Face over Fishing," 29 Jan 1973. ". . . accounts of their marital problems": *Washington Post,* "Indian Leader Says 2 Villages Target of Government Spying," 1 Sept 1973. Agreement between Evans and Indians to suspend arrests and drop weapons: Wilkins (2011). Flooding at Frank's Landing: Billy Frank Jr. Files, File No. 2, Frank's Landing, 130-1008, Bureau of Indian Affairs. "He would go off by himself," description of loss at Frank's Landing: *Seattle Times,* "High Water Wrecks Two Buildings near Olympia," 1 Mar 1972. Description of house pulling apart and "I told them": letter from John Vaninetti, Real Property Management Officer, to G. M. Felshaw, Superintendent, Western Washington Indian Agency, Billy Frank Jr. Files, Bureau of Indian Affairs, 17 Feb 1965. "I've stood on these banks": *Tacoma News Tribune,* "Franks Landing Washing Away"; "Help Tied in Red Tape," 21 Jan 1976; "We demand affirmative": Bureau of Indian Affairs, letter from Billy Frank Jr. to Francis Briscoe, 23 Jan 1976. Background of flooding and request for assistance, and "Frank's Landing is Indian Land": Frank's Landing on the Nisqually River, Request for Assistance, Bureau of Indian Affairs.

CHAPTER 9. THE SHELF LIFE OF TREATIES

U.S. v. Washington, 384 F.Supp.312 (1974); *United States v. Winans*, 198 U.S. 371 (1905). ". . . case to end all cases": Stuart Pierson, interview, 21 Mar 2011. "The Nisquallys didn't have": Wilkinson (2010). "represent the rights and legitimate": Hank Adams, letter to U.S. attorney general; Wilkins (2011).. "If this lawsuit"and assessment of Boldt: Pierson interview (2011); Wilkinson interview (2011); Ziontz (2009). Boldt assigned to pay board: Frank interview(2010). ". . . put on that table": *New York Times*, "American Indians Struggling for Power," 11 Feb 1979. "The hardest part of this case": Pierson interview (2011). Sohappy to Martin Luther King Jr.: Bill Morlin, "Fishing Rights Leader Freed: Sohappy Dedicates Rest of Life to Improving Things for Indians," *Spokesman-Review*, 18 May 1988. "We had strong disagreements": Al Ziontz, Presentation, Seattle Public Library Northeast Branch, 13 Apr 2010. "I don't have to sit down": Pierson interview (2011). ". . . between 1965 and 1970 chum had the best escapement record": *Seattle Times*, "No Holiday in Indian Fish Trial," 3 Sept 1973. Opening arguments, *U.S. v. Washington*: *Seattle Times*, "Suit Asks Decision on Indian Fishing Rights," 27 Aug 1973. "It is impossible to acquire" and "From the time I started": Testimony of Walter Neubrech, *U.S. v. Washington*, Exhibit G-16. "This is how I make my living": Testimony of Billy Frank Jr., *U.S. v. Washington*, 10 Sept 1973; *Seattle Times*, "State Stealing Nets since 1960s, Indian Tells Trial," 11 Sept 1973. "I watched his expression": Ziontz (2010). "I don't know why": *Seattle Times*, "Judge Criticizes State Witness in Indian Trial," 8 Sept 1973. "If you've ever made love": Cohen (1986). Lena Hillaire: Frank interview (2010); Adams interview (2010); Bennett interview (2010); Testimony of Lena Hillaire, *U.S. v. Washington*, 99173 Vol. 13 original trial, 11 Sept 1973, pp. 2853-2868. "I hope this place isn't rigged": Charles Wilkinson, *Blood Struggle: The Rise of Modern Indian Nations* (New York: W.W. Norton, 2005). "I know Slade personally": Ziontz (2010). "I think he": Mike Grayum, interview, 9 Mar 2011.

CHAPTER 10. STORM

Backlash to the Boldt Decision: *New York Times*, "American Indians Struggling for Power" and "They Would Have Shot Judge Boldt," 11 Feb 1979; Frank interview (2010). "I was burned in effigy" and "Sometimes I get": *New York Times*, "American Indians Struggling for Power and Idntity," 11 Feb, 1979. Fallout from the Boldt decision: Hank Adams and Billy Frank Jr., 10 Sept 2010, Wa He Lut Indian School, Lacey. "under the guise of": *Seattle Times*, "Shot Fisherman Still Serious," 26 Oct 1976. "It was complete anarchy": Grayum interview (2011). "The trouble was": Evans interview (2010). On changes to fishing restrictions after the Boldt Decision see, Associated Press, "War over the Boldt Fishing Decision," *Daily Olympian*, 17 Oct 1974. "It was kind of a shock": John Westerhome, Telephone interview, 2011. "Judge Boldt made a decision": Frank interview (2010). Description of the formation of the Northwest Indian Fisheries Commission: Frank interview (2010); Adams interview (2010). "And it was Billy," "I don't know how long," "I was going," and U.S. Fish and

Wildlife internal reaction to the decision: Grayum interview (2011). ". . . brandishing clubs and handguns": Letter from Survival of the American Indian Association to J. Stanley Pottinger, Civil Rights Division, U.S. Attorney's Office, 8 Feb 1975. Incident involving fog mace: *Seattle Times*, "Indians Seek Probe into State Actions," 8 Feb 1975. ". . . that the Washington Game": Letter from Survival of the American Indian Association to Pottinger, 8 Feb 1975. "It has been recalcitrance": U.S. Court of Appeals, Ninth Circuit, 520 F.2d 676 4 Jun 1975, As Amended on Denial of Rehearing En Banc 23 Jul 1975. "We're totally disgusted": *Daily Olympian*, "Fisherman 'Disgusted,'" 27 Jan 1976. "You came in": as related by Jim Waldo, Billy's 80th birthday party, 12 Mar 2011. "We're treating this": Jim Waldo, interview, 31 May 2011. Fisheries Department reaction and Jim Tuggle account: Haw interview (2010). ". . . unwarranted shooting": *Seattle Times*, "Shot Gillnetter Sues for Damages," 18 Oct 1976. "I would have done a lot": *Seattle Times*, "Candidates React Angrily to Shooting," 26 Oct 1976. "Washington state legal officials": *Washington Post*, "Salmon Is the Loser in Long Fishery War," 5 Sept 1979. "I don't think a fish": *New York Times*, "Interests Collide over Puget Sound Fishing," 28 Oct 1976. "You go back" and "After the Boldt Decision": Frank interview (2011). "After the Boldt Decision there was the Magnuson Act": Department of Commerce, Marine Protected Areas Federal Advisory Committee, Arlington VA, 15 Feb 2005, p. 242. "The Pacific Regional Council, Trail of Self Determination": Sugar Frank interview (2011); "We will be trying": *Seattle Times*, "Indian-Led Caravan Begins Trek to D.C.," 19 Mar 1976. "Because the calvary," "We stayed with," and "I would never take": Sugar Frank interview (2011). Changing of the guard at the Northwest Indian Fisheries Commission: Adams interview (2010); "My past is in the past": Northwest Indian Fisheries Commission, "NWIFC Sees Three New Commissioners," Newsletter, 23 Mar 1977, pp. 1-3. "John Ides just retired": Adams interview (2010). "He has a great love": Bennett interview (2010). "They started to know": Adams interview (2010). *Frank v. Morton*, and "People became enrolled": Walter interview (2010)."We did a letter": Adams interview (2010). Death of Maureen Frank: Kautz interview (2010); Adams interview (2010). Adoption of Tanu Frank and reunion with birth family: Tanu Frank (John Elliott), interview, 6 Jan 2012; Billy Frank Jr., interview, 6 Jan 2012.

CHAPTER 11. THE POLITICS OF SALMON

For background on Slade Gorton, including "I find racism appalling," see, John C. Hughes, *Slade Gorton: A Half Century in Politics*. (Olympia: Washington State Heritage Center 2011); "If the Indians were paid": *Seattle Times*, "G.O.P Differ over Indian Fishing Rights," 13 May 1976. "Now that Judge Boldt" and "Not only have we been given": *Seattle Times*, "Indians Accuse Slade Gorton of 'Double Talk' on Fishing Rights," 13 May 1976. "The fishing issue": *Seattle Times*, "25 Years after the Boldt Decision: The Fish Tale That Changed History," 7 Feb 1999. "If you want to right," : *Seattle Times*, "Absentees to decide 2nd District," 3 Nov. 1976 and Certification of 1976 contest, Lloyd Meeds v. John Garner: www.sos.wa.gov/elections. "He was a lawyer": Waldo interview (2011). "Somewhere in my paperwork": Keefe interview (2011). "The Supreme Court": Waldo interview (2011); "Yesterday's decision": *Seattle Times*, "Indians to Seek Federal Control of State Fishery," 10 Jun 1977. "Judge Boldt has great": *New York Times*, "Interests Collide over Puget Sound Fishing." "Federal takeover of fishery": Frank interview (2010). "I've never seen an Indian": *Seattle Times*, "Both Sides Unhappy with Boldt Rulings," 2 Sept 1977. ". . . depriving tribes of": Letter from Billy Frank Jr. to Leo Krulitz, Billy Frank Jr. Files, Bureau of Indian Affairs, 27 Aug 1977, to the President of the United States, 2 Sept 1977. Five percent reduction as "sucker bait": *Seattle Times*, "Both Sides Unhappy with Boldt Rulings," 2 Sept 1977. "We ended up taking": Waldo interview (2011). "They were just raping": Frank interview (2010). "183,000 salmon had been" and "Non-Indian fishermen": Mason Morisset, "Boldt from the Blue: The Salmon Wars" in George Scott, ed., *Turning Points in Washington's Public Life* (Folsom: Civitas Press 2011, p.131. "The state would announce" and ". . . isn't worth the powder": Northwest Indian Fisheries Commission, Tribal Report to the Presidential Task Force on Treaty Fishing Rights in the Northwest, 28 Oct 1977, vol 3, p. 124.. "There's a new breed" and "We are here": U.S. Civil Rights Commission, Oct 1977, Washington State Library "We are here": *Seattle Times,* "Indians Charge Federal Neglect," 21 Oct 1977. "As you know": U.S. Commission on Civil Rights, *Indian Tribes: A Continuing Quest for Survival* (Washington, D.C: Government Printing Office, 1981), p. 72. "We came out with this": Waldo Inteview (2011). "We realize that" and "We feel the general concepts": *Seattle Times*, "Reaction Negative on Fishing Plan," 20 Jan 1978. "We don't like": Waldo interview (2011). "Of course, federal" and "There were probably": Harjo interview (2011). "This case might make sense": oral argument of Mason Morisset, *Washington v. Fishing Vessel Ass'n*, 443 U.S. 658 (1979). "I think the important": *Seattle Times*, "Supreme Court Now in Historic Countdown on Boldt Decision." "The state's extraordinary": *Puget Sound Gillnetters Association v. United States, District Court* 573 F 2d (9th Cir. 1978), 1126. "I don't think": *Seattle Times*, "Fishermen Upset by High-Court Decision," 2 July 1979. ". . . the salmon is the": *Washington Post*, "Salmon Is the Loser in Fishery War," 5 Sept 1979.

Chapter 12. Bridge Builder

This chapter draws heavily on 2011 interviews with Tom Keefe and Bill Wilkerson. Warning: *Seattle Times*, "A Call to Save This State's Salmon," 18 Sept 1978. "In 1964, both" and "By the end": Adams interview (2010). "He is scrupulously": www.historylink.org, 14 Oct 2003. "Can't you load up": *Seattle Times*, "He Loved This State: Warren G. Magnuson," 21 May 1989. Phase II: see *U.S. v. Washington (Phase II)* 506 F. Supp. 187 (W.D. Wash. 1980). Reaction to decision: *Seattle Times*, "Big Business Enters Indian-Fishing Issue," 8 May 1981. "I encouraged the": Jacqueline Storm, *Land of the Quinault* (Taholah: Quinault Indian Nation, 1990). "We're going to" and "Then something": *Spokesman-Review*, "Colville Tribes Pull Money from SeaFirst," 22 May 1981. NCAI meeting and Seafirst gathering: Frank interview (2011). "What's the harm," "At that time," "Well, what happened," and "Billy has no": Waldo interview (2011). "It was an": *Seattle Times*, "Summit of Indians, Executives Praised," 24 Nov 1981. "If I hadn't been here" and "We don't need": *Seattle Times*, "Negotiation, Not Litigation," 1981.

CHAPTER 13. RESILIENCE

"The couple had a hard": Walter interview (2010). "I did what I had to do": Frank interview (2010). "She was like a force": Patricia Zell, interview, 6 Sept 2011. "I knew Sue": Wilkerson interview (2011). "Billy is twenty years" and "He screamed from": Keefe interview (2011). "She loved kids": Kautz interview (2010). "He was in pain": *Daily Olympian*, "Willie Frank: His 104 Years along the Nisqually," 19 Jun 1983. "While some of his family": *Daily Olympian*, "Mourners Bid Final Goodbye to Willie Frank," 22 Jun 1983. "Dad gave us": *Spokane Chronicle*, "Willie Frank: An Indian of the Old Ways," 21 Jun 1983. "He didn't rob us" "I'm no stranger to" and "This is the land": Suzanne Hapala, "End of an Era," *Seattle Times*, 22 Jun 1983. "That's the only thing": Willie Frank III interview (2010). "I knew Dad would pick": *Tacoma News Tribune*, "Tribes Gather to Eulogize Bill Frank," 22 Jun 1983. "To the editor": *News Tribune*, "Willie Frank's Dreams Remembered," 3 Jul 1983. "It was a different": Frank interview (2010). "I remember starting" and "I had friends": Willie Frank III interview (2010). "I can remember Billy": Walter interview (2010). "Even when she was sick" Tanu Frank (John Elliott) interview (2012). "When old man Bill": Kautz interview (2010). "We had a good life": Frank interview (2010).

CHAPTER 14. THE NEGOTIATOR

"Look for answers " and "We could have": Walter interview (2010). "Can you name another": Wilkerson interview (2011). "So many, in fact": *Aberdeen Daily World*, "The Treaty: Time to Fish or Cut Bait," 3 Dec 1984. "It was our stocks": Wilkerson interview (2011). "We have been": *Seattle Times*, "Chinook Crisis," 6 May 1984. "What brought it home to me": *Washington Post*, "Salmon Is the Loser in Long Fishery War," 5 Sept 1979. "Today, salmon recovery": Charles Wilkinson, Hearing before the Committee on Indian Affairs, U.S. Senate, 4 Jun 2003. "And we had, " "Judges and lawyers," "He was the tribal," and "He always knew": Wilkerson interview (2011). "The president really did" and "This is the best": *Seattle Times/ Seattle Post-Intelligencer*, "Salmon Accord Rreached: U.S., Canada Strike 'Best Deal Possible,'" 16 Dec 1984. "Everybody gives a little": *Seattle Times*, "Years of Bitter Feuding End with Stroke of Pen Tomorrow," 17 Mar 1985. "To make this": *Seattle Times/Seattle Post-Intelligencer*, "Seiners Say They're 'Big Losers,'" 16 Dec 1984. Dispute between Billy Frank Jr. and the Nisqually Tribe and "I've got the bigger": Frank interview (2012). "On average each": Washington Forest Protection Association, "The Everyday Use of Our Working Forests," www.wfpa.org/page/forest-products-and-jobs. "They were drawn": Adams interview (2010). "He was very" and

"He's made himself": Wilkerson interview (2011). "Us Indians are": Frank interview (2010). "The river is healthy," "It looked like everybody," and "I told people": *Seattle Times*, "Divided Interests Make a Deal," 17 May 1987. "I'll never forget": PBS, "Salmon Streams' Struggle Continues 40 Years After Clean Water Act," www.pbs. org/newshour/bb/environment/jan-june09/salmonwars_05-22.html, 22 May 2009. "Come to us" and "The biggest war": Wilkerson interview (2011).

CHAPTER 15. CLEAR CREEK HATCHERY

Diverse ecosystems in North America and "We live along": Frank interview (2010). "My eyes sparkle"; David Gordon *Nisqually Watershed, Glacier to Delta; A River Legacy* (Seattle: Mountaineers Books, 1995). 77 degrees and salmon eggs: U.S. Fish & Wildlife Service; Walter interview (2010); Frank interview (2010). Hatchery overview and its role in the watershed: David Troutt, interview, 2011; "An example is the": Northwest Indian Fisheries Commission, *Treaty Rights at Risk* (Olympia 2011). "Fundamentally, the salmon": Jim Lichatowich, *Salmon without Rivers* (Chicago: Island Press, 1999), pp. 7-8.

CHAPTER 16. SUBMERGED

Highest flood ever recorded: National Weather Service, "Washington's Top Ten Weather Events of 1900s," www.wrh.noaa.gov/pqr/paststorms/washington10.php. "The whole of Frank's Landing": Keefe interview (2011); Frank interviews (2010, 2011). "Whatever my feelings,": *Kitsap Sun*, "Wa He Lut School: Indian School Rebuilt After Floods," 12 Jan 1998. Descriptions of flood, aftermath, and school construction: Keefe interview (2011); Frank interview (2011); Adams interview (2011). Tanu Frank reconnecting with his birth family: Tanu Frank interview (2012); Billy Frank Jr. interview (2012)

CHAPTER 17. THE TOUGH GUY

"People supporting Ken": Susan Gilmore, "Fishing Resurfaces in Governor's Race: Old Tribal-Rights Decision Fans Controversy," *Seattle Times*, 16 Oct 1992. "One of the things": Norm Dicks, interview, 25 Apr 2011. "We are not interested": Northwest Indian Fisheries Commission, Spring Newsletter, 1997. "A basic part of Indian law" and "Yes, I have": Wilkerson interview (2010). "For too long" and "Signing the treaty": *Chicago Tribune*, "Tribes to Direct Own Wildlife Protection," 6 Jun 1997. "If that level" and "Where's Billy?": Wilkerson interview (2010). "The fight is fair and square" : *Indian Country Today*, "'Dump Gorton' Is Important Campaign for Indian Country," 7 Jun 2000. ". . . rounded up the Navajos": *New York Times*, "Backlash Growing as Indians Make a Stand for Sovereignty," 9 Mar 1998. "The doctrine places" and "The primary sponsor": Reuters, "American Indians Fight for Treaty Rights," 4 Sept 1997. "Whether he knows": Timothy Egan, "Backlash Growing as Indians Make a Stand for Sovereignty," *New York Times*, 9 Mar 1998. "Thanks to Slade": Adele Ferguson, "Gorton Not Anti-Native American," *Ellensburg Daily*

Record, 15 Mar 15, 2000. "The defeat of Slade": First American Education Project, "Gorton's Loss—Indian Country's Victory," www.yvwiiusdinvnohii.net/News2000/ 1100/FAEP001126Gorton.htm, 26 Nov 2000. "You don't want": Unidentified elder, interview, 26 Jan 2011. "He was fun": Jim Johnson, interview, 30 July 2010.

CHAPTER 18. "YOU WERE ALWAYS THERE FOR ME"

Trip to Hawaii related by Billy Frank Jr. and Patricia Zell. "They were getting daily": Zell interview (2011). "I mean, all my": Willie Frank III interview (2010). "On her death bed": "Sue Crystal, Adviser to 2 Governors, Died August 25, 2001," academic. evergreen.edu/projects/ehealthinstitute/SueCrystal.htm. "When Susan died" Tanu Frank interview (2011).

CHAPTER 19. THE CATALYST

"I've sat you next to": Wilkinson (2000), p. 93. "Presidents, we just": Frank interview (2010). Washington D.C. elevator scene: Grayum interview (2011). "If he'd been": Dan Inouye, Telephone interview, 2010. Canoe ride with Inouye, "You have to," and "When the waitress": Zell interview (2011). Background on Wisconsin treaty fishing rights: www.mpm.edu/wirp/icw-110.html; 700 F. 2d 341-*Lac Courte Oreilles Band of Lake Superior Chippewa Indians v. P Voigt United.*"No respect is given": *Washington Post*, "Wisconsin Fights Annual Fishing War: Chippewas Exercise Spearfishing Rights in Midst of Media Circus," 24 Apr 1990. Fallout from 1983 court opinion: *Time*, "Walleye War," 30 Apr 1990. Washington's role in dispute: Zell interview (2011). "Casting Light upon The Waters": www.act31resources.com/MainNavigation/Products/tabid/85/CategoryID/0/List/1/Level/a/ProductID/18/Default.aspx. "Wisconsin doesn't have": *Masinaigan*, "Potentials of Co-Management," Jan/Feb 1990. "He was a voice": Sue Erickson, interview, 26 Sept 2011. "We went there": Billy Frank Jr., page 242, Department of Commerce, Marine Protected Areas Federal Advisory Committee, 15 Feb 2005, Arlington Virginia, pp. 229-46. Nominee for the 2010 Nobel Peace Prize: Letter from Dan Inouye, U.S. senator, Hawaii, to the Nobel Peace Prize Committee, 29 Jan 2010. "Dubbed the walls of death": *New York Times*, "Agreement Is Reached at the U.N. to End Use of Drift Fishing Nets," 4 Dec 1989. "There's nothing phony": Jolene Unsoeld, interview, 2011; "These are our first," "This is the soul," and "I went through": Billy Frank Jr. and Michael Harris, "This Is Indian Country," www.babywildfilms.com, 2008. Spill impact: Christine Dell'Amore, "*Exxon Valdez* Anniversary: 20 Years Later, Oil Remains," *National Geographic*, 23 Mar 2009. "You could cut it ," "Why the hell ," and "You're the guy": Royce Pollard interview (2010). "We want to get the": Billy Frank Jr., page 242, Department of Commerce, Marine Protected Areas Federal Advisory Committee, 15 Feb 2005, Arlington Virginia, pp. 229-46.

CHAPTER 20. OPERATION CHAINSMOKER

For background on the Landing, *Nisqually Indian Tribe v. Governor Gregoire,* Response Brief of Appellees Frank's Landing Indian Community and Theresa Bridges, no. 09-35725, p. 14 of 68. "We [the families] don't get no": Frank interview (2010). For the U.S. Supreme Court case, see *Washington v. the Confederated Tribes of the Colville Indian Reservation* (1980), supreme.justia.com/us/447/134/. "This is the way the U.S. government" and "There will be very": *Washington Post,* "Indians Losing Cigarette-Sale Economic Base," 24 June 1980. Description of process to establish compacts between the State of Washington and Indian tribes: Adams interview (2010); Frank interview (2010). For an explanation of the taxation of cigarettes in Washington State, see Department of Revenue, Cigarette Tax, Sept 2011, dor.wa.gov/Docs/Pubs/CigarTax/CigaretteTax.pdf. "They started a task force": Frank interview (2010). "ATF takes these investigations": "Guilty Pleas in Cigarette Tax Case," seattlepi.com, 20 Nov 2008. "They confiscated everything": Frank interview (2010). "They scared the": *Ranting Raven,* "The Swoop on Frank's Landing," 7 Aug 2007. "We always contend": Frank interview (2010). "conspiring to traffic in": "Smoke Shop Owners Plead Guilty to Conspiring to Traffic in Contraband Cigarettes and Structuring $2.1 Million of Cash Transactions," Press Release, U.S. Attorney's Office, Western District of Washington, 13 Aug 2008. "They threatened to indict": Adams interview (2010). "There's no difference between": *High Country News,* "Cigarette Wars: Northwest Indians Want No Taxation in Their Sovereign Nations," 17 Aug 2009. "The Congress acted in": written statement, Patricia Zell, attorney [2011]. "Our issue is with": Cynthia Iyall, interview, 4 Nov 2010. "The way I look at it": Willie Frank III interview (2010). "For three years": Billy Frank Jr. interview (2010).

CHAPTER 21. HARD TRUTHS

"What do we tell our,": Frank interview (2010). State of Hood canal:, Jan Newton, The Hood Canal Dissolved Oxygen Program, University of Washington, Sept 2010. Dead zones around the globe: World Resources Institute; "New Web-Based Map Tracks Marine 'Dead Zones' Worldwide," www.wri.org/press/2011/01/new-web-based-map-tracks-marine-dead-zones-worldwide. "I used to swim in the": Historylink.org.; "Poison is going down": Frank interview (2010). "have increased 30-fold": Committee on Environment and Natural Resources, *Scientific Assessment of Hypoxia in U.S. Coastal Waters,* Interagency Working Group on Harmful Algal Blooms, Hypoxia, and Human Health of the Joint Sub committee on Ocean Science and Technology, Washington DC, 2010. "They look at the sound": Northwest Indian Fisheries Commission, "Being Frank: The Map," 15 Sept 2006. "An unhealthy Puget Sound means": *Port Orchard Independent,* "Now's the Time to Be Bold about Puget Sound," 15 Dec 2008; *Bellingham Herald,* "Now the Time to Be Bold about Puget Sound," 8 Jan 2009. Twelve-year study: Washington Department of Ecology, www.ecy.wa.gov/biblio/0503016.html and www.ecy.wa.gov/news/2011/304.html. Chinook,

12th year on Endangered Species List see nwr.noaa.gov/ESA-Salmon-Listings. "The status quo": Hearst Newspapers Division, "We Have to 'Tell the Truth' to Save Orcas and Puget Sound," 4 Apr 2007. "They don't want to hear": Frank interview (2010) and "Many resources in the": Testimony of Billy Frank Jr., U.S. Senate Subcommittee on Fisheries, Wildlife and Water, 21 Sept 2005. "Common sense would": *Yakima Herald-Republic,* "Yakama Nation Joins Tribes' Suit over Culverts That Block Salmon," 17 Jan 2001. "The judge's order": *Seattle Post-Intelligencer,* "Tribes Win Ruling on Salmon, State Ordered to Fix Culverts for Salmon Passage," 22 Aug 2007. "I'm 78 right," "The problem is," and "There's so much: *Seattle Times,* "Tribes Take Salmon Battle into State's Road Culverts," 20 Oct 2009. "We have to be": Hearing before Committee on Indian Affairs, U.S. Senate, 29 Apr 2004. "We've got to reach": Frank interview (2010); "Fishermen are being punished": Northwest Indian Fisheries Commission, "Punishing Fishermen Ignores the Big H: Habitat," 5 Apr 2006. "There's no fish there anymore" and following quotes: Frank interview (2010)."That's the enemy": unidentified fisherman, Frank's Landing, 2010. "They're just eating" and "The most sea": Frank interview (2010). "I got one on": *Virginian-Pilot,* "Sea Lions Still Threaten Salmon as Hazing Effort Falls Short," 24 Jun 2007. Growth of sea lion population since 1983: Alaska Fisheries Science Center, National Marine Mammal Laboratory. "Sea lions have": Humane Society, "Bonneville Dam Sea Lions under Seige," www.humanesociety.org, 13 Sept 2011. "This is not an easy": *New York Times,* "Salmon-Eating Sea Lions Sentenced to Die," 15 May 2011. "As Northwest residents": Doc Hastings, "Protecting Salmon from Predatory Sea Lions," hastings.house.gov/News/DocumentSingle.aspx?DocumentID=225494, 4 Feb 2011. Elwa Dam Removal: www.nps.gov/olym/naturescience/elwha-ecosystem-restoration.htm. "All of those who": BellevueReporter.com, "There Are a Lot More Elwhas out There," 7 Oct 2011. "We're taking the dams": Frank interview (2010).

CHAPTER 22. DREAMS AND LEGACIES

"I live here": Frank interview (2010); Wilkinson (2000), p.4. Billy's 75th birthday: Wilkinson (2010). "He's the exception": Willie Frank III interview (2010). "These really wonderful": Keefe interview (2011). "I don't know" and "the son I never had": Adams interview (2010). "From my one personal": Grayum interview (2011). Joel Pritchard's top ten list: Adele Ferguson, "Have You Ever Thought about Running for Office?" *Ellensburg Daily Record,* 1 Aug 2002.; "On this fishing trip": Wilkerson interview (2011). "I guess I would": Evans interview (2010). "No matter how": Waldo interview (2011); Willie Frank III interview (2010). "He just doesn't": Sugar Frank interview (2010). "I know the other": Bennett, interview (2010). "What's happening now": Frank interview (2010); Adams interview (2010). "So many generations": Iyall interview (2010). ". . . natural ability": Tanu Frank (John Elliott) interview (2012). "He made Indians": Hvalsoe Komori interview (2010). "What I tell my kids": Frank interview (2010). "I don't believe": N. Bruce Duthu, *American Indians and the Law* (New York: Penguin Group, 2008).

Select Bibliography

Interviews and Oral Histories

Interviews by the Author

Hank Adams. 1, 22 Apr 2010, Lacey, WA.

Peter Bergman and Frank Haw. 7 Apr 2010, Tumwater, WA.

Carol Burns.

Norm Dicks. 16 Jun 2010, Telephone Interview.

Herman Dillon Sr. 9 Sept 2010, Tacoma, WA.

Dan Evans. 22 Nov 2010, Washington Athletic Club, Seattle, WA.

Billy Frank Jr. 26 Feb, 9-10 Mar 2010, Northwest Indian Fisheries Commission, Lacey, WA. 14 Jun, 10 Sept 2010, Wa He Lut Indian School, Olympia, WA. 3 Sept 2011, Northwest Indian Fisheries Commission, Lacey, WA.

Willie Frank III. 28 Oct 2010, Panera Bread, Lacey, WA.

Willie Frank III and Sugar Frank. 20 Jun 2011, Panera Bread, Lacey, WA.

Tom Keefe. 19 Jul 2011, Telephone Interview.

Mike Grayum. 9 Mar 2011, Northwest Indian Fisheries Commission, Lacey, WA.

Suzan Harjo. 4 Jul 2011, Telephone Interview.

Susan Hvalsoe Komori. 28 Apr 2010, Telephone Interview and Electronic Message.

Cynthia Iyall. 4 Nov 2010, Nisqually Indian Reservation, Lacey, WA.

Jim Johnson. 30 Jul 2010, Temple of Justice, Olympia, WA.

Georgiana Kautz. 13 Jul, 2 Dec 2010, Norma's Burgers, Lacey, WA.

Stuart Pierson. 21 Mar 2011, Telephone Interview.

Jim Waldo. 31 May 2011, Telephone Interview.

George Walter. 1 Dec 2010, Olympia, WA. 23 Mar 2011, Washington
    State Library, Tumwater, WA.

Charles Wilkinson. 16 Apr 2010, Olympia, WA.

Bill Wilkerson. 18 Aug 2011, Lacey, WA.

Patricia Zell. 6 Sept 2011, Cutters Point Coffee, Lacey, WA.

Other Interviews and Oral Histories

Maiselle Bridges. Interview with Llyn De Danaan. 1 Aug 2000.

Angeline Frank. Oral History with Winona Weber. University of
    Washington Special Collections. 1980.

Billy Frank Jr. 12 Mar 2011. 80th Birthday Celebration. Little Creek
    Casino Resort.

Mary Miles Frank. Oral History with Kathy Bruneau. Center for Pacific
    Northwest Studies, Western Washington University. 1980.

Willy [sic] Frank. Oral History by Judith Espinola. In Voices of Wash-
    ington State: Collection of Washington State Slides and Tapes.
    Washington State Library. 1979

Willie Frank and Paul Leschi. Interview by Carol Burns. 1969.

Alvin Ziontz. Northwest Historians Guild. Seattle Public Library
    Northeast Branch. 13 Apr 2010.

SECONDARY SOURCES

American Friends Service Committee. *Uncommon Controversy: Fishing
    Rights of the Muckleshoot, Puyallup, and Nisqually Indians*. Seattle:
    University of Washington Press, 1975.

Amoss, Pamela T. The Fish God Gave Us: The First Salmon Cere-
    mony." *Arctic Anthropology*. 24, no. 1 (1987).

Barsh, Russel Lawrence. *The Washington Fishing Rights Controversy*.

Seattle: University of Washington Graduate School of Business Administration, 1979.

Brando, Marlon. *Songs My Mother Taught Me*. New York: Random House, 1994.

Chavers, Dean. *Racism in Indian Country*. New York: Peter Lang, 2009.

Clark, Norman. *The Dry Years: Prohibition and Social Change in Washington*. 1965. Rev. ed., Seattle: University of Washington Press, 1988.

Cohen, Fay G. *Treaties On Trial*. Seattle: University of Washington Press, 1986.

Deloria, Vine. American Indian Policy in the Twentieth Century. Norman: University of Oklahoma Press, 1992.

Garrett, Epps. *To an Unknown God: Religious Freedom on Trial*. New York: St. Martin's Press, 2001.

Harmon, Alexandra. *Indians in the Making*. Berkeley and Los Angeles: University of California Press, 1998.

Hughes, John C. *Slade Gorton: A Half Century in Politics*. Olympia: Washington State Heritage Center, 2011.

Jaunal, Jack W. *Images of America: Fort Lawton*. Charleston: Arcadia, 2008.

Josephy, Alvin M. *Now That the Buffalo's Gone*. Norman: University of Oklahoma Press, 1984.

Llyn De Danaan. *Katie Gale's Tombstone: Landscape, Power, and Justice on Nineteenth Century Oyster Bay*. Forthcoming.

Prucha, Francis Paul. *American Indian Treaties: The History of a Political Anomaly*. Berkeley : University of California Press, 1994.

Richards, Kent D. *Isaac I. Stevens: Young Man in a Hurry*. 1979. Report, Pullman: Washington State University Press, 1993.

Shreve, Bradley. "From Time Immemorial." *Pacific Historical Review* 78, no..3 (2009).

Wilkins, David E. *The Hank Adams Reader*. Golden, CO: Fulcrum, 2011.

Wilkinson, Charles. *Blood Struggle: The Rise of Modern Indian Nations*. New York: W.W. Norton, 2005.

Wilkinson, Charles. *Messages from Frank's Landing.* Seattle: University of Washington Press, 2000.

Williams, Herb C., and Walter Neubrech. *An American Nightmare.* Seattle: Outdoor Empire, 1973.

Woods, Fronda. "Who's in Charge of Fishing?" *Oregon Historical Society* 106, no. 3 (2005).

Ziontz, Alvin. *A Lawyer in Indian Country.* Seattle: University of Washington Press, 2009.

Government Reports and Documents

American Indian Issues in the State of Washington. Hearings before the United States Commission on Civil Rights, Vol. 3. Hearings held in Seattle. 1977.

Lane, Barbara. *Political and Economic Aspects of Indian-White Culture Contact in Western Washington in the Mid-Nineteenth Century,* Vol. 1., Report for U.S. Justice Department, May 1973.

Northwest Indian Fisheries Commission. *Report to the United States Presidential Task Force on Treaty Rights in the Northwest.* 1977.

Puyallup Tribe v. Dept. of Game, 391 U.S. 392 (1968).

Puyallup Tribe, Inc. v. Department of Game, 433 U.S. 165 (1977).

U.S. v. Washington, 384 F.Supp.312 (1974).

U.S. v. Washington (Phase II), 506 F. Supp. 187 (W.D. Wash. 1980).

U.S. v. Winans, 198 U.S. 371 (1905).

Washington v. Puyallup Tribe, 414 U.S. 44, 94 S.Ct 830, 38 L.Ed.2d 254 (1973).

Washington v. Fishing Vessel Assn., 443 U.S. 658 (1979).

Other Resources

HistoryLink, www.historylink.org

National Oceanic and Atmospheric Administration, www.nmfs.noaa.gov

Northwest Indian Fisheries Commission, www.nwifc.org

Survival of the American Indian Association, Olympia, WA

U.S. Fish & Wildlife Service, www.fws.gov/pacific

University of Washington Special Collections, www.lib.washington. edu/specialcollections

Washington State Archives, www.sos.wa.gov/archives

Washington State Library, www.sos.wa.gov/library

Washington State Secretary of State, Elections: www.sos.wa.gov/ elections

Yelm History Project, www.yelmhistoryproject.com

Index